Matthew 25 Christianity

Matthew 25 Christianity

Redeeming Church and Society

Donald Heinz

CASCADE *Books* • Eugene, Oregon

MATTHEW 25 CHRISTIANITY
Redeeming Church and Society

Copyright © 2022 Donald Heinz. All rights reserved. Except for brief quotations in critical publications or reviews, no part of this book may be reproduced in any manner without prior written permission from the publisher. Write: Permissions, Wipf and Stock Publishers, 199 W. 8th Ave., Suite 3, Eugene, OR 97401.

Cascade Books
An Imprint of Wipf and Stock Publishers
199 W. 8th Ave., Suite 3
Eugene, OR 97401

www.wipfandstock.com

PAPERBACK ISBN: 978-1-6667-3367-9
HARDCOVER ISBN: 978-1-6667-2853-8
EBOOK ISBN: 978-1-6667-2854-5

Cataloguing-in-Publication data:

Names: Heinz, Donald, author.

Title: Matthew 25 Christianity : redeeming church and society / Donald Heinz.

Description: Eugene, OR: Cascade Books, 2022 | Includes bibliographical references and index.

Identifiers: ISBN 978-1-6667-3367-9 (paperback) | ISBN 978-1-6667-2853-8 (hardcover) | ISBN 978-1-6667-2854-5 (ebook)

Subjects: LCSH: Christianity and politics—United States. | Bible. Matthew—Criticism, interpretation, etc. | Bible. Matthew—Influence.

Classification: BR516 H50 2022 (print) | BR516 (ebook)

New Revised Standard Version Bible, copyright 1989 National Council of the Churches of Christ in the United States of America. Used by permission. All rights reserved worldwide. Hymns by Carolyn Winfrey Gillette uses by permission. All rights reserved.

"When did we see you hungry Lord" c1998
"Whatever you do" c2008
"God, how can we comprehend" c1999

Dedication

To Pope Francis, patron saint of the least of these:
"I seek bishops who are shepherds living with the smell of the sheep."

"Just as you did it to one of the least of these who are members of my family, you did it to me" (Matthew 25:40).

"Go therefore and make disciples of all nations . . . teaching them to obey everything that I have commanded you" (Matthew 28:19–20).

Contents

Preface: Matthew 25 Could Be a New Religious Movement ix
Introduction: A Field Guide for Taking Matthew 25 Public xxvii

PART I: *Rediscovering Good News to the Poor in the Gospel of Matthew*

1. The Bible as the Founding Text of New Religious Movements 3
2. The Message of Matthew Then and Now 12
3. Contextualizing Matthew 25 in the Bible and Christian History 25
4. Can Matthew 25 Be Heard Today? 41

PART II: *Taking Matthew 25 Public Today*

5. Prophets Can Turn New Religious Movements into Church-Wide Reformation 69
6. Focusing Matthew 25 on the Kindling of the *Church Gathered* 82
7. Focusing Matthew 25 on the *Church Sent*: Text to Context, Word to World, Gospel to Social Gospel, *Christian* Social Gospel to *Societal* New Deal 107
8. There and Back Again: A Short Meditation on a Long Pilgrimage 152

Epilogue 159
Bibliography 171

Preface: Matthew 25 Could Be a New Religious Movement

IN THE ACCOUNT FROM 2 Kings 22–23, King Josiah is ruling the southern kingdom of Judah in the seventh century BC, as rival gods are gaining Israel's political allegiance and Israel is ripe for national reform. The diagnosis is they have lost touch with their origin stories. The exodus, like covenantal justice, has become a discarded image. Meanwhile, the Temple of Solomon is due for repair as part of national renewal. In a back room where sacred relics of the past had been stored, there is a remarkable discovery. The high priest exclaims that he has found the book of the law in the house of the Lord (probably the book of Deuteronomy). When it is read aloud to the king, he tears his clothes, repents, calls for it to be read aloud to the people, demands a national reformation, a rebuke of the present national course, and repeat performances of God's ancient covenant.

Imagine that today spiritual leaders come upon Jesus' inaugural address in Luke's account of his first visit to the synagogue in Nazareth. It is a breathtaking, change-making historical Jesus story. He opens the book of the prophet Isaiah and reads: "The Spirit of the Lord is upon me, because he has anointed me to bring good news to the poor. He has sent me to proclaim release to the captives and recovery of sight to the blind, to let the oppressed go free, to proclaim the year of the Lord's favor." Then Jesus closes the book and challenges his audience to see what is happening. "This is coming true today," Jesus says.

Imagine, again, that spiritual seekers today come upon Jesus' astonishing story in Matthew 25 about all the world gathered at the end of the age before Christ as judge. The final test is whether people have been able to see the crucified and risen Christ present "in the least of these"—the hungry, the homeless, the stranger, the naked, the sick, the imprisoned.

How the world responded to these is how they have seen and grasped and responded to Christ and his kingdom.

Today's religious movers could become convicted and then converted and then commissioned by this story that Matthew places in Holy Week, as Jesus is on the way to resurrection and elevation as king by way of the cross. Soon others will overhear these astonishing wake-up stories and run with them.

Religious movers often turn into religious movements, which leave permanent legacies in the life of the church and occasion new reformations. It keeps happening down through Christian history. Is a *Matthew 25 Christianity afoot*?

The history of Christianity can be seen as a succession of new religious movements that grew up periodically and carried Christian theology and practice forward to new solutions to the crises and opportunities of new days. Something similar has happened across many world religions, for example Buddhism. Historians argue whether it was great individuals or unique circumstances that fomented radical change, and the easy solution is to say it was a combination of both—heroic individuals interacting with ripe times. But the times are often more perilous than promising, and so determined movers and shakers and prophets and sometimes martyrs are required. Farsighted seers are grasped by compelling biblical *texts*, and then carry them forward into new *contexts*.

Consider how it happens. Spiritual seekers ransacking Christian traditions are struck with new understandings of the gospel as the solution to their religious angst, and meanwhile solve sometimes the problems of their age as well. Perhaps the Protestant Reformation was in some ways an accident of Luther's rediscovery, in a monastic cell, of St. Paul's gospel of grace and its centrality to the New Testament and the early Christian movement. After resolving his own spiritual dilemma about meriting divine acceptance, Luther "took it public" and turned Christendom around.

Over time, farsighted Christians have turned their own deep religious experiences into a mandate to take up Jesus' last words in Matthew, "Go into all nations and preach the gospel to all people." Coincidentally, they also recognized in Matthew a manual for obedient and costly discipleship and took it as their own religious map—from information to formation. The stories of such Christians have produced a vast literature on "missionary Christianity" and occasioned over time the new field of missiology.

PREFACE: MATTHEW 25 COULD BE A NEW RELIGIOUS MOVEMENT

In the 1970s I wrote my dissertation on the emerging Jesus Movement in the San Francisco Bay area, and I tracked their subsequent life course. Newly emerged from hippie culture on the beaches, Jesus Movement activists felt called to turn their own radical religious conversion amidst new social and cultural circumstances into a legacy that changed the face of West Coast evangelicalism, by bringing new blood into a Christianity in need of cultural transfusion and new religious vision. And not just guitars! The sociological literature on religious movements traces how, across all world religions, new movements rise up in opportune moments and change the course of religious traditions, equipping them for radical change as a new and necessary environmental response. This is the *new religious movement model, from movers to movements,* for understanding, magnifying, and institutionalizing Jesus' mandate in Matthew 25 to see and find him and to grasp the presence of the kingdom of God "in the least of these"—altogether creating a new kind of human community on earth. "Thy kingdom come" is the continuing reminder sedimented into the life of the church. (We are still waiting for the rediscovery in American Christianity that the juxtaposition of "give us our daily bread" and "forgive us our debts" evoke *bread and debt relief* as the most ancient dilemmas of the poor.)

In all this one may glimpse what has come to be called a *hermeneutical circle*, in which the discovery of a revolutionary text becomes the rediscovery of self, and then bounces off a larger context. Self-confident probers of a biblical text discover the text probing them. New relationships emerge between reader, text, and context. A seeker comes across a text in a moment of discovery, and then is discovered and uncovered by that text. The discoverer does not remain in charge of the text by holding it at a distance. There is a circularity of understanding, from text to context to self and back again. Meanwhile, it needs to be said today amidst the moral failings and privileges of contemporary Christianity, the church must "out" its complicities in life-changing acts of repentance before the newly discovered gospel is preached to the neighbors.

Near the end of the Gospel of Matthew, in the context of what Christianity came to call "Holy Week," Jesus tells a remarkable story. It is judgment day. All of humanity is lined up to pass muster, to give evidence of authentic faith, to pass the test of true discipleship, to determine whether they have truly met the challenge of seeing Jesus whenever and wherever he appeared—not conveniently postponed to the end of time to avoid disturbing the present. Jesus points them to the homeless who needed to be housed, the hungry who needed to be fed, the thirsty who needed a drink, the imprisoned who needed to be visited, the sick who needed to be healed—as dates with the *parousia,* the always coming arrival of the Son of Man. Then the test question: Did you see Jesus himself in all "the least of these"? Or did you pass on by? Did you fail to notice God on the road to Jericho? Did you not have eyes for God's moves? Did Christ's appearances go unnoticed? Judgment falls upon all those who lacked vision or will to see the presence of the kingdom of God on earth, a kingdom ruled by the one who went to the cross on the way to resurrection and then exaltation. Do Christians see that *the reign of God takes up social space* and respond accordingly? Today there are signs that this biblical text from Matthew is being rediscovered. And it is occasioning self-reflection and repentance and conversion across church, society, and country. Will Matthew be magnified by new religious movements for social justice? Will determined and transformed investors carry Matthew 25 into government and society as an "initial public offering"? Or will signs outside church buildings regretfully confess, "Nothing to see here"?

To get into the practice of eschatological expectation, consider now the rich history of Christian movers who turned their personal transformations into new Christian movements, who richly implanted the gospel on Christian soil and often went on to plant it in fields beyond churchly precincts. The patron saint of "initial public offerings" as a dimension of a new religious movement that takes off is the apostle Paul, who understood his religious conversion as turning him into an instrument of the God of Israel, now "going public" across the world and opening Paul's vision and missionary activity to the eschatological harvest of the Gentiles, far beyond the secluded precincts of Judaism. Christ's death and resurrection became God's instrument for reconciling with the world. Paul's theology and missionary drive became the most famous, and defining, initial public offering in the history of Christianity—fulfilling the dreams of Old Testament prophets in which God offers a universalizing divine covenant and "friends" the entire world—a Facebook dream.

Paul's conversion story is iconic. St. Paul was a devout Jew engaged in persecuting the new Christian movement that had emerged through Jesus Christ beyond Second Temple Judaism. Paul's supernatural and revelatory "conversion" happened on the defining *road to Damascus,* on which Paul was traveling as commissioned by the high priest in Jerusalem to take Christians prisoner and return them to Jerusalem for interrogation and possible execution. Paul's mission was interrupted and redirected as the risen and ascended Christ thunderously called Paul by name from heaven, knocked him to the ground, rendered him temporarily mute, claimed him as his own, and sent him on a new mission across the Gentile world.

Paul saw Jesus as Lord (*kyrios*), the true Messiah and Son of God promised beforehand through the prophets of the Old Testament and now embodying God's new covenant with all of humanity. Christ as Lord of all was being recognized in the earliest Christian confession, *kyrios christos*. New Christian believers would become one with Christ's death and resurrection by their baptism. By grace through faith the new Christians would live their new religious life in emerging communities as the new colonies of heaven. As the missionary founder of such communities, Paul was chosen to take the message of this all-encompassing grace through the crucified and risen Christ public, reaping an *eschatological harvest* across the Roman world.

Paul came to see that the grace of God revealed in the death and resurrection of Christ had turned his life around and moved him beyond the boundaries of Judaism to God's mission to the world. In the Wall Street metaphor I have proposed as a way of seeing what was happening, Paul turned God's personal investment in his call to Paul into Paul's "initial public offering" (IPO) of the new Christianity to the Roman world—generating ever new religious capital along the way. An individual investor newly converted deliberately seeks the input of many additional investors and the accumulation of sufficient capital for a worldwide effort. Paul's New Testament letters are the evidence for the new communities he left in his wake.

Nearly four hundred years later, following a series of daring thinkers in Christianity's fertile patristic period, St. Augustine emerged to voice Christianity's future in the midst of challenging times. The sack of Rome in 410 by the Visigoths, warring Germanic tribes, represented the first time in eight hundred years that the "eternal city" of Rome had fallen to a foreign power. Christianity was blamed by the civic intelligentsia for fatally weakening the empire. Having been converted and given his life to Christ after his personal investment in Pauline Christianity, Augustine, with ever increasing stature as an early church father, proclaimed Christianity as the solution to, not the cause of, a civilizational crisis. His legacy was the development of Western philosophy and Christian theology. St. Jerome said Augustine "established anew the ancient faith." As the Western Roman Empire began to disintegrate and with the future of Christianity in doubt, Augustine imagined the church as a spiritual City of God, distinct from the material Earthly City that Rome had been. While defending the church, he proposed a theology of history and a project of civilizational meaning by proposing that true meaning and an authentic future are achieved by the object of a community's love, a directed love that creates ultimate meaning and institutionalizes it in the Christian community in the course of earthly life. Augustine's teachings on salvation and grace became permanent deposits in the treasury of medieval and reformation Christianity. His personal religious investment in crucial Christian texts turned into a "public offering" fit for the establishment of a European Christian civilization.

No one solution is permanent because the times change and "new occasions teach new duties." In the sixth century St. Benedict feared that the essential uniqueness of Christianity and the treasure of the church was in danger of dissolution in challenging times. How to retrieve the essence of the faith and develop institutional means of preserving it? What became Western monasticism was Benedict's solution, from mover to movement. What he treasured personally became what he was able to institutionalize and pass on. His personal investment became his public legacy. (Curiously, the best-selling contemporary book *The Benedict Option* was written by an extreme neoconservative who sought to save Christianity from homosexuality and abortion by admitting it had lost the culture wars and responding by retreating and regrouping the Christian movement for the challenges of a new age.)

At the turn of the thirteenth century, St. Francis of Assisi inaugurated one of many monastic renewals that serially arose as reform movements across the Middle Ages, through which monasticism continuously reformed and replenished itself—and Christianity. Francis founded the Franciscan order of itinerant monks, from which also emerged the Poor Clares order for women, and which left behind a distinct and revolutionary legacy of valorizing and caring for the poor as a spiritual practice. Francis identified with the poor, the hungry, the sick, and with nature itself, as in "brother sun, sister moon." He epitomized the "corporal works of mercy" that Jesus had evoked in Matthew 25, such as feeding the hungry, clothing the naked, visiting the sick and imprisoned. He popularized nativity scenes, often in unexpected locations, as a way of bringing Christ and the Holy Family down to earth again, to villages, to countrysides. In effect, Francis taught artists and commoners and the church itself *how to see, and what to see*, and left a compelling Franciscan material culture as a mark of the church. It is said that he "saw sacramentally," clothing creation with incarnation. The mover Francis became the movement Franciscans. His spiritual attentiveness and identification with Christ brought the stigmata of the humble and suffering Christ onto his own body. The Franciscan legacy still lives eight hundred years later, as in the present Pope Francis.

In the sixteenth century, Martin Luther's rediscovery and personal investment in the theology of St. Paul and his subsequent resolve to "take it public" became so radical and far-reaching that it needed to be called the Protestant Reformation. The mover Luther became the Reformation movement. Luther believed what was good for his own faith and religious life would be good for Christendom—both church and society. Luther had his eye on himself and the monastery and the church, initially, but already by 1520 turned his attention to society and the public realm, as evidenced in his compelling tract "Address to the Christian Nobility of the German Nation." Luther did not imagine the church to be the state, or vice versa, but called Christians in both realms to divine accountability for the social welfare of the world. He envisioned the presence of God both in the church and the world and he called for a "priesthood of all believers" to be active in both "kingdoms." Later in this book I will use this move of Luther to justify both a churchly "social gospel" and a worldly "new deal" with many suggestions for mandates of Matthew 25 today.

Luther offered shares of his private and radicalized monastic spirituality as a public option for an age in crisis. His "initial public offering" (IPO) required the largest accumulation of shareholders via the printing press and the greatest output of pamphlets and books that Europe had ever seen, including a translation of the text of the Bible into German so foundational that it transformed German language and culture. He made God speak German, as missionaries to all indigenous cultures today labor endlessly to help people hear God speaking with their own voice. He took the New Testament gospel public and planted it in German culture and society, as documented in the book *Brand Luther: How an Unheralded Monk Turned His Small Town into a Center of Publishing, Made Himself the Most Famous Man in Europe—and Started the Protestant Reformation.* The Protestant Reformation depended on "Brand Luther" and the manipulation of the printing press for the largest and most saturating public offering ever achieved. Or possible. Massive capital investment followed. The artists Lucas Cranach and Albrecht Durer provided compelling images to illustrate Lutheran theology and spirituality and catch the attention of the public.

All in all, Luther did more for printing campaigns as a means for taking religious reform public than the printing press did for him. He also single-handedly returned the letters and theology of St. Paul to a primacy they had not seen since the days of early Christianity. He marketed Paul as what late medieval and early Renaissance Christianity most needed. Luther wrote: "I beat importunately upon Paul at that place, most ardently desiring to know what St. Paul wanted. At last, by the mercy of God, meditating day and night, I gave heed to the context of the words in Romans. There I began to understand the righteousness of God is that by which the righteous lives by a gift of God, namely by faith." (It tickled us Lutheran prep school boys to imagine that Luther's religious breakthrough may have coincided with the unlocking of his bowels after a grievous period of constipation.) While Luther's legacy is chiefly about *what* he discovered, modern Christians could benefit from considering *how* he discovered it. He beat on the texts, he shook them until they yielded their message for his own transformation. Justification by grace through faith mediated by Scripture became the essence of Protestant Christianity. Perhaps Luther also implied that what was good for him in the monastery and in the pulpit was just what Christianity needed as the times were changing at the end of the Middle Ages. As we know from the ways of Wall Street five hundred years later, the enthusiastic and shrewd issuance of public shares allows private investors to raise capital from public investors and achieve a widespread buy-in. The Protestant Reformation was an early model of a massively successful IPO. To allude in passing to social and economic effects of religious movements to this day, consider the social democracies of Germany and Scandinavia, whose moral outreach to the good of an entire social democratic system far exceeds that of American (individualistic) capitalism.

But perhaps Luther did not completely resolve the religious crisis of every age for all time? In the eighteenth century John Wesley inaugurated yet another new religious movement, Methodism, which brought what he saw as the shortfall of Lutheran *justification* to completion in Wesleyan *sanctification*. While the seven "corporal works of mercy" had established themselves as vital "marks of the church" in medieval Catholicism and left behind a material culture built on Jesus' story in Matthew 25, in which these good works are done as if to Jesus himself, it was Wesley who created an entire Protestant theology to undergird the admonitions of

Matthew 25. Luther had made preaching the gospel and administering the sacraments the two essential "marks of the church." Wesley added the sanctified life envisioned in Jesus' story about seeing and finding him "in the least of these." Corporal works of mercy, too, would become "marks of the church."

It is said that Wesley, an ordained pastor and preacher, took Anglicanism outdoors. As we have seen of many founders of new religious movements, they grew outward from a powerful personal religious experience or conversion. In Wesley's case, he found his heart "strangely warmed" while listening to a devotional reading of Martin Luther's preface to his commentary on St. Paul's Letter to the Romans. Wesley's revival movement followed his own conversion. At his death he was "the best loved man in England." His legacy began to be called the "Wesleyan Manifesto," a kind of midrash on the "works of mercy" Jesus evokes in his last judgment story.

Before concluding with Bonhoeffer and King, let us pause to look back at illustrious women self-ordained for change. Alongside St. Francis in the thirteenth century, Poor Clare of Assisi created orders of nuns in the Franciscan movement, whose monasteries left a unique imprint on Catholic Christianity. In a new book on Clare, Margaret Carney draws special attention to Clare's significant contribution to the Franciscan world in the many years following Francis's death. Far from merely reflecting Francis's light, Clare had her own charism, "a gift bestowed by the Spirit of the Lord and given to her in a fullness and forcefulness that was hers alone." A century before, Hildegard of Bingen saw visions, turned them into musical composition as well as means of intimidating male superiors, moved her monastery to escape male domination, and received special authorization for theological discourse on her own. The Catholic Church only caught up with her in 2010, when she was canonized. There are more surviving chants by Hildegard than by any other composer from the entire Middle Ages, and she is one of the few known composers to have written both the music and the words. In the twentieth century Mother Teresa took Matthew 25 more seriously than almost anyone, and her preoccupation was with "the poorest of the poor." The order she founded consists of five thousand sisters from all over the world, who oversee homes for people who are dying, as well as soup kitchens, mobile clinics, counseling programs, orphanages, and schools. At the same time, Dorothy Day, a lay woman out and then in with Catholicism, epitomized the Catholic Worker Movement and insisted that Christians be in direct contact with the poor, and established shelters, in which she herself also lived, for the homeless. All these women slowly changed the church's mind about what could be expected of women.

On the grand stage, as the Nazi era was on the verge of provoking World War II, a German Lutheran pastor and theologian, Dietrich Bonhoeffer, emerged as one of the leaders of new religious movements that arose to meet the crisis of their age. At the beginning of Hitler's reign, in 1933, the Pastors' Emergency League (*Pfarrernotbund*) arose to unite the clergy against the anti-Jewish "Aryan paragraph" proposed by the Nazi regime as the official position and practice of all German Protestant churches. Against the self-designated "German Christians" (*deutsche Christen*) who proposed a nationalist-aggrandizing theology of German people/German blood/German fatherland, the 1934 Barmen Declaration drew a line in the sand between Christianity and an idolatrous nationalism and insisted only the Bible (certainly not Hitler's ravings) could be a source of new revelation. A year later this Christian resistance movement evolved into the Confessing Church (*bekennende Kirche*), which proposed that perilous times must become for Christianity a confessional status (*status confessionis*), a make-or-break time that requires an explicit confessional declaration of what is at stake for the church and the gospel in that moment. Even today it is typically Lutheran to inquire, when facing "Bonhoeffer moments," "How is the gospel at stake here?" (Ordaining women clergy or blessing gay unions would *not* be examples of the gospel being at stake, except in the very conservative Lutheran Church–Missouri Synod.)

Since those times, some have coined the term *Bonhoeffer moment* to describe times that demand a new statement of Christian theology and principles that are antithetical to the dominant political and cultural norms of the day. A martyred mover became a compelling call for churchly movement. A Bonhoeffer moment emerges when the demands of obedience to Jesus have been accommodated and adjusted and dressed down to the requirements of current society and politics. A Bonhoeffer moment arises when the ravings of a dictator like Hitler must be rejected in the name of an unmistakable New Testament gospel. During and after the presidency of Donald Trump some neoevangelicals and many mainstream Protestants and Catholics called for a far-reaching and vigorous response to the attempts by Trump to commandeer the Christian Right (functioning like the German Christians under Hitler) for his own purposes. Or for the attempt of the Christian Right to attach Trump to their own causes, as when a billboard in Texas astonishingly pictured Trump's image alongside the hallowed incarnational words from the Gospel of John, "The Word became flesh and dwelt among us." Only the recognition of a Bonhoeffer moment, which has not yet come for the majority of evangelicals, would be adequate to take on a new religious nationalism in which Trump was functioning as the golden calf. A common Facebook trope making internet rounds in 2021 reads: "The magnification of Trump by American evangelicals will haunt Christianity for generations."

Bonhoeffer had become deeply immersed in the Gospel of Matthew, and out of that personal encounter and investment came his famous book *The Cost of Discipleship*. The book was first published in 1937, coinciding with the triumph of Nazism in Germany. It was against this background that Bonhoeffer's theology of costly discipleship developed, which ultimately led to his martyrdom. Bonhoeffer famously contrasted "cheap grace" with "costly grace." *Cheap grace* is the preaching of forgiveness without requiring repentance, baptism without church discipline, communion without confession, grace without discipleship, without the cross, without Jesus Christ, living and incarnate. *Costly grace* confronts us as a gracious call to follow Jesus, it comes as a word of forgiveness to the broken spirit and the contrite heart. It is costly because it compels a person to submit to the yoke of Christ and follow him; it is grace because Jesus says: "My yoke is easy and my burden is light."

Incidentally, Bonhoeffer had intended to travel to India to study under Gandhi, but felt called by God to remain in Germany for the crisis at hand. Martin Luther King was also deeply influenced by the Gandhian strategy of nonviolent resistance and civil disobedience. This coincidence between Bonhoeffer and King suggests to me that a revolutionary embrace of Matthew 25 and the social gospel it implies may also call for strategies borrowed from the world or from other religions.

In the middle of the twentieth century there emerged what some have called a "second black social gospel," a successor to the reconstruction movement that followed, all too briefly, the Civil War and that some see as an earlier black social gospel movement. Although the civil rights movement that began in the 1960s was not exclusively a "new *religious* movement," Rev. Dr. Martin Luther King Jr., icon of the black church, in the years from 1955 until his assassination in 1968, made its origins in black Christianity unmistakable. King became the ultimate story in our time of a great mover evolving into a great movement. The Jesus of the New Testament, with whom King was intimately related and who was the beating heart of the black church, became the driving force of King's movement for civil rights, with nonviolent resistance and civil disobedience, derived especially from Mahatma Gandhi but congruent with Jesus' own ministry, as its strategy for effecting social change. King's personal investment grew from the socially located investment of the black religious experience. While the black church had mostly been marginalized and indeed isolated from white Christianity, King almost single-handedly *took it public* and made it visible nightly for several years on the evening news that white people watched and could not avoid. With remarkable savvy, King turned his movement into an *initial public offering*. One could say he became a master at attracting wide Christian and then also secular investors who found his message compelling and the draw of his movement irresistible. The Southern Christian Leadership Conference achieved a unique moral authority across the country. The popular crusades of the white evangelist Billy Graham were an early influence.

King helped organize the 1963 March on Washington, where he delivered his famous seventeen-minute "I Have a Dream" speech on the steps of the Lincoln Memorial. He imagined what it would take to *bring together a Christian social gospel and social justice in an American democracy.* King welded his own religious inspiration to the political dreams of the founding fathers when he intoned, "It is a dream deeply rooted in the American dream. I have a dream that one day this nation will rise up and live out the true meaning of its creed: 'We hold these truths to be self-evident: that all men are created equal.' I have a dream that one day on the red hills of Georgia the sons of former slaves and the sons of former slave owners will be able to sit down together at the table of brotherhood. I have a dream that one day even the state of Mississippi, a state sweltering with the heat of injustice, sweltering with the heat of oppression, will be transformed into an oasis of freedom and justice. I have a dream that my four little children will one day live in a nation where they will not be judged by the color of their skin but by the content of their character. I have a dream today. I have a dream that one day, down in Alabama, with its vicious racists, with its governor having his lips dripping with the words of interposition and nullification; one day right there in Alabama, little black boys and black girls will be able to join hands with little white boys and white girls as sisters and brothers. I have a dream today." This is thought to be one of the finest *public* speeches in American oratory. In 1964 King won the Nobel Peace Prize for combating racial inequality through nonviolent resistance. And for a compelling moral call to all investors. Very importantly, he brought together Christian theological moral aspirations with the political aspirations drawn from natural law by the founding fathers. It is this collaboration that drives the later argument of this book.

King's religious and societal vision kept expanding. Against the advice of many, he eventually found it necessary to make the connection between poverty and civil rights and capitalism and American colonialism. *He connected the Christian social gospel to a new deal for society.* And so on April 4, 1967, in a famous appearance at New York City's Riverside Church, King delivered a speech titled "Beyond Vietnam: A Time to Break Silence." He spoke strongly against the US role in the war, arguing that the US was in Vietnam "to occupy it as an American colony" and, as if he were John the Baptist redivivus, calling the US government "the greatest purveyor of violence in the world today." He connected the war with economic injustice, arguing that the country needed serious moral change: "A true revolution of values will soon look uneasily on the glaring contrast of poverty and wealth. With righteous indignation, it will look across the seas and see individual capitalists of the West investing huge sums of money in Asia, Africa and South America, only to take the profits out with no concern for the social betterment of the countries, and say: 'This is not just.'"

In 1968, King and the Southern Christian Leadership Conference organized the "Poor People's Campaign"—a trope that continues to this day—to address the Matthew 25 implications for issues of economic justice across the land. King traveled the country to assemble "a multiracial army of the poor" that would march on Washington to engage in nonviolent civil disobedience at the Capitol until Congress created an "economic bill of rights" for poor Americans. (Imagine the contemporary recovery of a Christian social gospel morphing into a New Deal in American society and culture, a subject this book invokes.) King was planning a national occupation of Washington, DC when he was assassinated in Memphis, where he had gone to lead a strike on behalf of garbage workers.

A day before his death, King delivered his "I've Been to the Mountaintop" address, anticipating his own death: "And then I got to Memphis. Well, I don't know what will happen now. We've got some difficult days ahead. But it doesn't matter with me now. Because I've been to the mountaintop. Like anybody, I would like to live a long life. I just want to do God's will. And He's allowed me to go up to the mountain. And I've looked over. And I've seen the promised land. I may not get there with you. But I want you to know tonight, that we, as a people, will get to the promised land. So I'm happy, tonight. I'm not worried about anything. I'm not fearing any man. Mine eyes have seen the glory of the coming of the Lord."

A few months before his death, King was speaking at his own Ebenezer Baptist Church about how he wished to be remembered after his death: "I'd like somebody to mention that day that Martin Luther King Jr. tried to give his life serving others. I'd like for somebody to say that day that Martin Luther King Jr. tried to love somebody. I want you to say that day that I tried to be right on the war question." Unmistakably echoing Jesus' words in Matthew 25, King went on: "I want you to be able to say that day that I did try to *feed the hungry*. I want you to be able to say that day that I did try in my life to *clothe those who were naked*. I want you to say on that day that I did try in my life to *visit those who were in prison*. And I want you to say that I tried to *love and serve humanity*." As do many today, he was expanding the "corporal works of mercy" in Matthew 25 to a larger vision of social justice: "Say that I was a drum major for justice. Say that I was a drum major for peace. I was a drum major for righteousness. But I just want to leave a committed life behind."

In the life of Martin Luther King, Matthew 25 began to come true. The "history of its effects" (a contemporary scholarly discipline) reached a new climax. King became the first "Matthew 25 Christian" in a movement that began to take off in the twenty-first century. And how do Matthew 25 saints fare? FBI director J. Edgar Hoover considered King a social radical and made him an object of continuing FBI investigation and spying from 1963 on—for possible communist ties. And he was assassinated. *Alas, King was made a martyr before he could achieve his dream of a social gospel tied to a social justice democracy. Alas, we are still very far from having arrived there, from Matthew coming true.*

Martin Luther King Jr. Day was established as a holiday in cities and states throughout the United States beginning in 1971. President Reagan made it a national holiday in 1986. The Martin Luther King Jr. Memorial on the National Mall in Washington, DC was dedicated in 2011. In a memorial stained glass window alluding to the Birmingham bombing, a crucified figure of a black Christ is depicted, his left hand raised in protest and his right in reconciliation. The inscription reads: "You do it to me," alluding to Christ's words in Matthew 25, "What you do to the least of these, you do to me." In this remarkable reversal of its usual meaning (works done for the poor are done for Christ), the killing of Martin Luther King and of four little black girls in Birmingham are seen as at one with the crucifixion of Christ. King wanted it to be remembered that he had died not grandly but for garbage collectors, the least of these.

With Bonhoeffer and King most recently still in mind, Matthew 25 Christians aspire to become a movement that could evoke "a pastors' emergency league" to respond to the crises of the time, a Christianity in a Bonhoeffer moment that requires unmistakable confession of what the Gospel requires. In his famous "Letter from a Birmingham Jail," King responded to a small group of local clergy who advised him that his nonviolent protest movement was unwise and untimely and condemned outsiders from the North who had come down to identify with the protestors. The critical clergy purported to be sensible Christians of good will who cautioned against extreme responses to white supremacy and economic injustice. (Today such sensible Christians are now the conservative Christian Right, dedicated to opposing social structural change in the country.) King insisted he was in Birmingham because injustice was in Birmingham. (Bonhoeffer returned to Germany from sojourns in New York and London because that's where he felt the call of God.) King was profoundly disappointed in white Christian moderates who insisted on going slow and ignoring the crisis of the age, who saw no emergency, who did not rise up in the confession the moment required. Where today is the Christianity that on occasions through the ages was boldly transformative and unaccommodating? Where is the church acting conspicuously as a nonconforming resistance movement? Christianity has never been called to be a theology of the status quo. That is the illusion of the once-born. As we have seen, Paul and Augustine and Benedict and Francis and Luther and Wesley turned their personal callings and investments into public movements that offered a reforming Christianity to their times. In responding to their own spiritual crisis, they helped resolve the crises of their ages.

This preface has discussed how religious change can happen, and has happened, as great movers evolve into significant movements that change the church, and even become "public offerings" to the world. Two metaphors help consider the question in the present, *whether it can happen again,* whether we might be looking at a new stage in the "history of Matthew's effects." The first is whether we are looking at the emergence of a new religious movement, with a new social gospel. We have seen what religious movements look like and how they emerged. What does it take for a new religious movement to magnify and institutionalize and leave behind fundamentally new approaches to the Christian message and practice that meet the challenges of the day, that turn ancient texts to new contexts, and change the course of the church for decades or centuries?

But I've also alluded to another way of seeing and accounting for religious change, for magnifying Matthew, and that one carries a church-ly social gospel beyond religious precincts into a New Deal for society, government, and economic systems. European social democracies have typically grown under Christian influence, as reflected in the German political parties, "Christian Democratic Union" (CDU) and "Christian Social Union" (CSU). Did they imagine concern for the least of these as a new form of social democracy? In recent decades there have arisen movements championing "socially responsible investments," which pioneered opportunities to benefit the environment or public health or worldwide poverty and were determined to go public with such callings as a way of attracting wider shareholder investment. The pitch was that investors could feel gratified morally as well as financially. So, religious and spiritual readers may be surprised to see me borrowing a Wall Street metaphor for individual investors attempting to attract new capital for their enterprises by imaginatively sponsoring "initial public offerings" (IPO) that become famously successful and achieve a widespread buy-in.

I propose this second metaphor, in addition to the trope of "new religious movements," as a way of understanding opportune moments for religious change that move from religion to social systems, from compelling texts to larger contexts. And that could involve both religion and society in creating nurturing communities that overcome the polarizations and moral deficits of the age. An unexpected contemporary conclusion is that today's progressive Left needs from religion the insistent modeling of a new kind of community that overcomes widespread polarization through a common social-capital-rich humanity, and a utopian vision that carries them beyond the imagination of can't-do-much-better late capitalism. Religion ambitious for social justice will practice collaboration with the academy and politicians and critical economists to institutionalize a great vision in social-political-economic systems rooted in natural law or historic Christianity.

This other illuminating metaphor, admittedly a strange bedfellow from Wall Street amidst the disciplines of theology and church history, is that of seeing a startling new investor appeal to an initial public offering, for taking the social gospel public. This second heuristic model is of private actors deeply immersed in objects of their investment who then determine to draw attention and commitment and new public investments that multiply social capital. Their strategy is to *take it public through an "initial public offering."* Who will broker Matthew 25 today? Who will take public Jesus' demands to come to the needs of the least of these—as to him? Who will make "corporal works of mercy" an indispensable sign of the church, of authentic Christianity? Who will turn the gospel into a social gospel in the church, and beyond the church turn a social gospel into a new deal for a social democracy?

The concern for the poor and the downtrodden, deeply embedded in God's own passions in the Old and New Testaments, has, on-again off-again, clothed the entire history of Christianity. Especially remarkable, and binding, are the red-letter lines from Jesus himself, whose inaugural sermon aims at *good news to the poor,* a message congruent with the Old Testament prophets and the covenant theology they kept fighting to renew. The specificities and name-calling of the prophetic vision make the most enthusiastic leftist vision of today seem anemic and bland. In an age when capitalism, even at its most benign, tramples on the poor and takes no notice of the underdog, and when progressive leftists falter for lack of imagination beyond the givens of capitalism and the polarization of society, the times demand both a religiously based vision and also a Christianity that fraternizes and aligns with the academy, with political visionaries, with visionary economic critics. (It would be visionary not to become utopian but just to get back to Eisenhower's platform.) The imagination of Matthew 25 must evoke a great arraignment of forces. Religion has something to teach the progressive Left about the crisis of civic belonging that goes beyond renewing capitalism. It is precisely this crisis that the Far Right answers with militant nationalism or white resentment. Religion strives to turn hostile strangers into families, into communities rich with moral capital. It joins radical inclusion with socialized goods.

So the book before you, as outlined in the Introduction, is a strategy for how it could happen, in view of how it has happened. How could new movers and new movements turn into a permanent shift in the whole church? How could Matthew become a manual for embedding a social gospel in the life of the church and then taking it public and achieving a public audience and public alignments and public, as well as churchly, capital.

The Introduction imagines and evokes a wide-ranging collaboration of religion and the public sector for the good of all. Of course, this will seem utopian, and many will denounce it as cultural Marxism, even a betrayal of Christianity, so a theology of hope and eschatological vision must be evoked as well. If utopia is the name for a vision of the kingdom of God, abundantly beckoned across the world in the Lord's Prayer, so be it. This sweep, from new religious movements retrieving biblical texts and implanting them in new contexts to committed investors taking religious stock public, could be the entirely new approach the age requires. This book proposes to be a strategy for making the possible probable, a field guide for carrying Matthew 25 to new completions, coming true in a new present, while resolving the crisis of an age.

But this book is not just a call for a Matthew 25 movement to emerge. *In fact, a distinctive Matthew 25 movement is already underway.* Over fifty years ago, as a product of the Jesus Movement and neoevangelical Anabaptism, Jim Wallis founded the Sojourners community and a magazine by that name. Wallis called Matthew 25 his "conversion story" and Sojourners hosts a Matthew 25 pledge to care for the least of these.

The leading international relief organization World Vision invites followers to a "Matthew 25 Challenge." Similarly, Matthew 25 Ministries is an international humanitarian aid and disaster relief organization, based in Ohio.

Of all Protestant denominations, the Presbyterian Church (USA) has led the way in adopting a Matthew 25 designation for all its social justice ministries. It invites its congregations to become "Matthew 25 churches." Meanwhile, the Southwest Synod of the Evangelical Lutheran Church in America calls its congregations to join a Matthew 25 movement. Likewise, an advocacy movement in Southern California concerned with immigrant issues calls itself a Matthew 25 movement. And the Poor People's Campaign led by Rev. William Barber marches under the Matthew 25 banner.

Other examples could be added. But perhaps the most important matter is seeing the present situation of gross inequality in America, driven by deregulated capitalism and characterized by gross neglect of the poor, as a kind of "Bonhoeffer moment" that calls for a confessing church to arise and embody an activist social gospel movement responding to these perilous times.

Introduction:
A Field Guide for Taking Matthew 25 Public

THIS BOOK POSES THE question, could Matthew 25 come true in our times? It proposes to be a *field guide* for a contemporary Christianity facing a Bonhoeffer moment in a society perilous for the least of these. The question is whether Christians can "see Christ" amidst the clamor. The book traces the course from Matthew 25 as a *seminal biblical text* into a *contemporary context* by way of new religious movements and prophetic figures. Astute commentators propose that the times call for a new social gospel. How will this come about? I propose taking personal investment in Matthew public, from movers to movements, to the church gathered and then the church sent, ultimately to become an initial public offering that could transition to a New Deal for a social democracy influenced by Christianity. (Not a theocracy.)

In June 2021, Rev. William Barber, a successor to the unfinished mission of Martin Luther King, began driving his continuing but not widely reported Poor People's Campaign toward a mighty climax in Washington in the summer of 2022. Originating in North Carolina, his campaign sees itself as "A National Call for Moral Revival." It calls citizens to become moral witnesses and to practice direct action and to call for a poor people's moral budget. It proposes to speak for the 140 million poor and low-income people in the nation—largely ignored, dismissed, and pushed to the margins of political and social agendas. It means to challenge the lie of scarcity, in the midst of moral abundance. It proposes "Moral Mondays," regular days set aside for lobbying the government. It helped sponsor a House Resolution on the need for a "Third Reconstruction"—building on the failed post-Civil War Reconstruction movement and the mid-twentieth century civil rights and Great Society movements.

While undoubtedly a Christian movement, its most visible efforts are as a progressive political movement, aligning with unions and other civic organizations. As such it may represent less the first focus of this book, individual Christian movers becoming new religious movements, than the second focus on Christian (and humanistic) values becoming public offerings to a just commonwealth.

As Barber's new effort began, President Biden released a two-minute video in close support of campaign goals like a fifteen dollar an hour minimum wage, expansion of health care benefits, protection of voting rights, and the right of workers to unionize. "I don't think we've ever been together at a time of such great opportunity to deliver dignity to our poor and low-wage workers and make ending poverty not just an aspiration, but a theory of change," Biden said in the video. Biden went on to say he and vice president Kamala Harris "will keep working with you and your Poor People's Campaign to answer that clarion moral call." Is this an early sign of renewed times, a new social gospel in the churches inspiring a collaboration that produces a New Deal for society as well? Could religion help effect a transformed community with abundant social capital supplanting the dead end of late capitalism? An unavoidable issue for this book is whether the immiserations and injustices of late capitalism constitute a Bonhoeffer moment to which Christianity must finally speak and for which it must develop social alliances.

The Preface to this book was a kind of history-as-manifesto, a rehearsal of how ancient biblical texts could migrate into new and urgent and perilous contexts, carried by Christian movers and movements. I proposed that modern recoveries of Matthew 25 can be compared to new religious movements that have periodically occurred in the history of Christianity. Unexpectedly, I also appealed to the Wall Street language of an initial public offering (IPO) to suggest how the church's social gospel could attract such a wide array of secular, as well as religious, investors that a churchly vision could attract widespread investment and accumulating social capital so as to migrate into a societal New Deal. How would we know if it's actually happening? How would we predict its success, or failure? How could we cheer it on? How could we join it? How could we become it?

FROM CHURCH GATHERED TO SENT, FROM NEW SOCIAL GOSPEL TO NEW DEAL

In this Introduction, I discuss how to proceed with such questions and what disciplines are required to name it and claim it. I offer a preview of the entire book's approach. Part I is a searching look at the Gospel of Matthew, including Matthew as a discipleship manual for the early church and especially Jesus' remarkable last judgment tale about seeing and finding him "in the least of these." Matthew is a call to see the kingdom of God and measure—and occupy—the social space it claims. A "history of Matthew's effects" considers how over the course of Christian history key biblical passages become founding texts of new religious movements through which they hitch a ride into new contexts and change the church and the world. This requires a grasp of the entire course of the Gospel of Matthew and then an argument that Matthew 25 is not a one-off, marginal to the entire biblical message, but deeply embedded in the entire course of the Old and New Testaments and deeply characteristic of the biblical God who makes a covenant with ancient Israel, and then in New Testament Christianity with the entire world and all of humanity. All along, and not as an outlier, there is God's passionate heart for the poor. Are we seeing, or are we prepared to see, Matthew dramatically *coming true* in our time? But this cannot reduce to a giddy vision for the night of the prom. I close Part I realistically discussing the chances of Matthew getting a hearing in early twenty-first-century American Christianity and culture. Is Matthew speaking such a strange language, such an exotic tongue, that no one today could understand it? Has the contemporary American context rendered itself immune to Matthew's text? Is the modern church also unable to hear it, opposed to heeding it? The "social location" of the churches and the culture is always in view.

In Part II I turn to strategies for taking Matthew public across the church and into society. A groundbreaking and transforming biblical text must be magnified and then embedded and institutionalized in the church first of all, and then possibly in new and often unwelcoming cultural and economic and national contexts. (Think of precisely this repeated process in the lore of Christianity moving northward through Europe in the Middle Ages, one idol after another falling.) New movements take prophets and missionaries who speak to their times and see beyond their times. Will readers of this book audition for such roles? Who will declaim Matthew from public stages in "revivals" of the play?

I take up "Matthew 25 Christians" and social justice Christians generally as new religious movements gradually embedding themselves in the *church gathered*, where through lectionary and liturgy and sermon and study and prayer Christian believers gradually acquire a new shape, a liturgical formation, a new intentionality, a new way of being a Christian community. And then move *from gathered to sent*.

If sufficiently magnified and embraced, could Matthew become a new *canon within the canon*, a new John 3:16 sign held up for all to see at football games? Will "faith formation classes" adopt Matthew as a discipleship manual? Will the newly invested begin to call themselves "Matthew 25 Christians" and even call it their conversion story? In Part II I turn to strategies for taking Matthew public across the church and into society. A groundbreaking and transforming biblical text must be magnified and then embedded and institutionalized in the church first of all, and then possibly in new and often unwelcoming cultural and economic and national contexts. Will "Matthew 25 congregations" and then special Matthew 25 designated ministries and programs and projects follow? (The evangelical relief organization World Vision is already attaching its mission to Matthew 25.)

I move then to the *church sent*—performative liturgy on the move, as in the exodus from Egyptian bondage, out the door and into the world and toward the promised land. Transformed by Matthew, will the church move from Word to world, from gospel to social gospel, even from social gospel to a New Deal for society and country? The church would have to sacramentalize the world as its territory, acknowledging the larger contours of Jesus' kingdom and the social space it occupies. The church would have to become a *nonconforming resistance movement*, but then risk partnering with politics and moving towards social justice as the social form of love.

Out in this new territory the church would have to become prophetic, raising pressing questions about the nature of a capitalist economy, and debt, and workers' unions. But would such a vision survive the test of "Christian realism"? Or is realism a false test that renounces utopian thinking as a way of adjusting the Christian vision down to the status quo?

The church's liturgies would have to become performative. The symbols of the culture, good and bad, would have to become subjects of "liturgical inculturation," brought indoors to the life of the church while it practices its sacramentalizing tasks. All the while the church would come to see that there is *no Christ without a kingdom*, no mission that does not occupy public space. Calvinists like to say that there is no square foot of earth that Christ does not claim. Will a contemporary secular society be conquered or seduced? The church would begin joint ventures with the academy, economic theorists, politics and government—not in search of theocracy but in collaborations for social justice and the common good and a value-laden society. This could lead to a social democracy with a New Deal.

In an epilogue I invoke a collaborative eschatology in which the church meets a descending kingdom of God on the road ahead. And this will require a Matthew 25 altar call. And finally a baptismal recommissioning for the mission ahead.

SOCIAL JUSTICE MOVEMENTS IN PERILOUS TIMES

How should this handbook, this field guide, proceed? A long time ago, in the 1970s, I wrote my dissertation on the Jesus Movement as part of a larger UC Berkeley project studying new religious movements in the San Francisco Bay Area. Our individual projects were exercises in the sociology of religion, as it was being taught and practiced in those days under the tutelage of Robert Bellah and Charles Glock. I adopted the sociological method of "participant observation" and lived alongside this new religious movement for two years. But I was not a disinterested observer. I was also a Christian and a Lutheran minister, hoping the Jesus Movement might thrive and make a significant contribution to the evolution of American Protestantism. I was also a Berkeley leftist, sympathetic with the particular manifestation of the Jesus Movement in Berkeley that tellingly called itself the Christian World Liberation Front. Once we all caravaned across the Bay Bridge from Berkeley to downtown San Francisco to picket Richard Nixon. I was reprimanded by the Secret Service for lack of respectful patriotism. "Get back on the sidewalk."

While analyzing the social location of various burgeoning cells of the Jesus Movement in California and trying to give an account of their origins and aspirations, I was also observing and noting how they might succeed (or fail) and the kinds of things that needed to happen, religious and sociological, if they were to make significant contributions to American Christianity rather than be written off as ephemeral and self-indulgent fads of the moment—hippie Christianity.

As a theologian adopting sociological methods, as so much of historical theology and biblical studies have been doing since the middle of the last century, I have become interested in the interplay of *text and context*. Context alludes both to the religious and social setting of original biblical texts and also to the situations in which they are newly appropriated over time. Modern theology, and especially Christian ethics, has been scrutinizing the social-cultural "locations" of contemporary Christian churches, as well as of new religious movements, attending to such dimensions as class, ethnicity, conservative and liberal, modern and traditionalist, spiritual and rational, believing and belonging. In the current moment, there is also special attention to Eurocentrism. (Lutheran postcolonialists, sometimes known as social justice warriors, recently denounced Lutheran parishes near the Mexican border in Texas for sponsoring annual bratwurst festivals.)

White supremacy, racism, and misogyny have become key variables to monitor. The current term *intersectionality* suggests an analytical framework for understanding how aspects of a person's social and political identities combine to create different modes of discrimination. Or privilege. It evokes multiple variables that lock together in a social construct. American gun culture, for example, is rooted in gender, class, ethnicity, political ideology, and God/religion. A remarkable fact, especially considering that religion is claimed as an undergirding of gun culture, is that this very set of variables also functions to marginalize (not support) "the least of these" and deliberately refuse them recognition.

How do our present social contexts determine or hem what a sacred text can be saying, or what we allow ourselves to hear, or what is particularly compelling? Biblical interpreters have recently urged a "hermeneutic of the poor" or even a "hermeneutic of the hungry" to control for the fact that most Bible studies take place with no poor or hungry people in the room, or anywhere in sight. Students can be trained to imagine the presence of the excluded. Or even invite them in. Their presence could become a necessary tool for interpreting texts that affect them, as well as the Christians who are reading such texts as their own.

As biblical studies and sociological reflection come together, the question arises how the *meanings of texts, arriving from their own original social locations, migrate into new contexts, how biblical texts can found new religious movements and then evolve along with them, and how religious movements, in turn, are carried by and become carriers of ancient texts migrating into new situations.* Where did self-designated "Matthew

25 Christians," or social justice partisans, come from, and where do they see themselves going? Biblical texts can speak to new contexts when the latter are urgently recognized and challenged as "Bonhoeffer moments," perilous times which demand new confessions of biblical truth, including, especially amidst the immiserations of free market capitalist ideology, *good news to the poor*.

In the twelfth century, for example, Francis of Assisi took to heart Christ's injunction to his disciples in Luke 9:3 as he sent them out on missionary journeys: "Take nothing for your journey, no staff, nor bag, nor bread, nor money." And so was born an itinerant monasticism known for its vows of poverty and its devoted presence among the poor. After Francis's death, his challenges to the material wealth of institutional Christianity became so dangerous that his legacy had to be reined in and the radical "spiritual Franciscans" denounced by the papacy. Will the obsession of "Matthew 25 Christianity" with the least of these bring similar challenges to church and society early in the twenty-first century?

In the fourteenth century, John Wycliffe and the English Lollards believed the church should aid people to live a life of evangelical poverty, imitating Jesus Christ. Wycliffe's incessant attacks on an over-endowed church eventually led to his excommunication. After his death, his body was exhumed, burned, and his ashes thrown in a river. *Sola scriptura*, and a proto-Protestant focus on particular biblical texts, can become the basis for a radical critique of churchly traditions, the lever and fulcrum that moves church and culture, as in Lutheran and other Reformation movements.

The sixteenth-century Anabaptists committed themselves to a literal interpretation of Jesus' Sermon on the Mount in Matthew 5–7 and thereafter renounced violence, oath-taking, the use of military force, and even participation in civil government. Their ecclesiology reflected a new religious movement understanding itself to be citizens of the kingdom of God and not of earthly governments. As Stanley Hauerwas, a modern admirer, likes to say, they longed to *become* the New Testament story they were telling, and the texts that shaped them contributed to a new Christian vocabulary and became the new language they spoke. The gospel required and was carried by such a new vocabulary. They would soon be widely persecuted by both Protestants and Catholics. Martin Luther had seized upon Paul's theology of faith alone and grace alone in Galatians and Romans as the answer to his personal religious struggles as a monk.

In his biography *Young Man Luther,* Erik Erikson argued that *in resolving his own existential crisis, Luther also resolved the problems of his age.*

This study will consider how the appropriation of Jesus' last judgment story became normative for the new religious movement calling itself *Matthew 25 Christians* and for all those newly dedicated to social justice. They found in it the answer to their own doubts and need for an authentic Christianity while also offering it as the proper response to the moral crisis of their age, one constituted as a *status confessionis,* a pregnant moment that requires a new statement of what Christians "believe, teach, and confess." They have sought to *magnify and institutionalize* (plant) Matthew 25 into new contexts. In this well-practiced manner, newly appropriated biblical texts can achieve super-canonical status and become a new *canon within the canon,* which is to say they are made to illuminate and interpret all other texts and suggest how the whole Bible should be read and interpreted in their light. Achieving this would mark significant success for the movement. Luther did the same thing with Galatians and Romans.

A biblical text founding a new religious movement is likely to drive that movement into new and perilous contexts in which the problems of an age are confronted and possibly resolved. In the past the contemporary context sometimes fought back, as in the case of the spiritual Franciscans, John Wycliffe and John Hus, and the Anabaptists, and the response was persecution. Today's calls for social justice are ridiculed as cultural Marxism and written off as outdated leftist slogans.

Sometimes a new religious movement defines a *moral crisis the age is unaware of or is determined to deny.* I will raise the question of whether the twenty-first century is even capable of hearing Matthew 25. Ayn Rand's legacy has been to exalt a libertarianism that exults in the disencumbered life and delegitimizes all calls for social responsibility. In considering the Matthew 25 Christians movement that is perhaps so far unnoticed by most and whose outcome cannot certainly be predicted, I note its social location in contemporary American churches and probable reasons for its emergence at this time in American society and political culture. As we examine how trenchant is its theological self-understanding, we may wonder whether it might succeed and even become a turning point in the history of American Christianity, as the social gospel movement at the beginning of the twentieth century became a distinctive contribution to world Christianity. Could this become yet another *Great Awakening,* a repeating occurrence in American religious history? How deeply must newly appropriated and revisioned biblical texts sink into the Christian consciousness of an age before they are *elevated to John 3:16 status* or the grace and justification canon of Paul and Luther?

Discovering what Matthew 25 Christians stand for is not guesswork, nor does it require a sermon from me. (I did not learn to preach such a sermon in Lutheran seminary!) Social justice Christians with an ear for Matthew 25 have discovered in this text their own voice, which speaks to their own context. It is not difficult to overhear what is being said. If you listen to Matthew 25 Christians preach at rallies or heed their manifestos or how they publicly demonstrate on "Moral Mondays," you will experience the recent residue of their understanding and appropriation of Jesus' last judgment story in Matthew 25. After fifty years as the founder of Sojourners, Jim Wallis, who called Matthew 25 his conversion story, is now migrating onto a university faculty to represent to the academy the concern with faith and justice.

But will the vaunted Matthew 25 claims turn out to be a one-off on the edge of biblical proclamation? Or will they reveal themselves to be fully rooted in the exodus and covenant theology at the heart of Old Testament prophetic affirmation, which reappears in Jesus' inaugural sermons and in the radical discipleship enjoined by the New Testament Gospels? "Widows, orphans, and strangers" has been called the holy trinity of Old Testament religion. *God's heart for the poor* permeates the entire Bible. While the "preferential option for the poor" characteristic of Latin American liberation theology had been written off by Christian conservatives (and even by Pope John Paul II) as a Marxian vestige to be resisted and held off from invading the church, Pope Francis, a true Franciscan, now pays attention to the *hundreds of verses* that worry about poverty and proclaim God's special love for the poor. As noted on the dedication page of this book, Francis likes to say that in appointing bishops he looks for shepherds who still have the smell of the sheep about them. Is the neglect of the poor and the hundreds of verses preoccupied with them elbowed aside with seven verses in the whole Bible about homosexuality a clue to the social location and moral obsessions of American Christianity? And how does the denigration of women fly in the face of Mary Magdalene's Easter morning commission to be an "apostle to the apostles"?

So *Matthew 25/social justice Christianity as a new religious movement and its prospects are the occupation and preoccupation of this book.* Which is to say an origin story about how new movers and movements came to take Christianity seriously, and were gripped by it, and made the concern with "the least of these" the cause of their religious life. And how they hope to change American Christianity and its political economy with this message. This is what all the commotion is about.

Matthew 25:31–46 is the story that Jesus tells about final exams on judgment day that all people will face. What will be the proof of the Christian pudding? Does the Greek word *parousia*, which in the Gospels, especially Matthew, connotes "presence, arrival, or official visit" allude to *being prepared to see* and respond to Jesus in unexpected places, to trace his distinctive presence in earthly life and his ultimate triumph and reign over all the earth from the Father's right hand? To see this Jesus, Matthew implies, is to take note of God's true preoccupations. You've heard the story: it is the end of the age and all people are lined up, like sheep and goats, before Jesus as the cosmic judge. A series of questions ensues and judgments are made. Did you see me among them, Jesus as King asks, when there were *homeless to be sheltered, naked to be clothed, hungry to be fed, thirsty to be given a drink, strangers to be welcomed, the imprisoned to be visited*? If you did these things for the least of these, you were serving me. Now you will inherit the kingdom prepared for you since the foundation of the world. If you missed them, however, you missed me, you never saw my presence, and will you ever?

In Luther's language, this is to see and act on a "theology of the cross" that finds Jesus among the least of these while walking the *via dolorosa*. This is not the "theology of glory" that celebrates a *rapture* in which self-satisfied Christians take off to glory ("If I'm raptured, take the wheel," bumper stickers used to admonish) and leave God's world behind. How astonishing if the American church misses the message of Jesus' tale, the new movement admonishes! Yet Matthew scatters warning clues throughout his narrative: Jesus' disciples keep missing the point of his method and mission. But repentance and change of heart and a new ethic are available to those who are graced to see. (Some activists audaciously claim that the poor are a means of grace for Christians learning how to see.)

The significance of this study does not depend solely on whether a new movement called Matthew 25 Christianity really takes off. The question is larger: Is there a new drive by Christians for social justice across the land in times of peril? Is the social gospel the times require now birthing? Have alert Christians been watching and waiting during the church's pregnancy with Matthew? Most tellingly, is American society (and the church) perhaps facing a moral crisis that Matthew 25 could diagnose and resolve? Is this the reason for the discovery and recovery of Matthew's proclamation of the true reign of God? Is it possible that a story about ultimate judgment based on seeing a deliberately unnoticed Christ, on the way to resurrection via the cross, and among the least of these, a clue to what a disengaged capitalist economy or a self-satisfied church see or fail to see on the human landscape?

Consider a small test case. Do American churches want to acknowledge their own social location that keeps them from noticing, at the beginning, the uniqueness of Matthew's "infancy narrative"? There a small refugee family flees from a powerful king and narrowly avoids being sacrificed for the policy of the state and the king's threatened interests. Only in the last ten years do Christmas cards and Facebook postings depict Mary and Joseph and the baby as endangered refugees fleeing along a border. If the church itself is coming to new awakenings, does it want to practice noticing the social location of American economics and culture? And practice "cross-class" readings of biblical texts? How do churches or politicians go about shielding themselves from what they do not want to consider? Do American Christians, defining religion as spiritual individualism, bow to a Christ whose kingdom takes up no social space—indeed, do they worship a "Christ without a kingdom"? Except of course for the appearance of Jesus in the believer's heart. Some wags have remarked that such a Christ gets a cross but no speaking parts. Matthew 25 pales next to sublime reflections on substitutionary atonement.

Matthew has been called a *discipleship manual*. Will it become a gift to the newly baptized and commissioned? It was Matthew that Bonhoeffer was reading when he took upon himself "the cost of discipleship." In today's language, discipleship represents a seriously *encumbered life*. By contrast, we live in a time of a *disencumbered culture* set free from all social responsibilities by a "small government" ideology that excuses us from any preoccupation with social justice and fails to think of the state as a political entity charged with achieving the good of the commonwealth. Fresh college graduates confronted, in their first jobs, with taking a position on the dilemmas of their age may fashionably plead *ironic detachment* as their excuse for the unexamined life. (I once had a student in my Religious Studies class, a business major, who told me he wanted to get all his moral reflection out of the way before graduating.)

In the analysis of Matthew 25 Christians, and of the Christian Left, defense and deliverance from Jesus' judgment story are guaranteed by the Christian Right. They say the Bible makes no claims about social justice, which, in fact, is an outworn leftist slogan. President Trump's MAGA was the golden calf that substitutes for exodus liberation theology. And many evangelicals are still wearing those hats. Indeed, American evangelicals in general, and most conservatives, claim a theological exemption from any use of the word *social*, lest it open the door to cultural Marxism. And so they limit sin mostly to *personal* sex and gender issues. Abortion policy is a *personal ethic* for carefully monitored women that does not occupy itself with the social and economic world in which newborns must flourish. Corporations have "nothing to declare" as they navigate cultural and economic customs or enter the confessional where social responsibilities come up.

An individualist and spiritualizing Christianity abstains from any *structural diagnosis* of the social and economic system. No analysis is called for to explain how the least of these are trapped and marginalized and forgotten. In a libertarian landscape there is no toxic waste to worry about accumulating in the public watershed. No Pauline "principalities and powers" undermine the Christian program. Pass on by. Nothing to see on the road to Jericho. Maybe thoughts and prayers are briefly wafted. *Amidst all this, a small group of Matthew 25-social justice Christians is using the "least of these" as an analytical tool for diagnosing the American social and economic system and determined to do something about it.*

So is Matthew 25, or the outcry for social justice, *destined to be the new thing?* Just in case, and to suggest how, this book aspires to connect the Matthew *text* to the American *context*. And to reflect on how biblical texts historically founded and drove new religious movements. And how new religious movements contributed to the evolution of biblical texts. (Consider Luther's effect on the role of Paul in Protestant Christianity. Lutherans own Paul. But has the time come for new acquisitions?)

Just in case, after introducing readers to Matthew and exploring whether Matthew 25 could even get a hearing in the twenty-first century, I propose two basic moves, which can also be seen through a sociological lens envisioning a new religious movement: *magnifying and institutionalizing (planting) Matthew* in the *church gathered* (the called religious community), and then again in the *church sent* (the community sent on mission to the world). *How might Matthew play, how might Matthew come true in new "effects," in the interplay between text and context, Word and world, gospel and social gospel, church and society?*

Why Matthew and why now? A particular textual tradition, or historical moment, sinks out of sight or reemerges as influential and conclusive in a given age. We forget and rediscover biblical and theological traditions. Sometimes one of the Gospels prevails—John for incarnational theology. Sometimes the Pauline letters. Or the Pentateuch. Especially among Protestants (Jews seem to prefer the Torah), the prophets *speak loudly*—too loudly for senator Dianne Feinstein. Those who do not prize prophets are likely to complain, "Nevertheless, they persisted." Any of these textual and historical traditions periodically rise or fall. And they become normative and highly influential in and through new religious movements. Consider how sociological and theological analysis of the Matthew 25 movement might proceed today:

1. Small groups of Christians, perhaps especially neoevangelicals and Anabaptists, are learning to take a recovered Matthew 25 seriously, even above the din of modern secularism and the indifference to the downtrodden in American politics and economics. Contemporary Bible study may break through prejudice and privilege and even play in the company of the poor.

2. Grasping Matthew's Gospel as a discipleship manual stemming from early Christianity *begins to shape the church internally into nonconformity with the world and externally into a resistance movement active in the public square.*

3. Matthew 25 might achieve John 3:16 status and become a new canon within the canon that determines what is normative and even preeminent to Christian self-understanding and warranting a new *social gospel* at the opening of the twenty-first century.

4. Gradually, they may team up with secular progressives trying to bring the social justice of the New Deal or Great Society back to life. This new understanding of a gospel with social rather than only personal significance may evoke alliances between the church and the new Left, between Christians and government, between theologians and social scientists who critique neoliberal capitalism as the normative economic system at the heart of market fundamentalism. This could happen in the service of the "least of these" in an economic culture that produces gross inequality, disparages the poor, and disencumbers itself from social responsibility. Ultimately this analysis and commitment could seek to deconstruct the old order and create a new one in which Matthew's Gospel comes to prevail as a necessary mark of the church and the pursuit of social justice across society. This could become part of the history of "Matthew's effects" down through Christian history. The weight and significance of texts change over time. By the time the book of James got

to the sixteenth century, Martin Luther was dismissing it as "an epistle of straw"—so far did it seem to depart from Luther's situated understanding of Galatians or Romans as "a canon within the New Testament canon," a norming text by which all others are illumined.

Soon enough, pastors and pundits, seminary professors and public theologians, book and essay writers, casual commentators on the religious Left and suspicious critics on the Right, *whether personally engaged or not*, will be weighing the Matthew 25/social justice movement—its origins, present course, and possible outcomes. Christian thinkers will be asking whether a single story in Matthew 25 can bear the weight of this new movement. How much can or should the contemporary church invest in this single text? Can Matthew 25 count as central to the entire biblical proclamation or is it just a momentary curiosity? It is useful to recall that Jesus' judgment story that drives this movement is preceded by a little parable about ten bridesmaids who are attendants at a wedding, charged with celebrating the arrival of the groom at the right time. When the right time comes, five of them are unprepared. Their lamps won't light. Stay awake and don't run out of oil for your lanterns is the concluding admonition. No doubt the Matthew 25 Christians would similarly want to admonish the readers of this book.

To entice my readers and interest them in going along for the ride and more, and also because genuinely religious issues are in the offing, and even the urgent evolution of American Christianity, I invite them to consider participant observation status, as I did with the Jesus Movement long ago. *Imaginative investment increases if this seems more than a mere intellectual or theoretical exercise in political theology or in the sociology of religion.* But note well: A diligent and all-embracing appraisal of the contemporary influence of the Matthew 25 meme should not be limited to the small movement of self-designated "Matthew 25 Christians," but must include all ambitious efforts to recover the moral power of a renewed social gospel, emphasizing especially social justice and the directed inclusion of "the least of these" into the viewpoint of Christianity, politics, economics, and culture.

HOW TO STUDY MATTHEW 25 AND SOCIAL JUSTICE MOVEMENTS IN THE PRESENT

The purpose of this book, then, is to take up on the ground disciplines for theological and sociological study and analysis. This book proposes to be a handbook for following the message of Matthew 25 as good news to the poor, a field guide to contemporary Christianity in church and society, a manual for public moral investments. *Biblical studies* specialize in the social and historical settings of ancient texts and how to interpret their proclamation theologically. *Hermeneutics* is the theory and methodology of interpreting biblical texts. Practitioners notice when sacred texts are anchored in a theological viewpoint and from it proclaim a message that makes claims on subsequent readers. They take care to see that the meanings of what texts are or can be saying are not determined ahead of time by the assumptions and social location of the modern reader. Or by the hands-off approach of Religious Studies faculty protecting their students from claims not announced in the syllabus. (Religious Studies departments in public universities in effect promise there will be no conversions!) A hermeneutical circle posits a back-and-forth in which the church and individual readers take up the Bible and then find the Bible taking up them. A text scrutinized talks back. A Christian examining a text discovers the text examining her. A *hermeneutics of suspicion* "outs" the social location of the modern church and uncovers its hidden assumptions of power and privilege and white supremacy and colonialism and sexism. A *hermeneutics of the poor* insists the poor be present, and in on the conversation, when we decipher a text regarding them. As we saw above, a cross-class reading of Matthew's infancy narrative does not fail to notice, even amidst the extravagance of a middle-class Christmas, that a desperate refugee family is fleeing across borders from a hostile state as God's kingdom arrives to challenge the domain of oppressive political power.

Ulrich Luz, having written a magisterial three-volume commentary on Matthew, subsequently wrote *Matthew in History: Interpretation, Influence, and Effects*. This short manual urged attending to *Wirkungsgeschichte*, the history of *Matthew's effects* across Christian and secular history. The early church spoke of "incarnational deposits" that would give evidence that Christ has not abandoned the world after his resurrection and great commission. The saints were considered such deposits. We can trace how Matthew (and Christ as King) came true over time and left evidence of that. Luther once mined the letters of Paul and brought forth grace and faith active in love as Christian essentials. He gave biblical writing pride of place by his assertion of *sola scriptura*. Bible-appealing Protestantism would become a new deposit of words once spoken and exemplified. Matthew 25 left its effects as "corporal works of mercy" in the material culture of medieval Catholicism. Many works of medieval art depict Christians feeding the hungry, clothing the naked, attending to the homeless, visiting the imprisoned—as enactments of their everyday Christian lives, dimensions of a necessary Christian agenda. When John Wesley mined Matthew 25, he found an emphasis on sanctification he thought Luther had neglected and made it a necessary "mark of the church." English departments study "reader-response theory" to account for how new generations of readers bring old texts to new completions. (Shakespeare and Milton keep evolving.) Are we prepared to see modern readers leverage Matthew to break through twenty-first-century self-congratulatory nationalism and capitalist privilege? *New religious movements happen when people begin telling new conversion stories and rooting them in rediscovered historic texts.* When Christ is discovered today among "the least of these," Matthew 25 is becoming normative to contemporary Christianity.

The *humanities and social sciences* track texts and new religious movements and continuously uncover the social location of contemporary Christians and the modern church. Sociologists of religion are not necessarily informed regarding theology and biblical studies, but in the last several decades of the twentieth century sociology was increasingly adopted as a partner discipline to biblical and historical scholarship. What cultural presuppositions determine or limit religious consciousness and understanding? Slaveholders once read the Bible without letting uncomfortable texts challenge their moral lives. Is this still going on? Philosophers teach us to *defamiliarize* texts and traditions that have been sanded down and made too comfortable over time. Scholars caution us about "common sense hermeneutics" that acclimate biblical texts to the American way of life so they do not disturb or unsettle our political and economic arrangements. Matthew 25 may turn out other than in our mother's Bible. Capitalism disencumbered from social responsibility reigns as the creed of market fundamentalism, while Wall Street claims it is doing God's business during the week. Hedge funds are God's economic strategy and the free market is God's right hand. What are the chances of hearing Matthew speak above this din?

A new religious movement that is rooted in the church will raise *ecclesiological questions* as well. Catholics, Lutherans, Methodists, Calvinists, and Anabaptists all have different views of the church, including what ecclesial structure, orientation towards the world, and self-awareness is most appropriate given their understanding of biblical proclamation and the church's mission and calling. Why are the "corporal works of mercy" derived from Matthew 25 necessary "marks of the church" for Catholicism and Wesleyan Methodism, but not for Lutheranism? Matthew has been called a manual for Christian discipleship, and most scholars agree that it early on became a kind of catechism for founding and acting out what it would mean to be the church at the end of the first century. Matthew's audience were probably a mixed Jewish-Gentile urban group of new disciples undergoing persecution and by no means easily acclimated to the world of the Roman Empire.

Drawing from ecclesiology and theology is the discipline of *religious social ethics*. When sixteenth-century Anabaptists or seventeenth-century Puritans felt called to be dissenters or nonconformists in the fixed world of European Christendom, they saw that being a certain kind of community with a certain kind of story with a certain vocabulary would become their ecclesiology. *Becoming the story* they were telling would define their self-understanding and relation to the world. When Calvinists determined to transform culture and to find Christ the King as sovereign in every sphere of life, considering no square foot unoccupied by the sovereignty of God, they were bravely setting out to change the world around them while also risking the possibility of cultural transformation drifting into cultural assimilation. Luther divided his theological ethic into two kingdoms, the church and the world—quite distinct from one another and risking what indeed became "Lutheran quietism." Wesley felt Luther stopped short of the challenge of justification followed by sanctification, so he made provision for the vision of Matthew 25 to be projected onto the world by the church. A Wesleyan social gospel would exemplify the sanctified life of the church. Eventually, the Salvation Army was born.

The advantage of identifying a theological or social ethic is that it persists in asking the question, before it can be forgotten or ignored, of how one should define the mission of the church in the world, how to characterize its "effects" within its own household as the *gathered church* and also its effects in the life of the world when it functions as the *sent church*. To elaborate a theological ethic, and to bring together the gathered and the sent church, I turn to the categories of *gospel* and *social gospel*, all the while mindful of those who insist they cannot really be separated or that there is no such thing as a "social gospel." *Or that when gospel and social gospel are conceptually separated, it is in some political or economic interest.* The kerygmatic gospel in the New Testament, with its claims and demands for decision, does not stop short of the real world in its self-understanding derived from the ministry of Jesus, crucified, risen, and exalted King. The kingdom of God, a fundamental category in Matthew, cannot be spiritualized away or postponed to the afterlife; it takes up space in this world, space in which a new earth is imagined and enacted. Acting out discipleship requires imagining and occupying new public space.

Finally, I appeal to *political and economic theory* to analyze the world that contextualizes the church and hems its social ethics, and in order to diagnose the political economy that is ignoring or even deliberately rejecting calls for a responsible government to achieve social justice across the land and the necessary attention to the least of these. Christians who hunger and thirst after righteousness will have to encounter those who hunger and thirst. The transition from gospel to social gospel cannot ignore the state of the public square and its constraints, especially its relation to the downtrodden—not only failing to lift them up but allowing their immiseration by an economic system and public culture disencumbered from all social responsibility.

The question arises, what must be required if a profoundly unequal economic system is to be deconstructed and a new one imagined? Not everyone among Matthew 25 Christians will agree with calls for partnerships that a social gospel church should seek when it leaves its safe religious precincts and enters the neighborhoods all around it. What allies in the critical intellectual traditions of the university and in progressive politics should the church pursue in the face of an oppressive economic system that claims to be an objective science populated by self-satisfied and unchallenged rational actors?

To heed Matthew 25 may call for new alliances between the church and secular progressives, between theologians and political economists, that could lead the way in developing vigorous critiques of Christian nationalism, the self-righteousness of the American dream, and the hegemony of a disencumbered capitalism that desolates the commons and immiserates the poor and working classes. *To be a Christian disciple is to be encumbered.* To that end there are calls all around to look to the *radical economic analysis* characteristic of contemporary capitalist critics. Will this mean alliances with the *secular Left* as well? And a recovery or new birth of leftist Christianity? And a more complex social gospel?

Part I

Rediscovering Good News to the Poor in the Gospel of Matthew

1

The Bible as the Founding Text of New Religious Movements

DISCOVERING AND BEING DISCOVERED BY A BIBLICAL TEXT

EVERY NEW RELIGIOUS MOVEMENT that is Christian is likely to be grounded in some new appeal to biblical texts. Monasticism, for example, was a spiritual vocation dedicated to an uncompromised imitation of Christ. Over time it embedded itself in long-lasting institutional structures, having caught an essential dimension of biblical Christianity and distilled it for church and society. It provided opportunities to retreat and regroup in order to retrieve and renew certain biblical distinctives and instincts in danger of being lost amidst the evolution of early Christianity. It regenerated a purer and less compromised form of Christianity that could survive social and cultural encroachments and become a new deposit of the incarnation amidst the decline of the Roman Empire and encroaching "Dark Ages." Its thriving over two millennia suggest the power of an *intentional movement* to answer the crisis of an age and embed its response in a changing church. It is important to notice that monasticism was much more than a movement of personal piety, even if it began that way among the "desert fathers," but a brilliant and successful instance of institutionalization, which is to say planting and embedding in the general culture. It is a movement that met the test of religious evolution and structural survival. Medieval monasticism, incidentally, became a structural instrument for the introduction and practice of the "corporal works of mercy" in the life of the church, evoked by Matthew 25.

The sixteenth-century Lutheran Reformation is the prime example of a new religious movement that emerged to reform an errant Christianity precisely by the intensive mining of normative biblical texts and the development of an entire theological worldview based on them—above all the New Testament writings of St. Paul to the Galatians and Romans. A rival Anabaptist movement arose to reject a culturally compromised European Christendom and appeal to a purer response to a biblical story that required dissent and nonconformity if it were to come true and if Christians were to *become the story* they preached. Adult believers' baptism, rather than acclimation to European civilization at birth, became its notable mark. And a reason for its persecution by all other Christians. Its legacy is still normative and practiced today among evangelicals and Anabaptists.

Eighteenth-century Wesleyan Methodism represented a self-knowing *completion* of the sixteenth-century Reformation and the insistence that Luther's doctrine of *justification* needed to find its purpose and fulfillment in the equally important life of *sanctification*. Matthew 25 was among the biblical sources for the "good works" that would characterize the practiced and perfected life in the Methodist movement.

So-called nineteenth-century European Protestant liberalism, represented by movers like Friedrich Schleiermacher, was an attempt to reimagine biblical texts in ways that enabled them to transcend the critiques of Christianity generated by the European Enlightenment. The religious feeling of "absolute dependence" as the essence of religion became a rejoinder to modernist self-confidence and cool rationalism.

The early twentieth-century American Pentecostal movement, the most dynamic movement of Christianity across the world today, self-consciously reclaimed the example of early Christianity by appealing to the New Testament book of Acts, with its story of the first Pentecost, a recovery of the history of revivalism, and the decisive role of the Holy Spirit (which the several American "Great Awakenings" had already done in the previous two centuries), speaking in tongues, and fervent religiosity.

Long ago St. Augustine, in a quiet moment in his garden, heard neighborhood children playing a game in which they kept crying out (in Latin), *Tolle, lege*—take and read. Hearing this as a mysterious admonition to take up the Bible and read it, Augustine opened himself up to what would become his conversion experience and with great intellectual effort left a still-living theological legacy to all of Christianity.

As Christians gripped by perilous times today hold the Bible in their hands, how do they consider whether a new religious movement is called for, whether the Bible is speaking to them anew and urgently, crying "Take up and follow"? They may consider the Bible's origins and the history of its meanings and effects over time. Could its texts be saying something new today, only discovered because changing times call for new hearings, as *new contexts evoke ancient texts?* In a time of gross economic inequalities and the immiserations of the downtrodden, some Christians came across Matthew 25, where they discovered an amazing story Jesus told about the last judgment. Together with all humankind disciples will meet "the least of these" as they stand in line waiting for a verdict about the meaning of their Christian lives. Did they ever see Jesus in and among people such as these?

These contemporary Christian readers have come to see Matthew 25 not as a singular one-off but contextualized in a larger liberation story begun by God in the exodus. It went on to a social covenant obsessed with *widows, orphans, and strangers.* Then prophets brought "covenant lawsuits" against the people of God when they fell short of the vision. All this was catching and then fulfilled in the New Testament appearance of Christ as King, whose unexpected appearances evoked religious transformations. As the story grips new discoverers, they realize the biblical proclamation is more about *formation* than *information.* This anticipates decision-making and change of life. Especially if they are in the Protestant traditions, they may honor the centrality of the Bible with some version of *sola scriptura,* which is to say the centrality of the Bible to Christian understanding and action. They join other Westerners, from Judaism to Christianity to Islam, in having inherited a "religion of the book." They may achieve Luther's insight that the Bible becomes holy and indispensable only when one responds to it as the Word of God making life-giving and life-changing claims.

To those in their grip, especially those desperate to hear something new and authoritative in bewildering times, trenchant biblical texts become God's act of free communication—*from God's voice to their heart.* If the times beckon for new understanding, then new religious movements are likely to move beyond "commonsense readings" or "feels right exegesis." The Bible arrives to disturb and unsettle. You enter an entire history of powerful divine-human encounters, not freeze-dried verses, and you discover how liminal religious life can be. Because the Bible can be bewildering and mystifying and used for suspicious purposes, many commentators historically and again in our times admonish: Hold the Bible accountable to Jesus Christ and the good news he brings. Also, do not assume that the text is automatically "on your side." It may be on the side of the poor. Or women. Or immigrants. Some of your previously unseen neighbors may be necessary to help you decode it.

If you are gripped by texts the times seem to require, you may parade them through the public square. Will new biblical meanings born by new religious movements pass American auditions? Will the news that God comes as a free gift to humanity play in a self-congratulatory Horatio Alger culture? New religious movements must often make their way amongst the wise who insist with respect to religion, "Nothing to see here." Ronald Reagan's son offers weekly, smirking commercials for "freedom from religion" and hellfire. Neither village idiots nor the well-endowed are seeking transformation. Or conversion. Preaching biblical texts means exposing the public claims of the text. Are you ready for this? *All preaching and every new religious movement is political. Keeping religion free of politics, and vice versa, will mean keeping a revolutionary Christ out of the church and out of society.*

OPENING UP TO MATTHEW'S GOSPEL

The message-proclaiming and claim-making Gospels invite readers to open up to them. Objectively distancing approaches to biblical texts are now out of vogue. The approach in many university Religious Studies classes has been to keep students safe from direct encounters with the religious claims of sacred texts—lest the department is seen as proselytizing and losing its stance of secular neutrality. But now the trend is to open the texts and ourselves to mutual engagement. Of such encounters new religious movers and movements are born. It is not unheard of for students to have their lives changed in college and reenter the world after graduation with a new sense of purpose.

"Narrative criticism," a contemporary way into the four Gospels and especially into Matthew, assumes the book is constructed to have certain kinds of effects on its readers. It is a story meant to catch up its readers and carry them along to some end. Stanley Hauerwas in his popular commentary on Matthew assumes that Matthew wants to tell a story and it is not his job to get in the way of it. He does not purport to be smarter than Matthew.

Matthew wants to make disciples of his readers and of the early church at the perilous end of the first century, as Jesus did with his disciples in the pregnant decades earlier. Matthew intends to picture Jesus as God's Messiah. Narrative criticism focuses on an original story to see how to make meaning in *our* stories, in our everyday experience. Matthew and also we and all storytellers thread meaning into human experience, into our biographies. Can we impose narrative order on our own lives—that could be called conversion—and turn them into discipleship? Pretty soon we are sharing these stories with each other and *a movement is born*. We begin to find common sequence and meaning in the narratives of our lives. Stories often have a beginning, middle, and end. In the process, character (and characters) arise, and also complications and climax and resolution.

As in the "reader-response theory" characteristic of literature departments, Jesus, Matthew, and all great texts can be understood to be speaking to ever evolving *implied readers*. For example, it speaks to present-day American Christians or spiritual seekers, just as it did to readers in various circumstances across history. We, among many others, are the readers living in the fraught times between the resurrection and the parousia, between the hour we first believed and the ultimate appearance of Jesus, the time when God's coming and our becoming achieve a collaborative eschatology in the universe—something very appealing to mystics and cosmologists. The drama is watching how great stories bring readers into conformity with the shape of the original storyteller's intentions. The story of final judgment in Matthew 25 seeks to pull readers into conformity with the shape of Jesus' life and the social space of the kingdom evoked every day in the Lord's Prayer. The essence of the New Testament *kerygma*, its gospel proclamation, is the cross and resurrection and kingship. All the other speeches are commentary on it.

The Gospel of Matthew is an entire tapestry, one that may come to be the backdrop of present life narratives—the quilt we are making to signify our lives or to give to the poor who are cold. Is Matthew's deep concern for the least of these the New Deal that Matthew 25 Christians would like to make the backdrop of their present age? Maybe readers will come to see Matthew's themes duplicating themselves in their own lives, or in the grand narratives of their times. Could Jesus versus the authorities of his day become today a plot in which Jesus and American nationalism compete? In the cross and resurrection God vindicates Jesus as King, the triumphant meaning of all, but the goats in Jesus' judgment story never grasped that as they ran by the least of these, chasing their own meanings in their own self-fulfilling narratives—they were running by the presence of Jesus. The judgment setting of Jesus' story in Matthew 25 wants readers to see that all narratives must come to final adjudication.

The point of the New Testament *kerygma* is that Jesus' announcement of the arrival of the reign of God still descends over readers' time and throws their lives into a crisis of decision. Matthew's story still counts today—something mere historical criticism (deliberately) missed and postmodernism minimizes in its abandonment of "grand narratives." For such critics it was enough to establish what used to be. As we are lately seeing, epidemics and insurrections can throw an entire age into crisis and dress our times with an apocalyptic dimension, in which ultimate questions are surfaced and penultimate arrangements and assumptions are tested.

Grand narratives, like Matthew's, hover over us with a sense of ultimacy—judging our times and proposing solutions to their dead ends. The common term for this in New Testament studies is "apocalyptic" and its dimension of ultimacy sets the gospel narratives into crisis mode. When apocalyptic time is seen to intersect with everyday time, a crisis is invoked. In Matthew's telling of the Christmas story, for example, Herod experiences a political crisis at the birth of Jesus. The apocalyptic stance of John the Baptist provokes a crisis for a second King Herod. In the course of Matthew's narrative, apocalyptic time is a disruption of readers' time by God's time, so that their lives may be redeemed and turned to new purposes. The new religious movement calling itself "Matthew 25 Christians" or so-called "social justice Christians" purports to be a response to modern times that carelessly immiserate the poor and deliberately celebrate the rich.

A disruption of present time by God's time is supposed to become the *momentous* time (*kairos*) for the redemption of the age, including our own age. But a religion that is private and personal, that stays out of the public square and makes no public claims, that runs away from the political—even God's own reign and claim—will not become the disruption that the kingdom of God assumes and requires. The coming of God to earth creates alternative worlds, alternative communities, alternative politics—not private spiritual sanctuaries.

Just before the discourse on "the least of these," Jesus tells a story that challenges hearers to live in the light of Jesus' coming. If you are uncertain of the times you are in, as the five foolish virgins who ran out of oil for their lamps were and so missed the arrival of the bridegroom, it is all the more important to live close to the script Jesus has announced. To make sure we keep seeing the King. But Jesus' little stories will make little sense if abstracted from the big story that is Jesus' proclamation of the arriving reign of God and the re-enchantment of the earth.

To conclude: Does the religious movement around Matthew 25 speak to the gross injustice of our times? Do Matthew's story and our story interlock? Is Matthew's story just what the times, and we ourselves, require? Where does American Christianity fit? What appeal is there to all who seek social justice? Is something much bigger afoot than just the small movement of self-designated "Matthew 25 Christians"?

OUTING ONESELF BEFORE PROCLAIMING MATTHEW TO CHURCH AND COUNTRY

Remember the last time you sat down to file your IRS tax forms for the previous year? Remember the total income figure about halfway down on page one? Remember deductions you claimed on a separate form, which then reduced the amount of your taxable income? I wonder if we sometimes read the Bible that way. So here we are reading Matthew, considering the benefits that come to us as disciples of Jesus (our gross income). Then we get to what Bonhoeffer calls "the cost of discipleship." That would be our discipleship tax! But wait. We surely have a right to our itemized deductions—amounts we claim which, when subtracted from our gross, will reduce our taxable income and hence reduce our taxes.

I'm wondering how many itemized deductions we bring to the biblical text, how many claims we make that can subtract from the total cost of taking the text seriously. *Jesus, let me follow you. But first let me consider my itemized deductions!* There's actually a story like that in Matthew 8, where someone being called to discipleship says, "First I must bury my dead and then I will follow." Jesus' reply is that discipleship does not allow any "yes, but's." True disciples are not allowed to suspend for a time their commitment to follow Jesus. No previous obligations may take precedence over discipleship. Like: first, let us get the economy running. Or, before we attend in our social policy to "the least of these," let us make our peace with the demands of late capitalism. Like: before I become a Matthew 25 saint, let me get my career established.

A question too rarely asked, but perhaps more common in new religious movements, is what biases and self-exemptions we bring to the text and how we can correct for them. The practice of interpreting Biblical texts can be tricky. Or self-serving. During one period in American history, Christian slaveholders practiced "commonsense readings" by which they adjusted the call of the gospel to their slaveholding way of life. These days it is common to refer to white racism as American Christianity's original sin. "Critical race theory" is currently denounced by all who defend culture and nation against charges of white supremacy. Does "white privilege" harden hearts as people study the Bible and figure out what it could be saying to them? Do "Black Lives Matter" when counting "the least of these" the church is called to serve? When contemporary theorists claim "there are no apolitical readings of the text" (or apolitical sermons), they mean that we inevitably and perhaps unknowingly bring to the text an entire spectrum of cultural and economic and nationalist readings that are likely to seep into what we say the text must mean.

Participants in the social justice movements write about a *hermeneutics of hunger*. Or a *hermeneutics of poverty*. These, when self-consciously practiced in the movement, refer to interpretive postures adopted that make it more likely we will let the text speak to us—perhaps through the voices of the least of these. So we are called to study Matthew 25 with the poor in mind, or with the poor and the hungry in the same room. Imagine bankers and those they are foreclosing on meet in the space around the altar, pass the peace, and then go up to the eucharistic table together. Could we allow our liturgical practice to inform and reform us before we join in the study of biblical texts? The Matthew 25 movement has noticed that when Jesus said, "The poor you always have with you," this became an escape clause for middle-class Americans (and politicians) waiting to adjust Christian discipleship down to the status quo. They urge us to *out ourselves* before we go next door to witness to the neighbors, or at the next church council meeting, or when examining political platforms.

Before the Matthew 25 movement, feminist Biblical scholars had developed a "hermeneutics of suspicion" to uncover and expose the extent to which biblical interpretation has been largely in the hands of white males. And so we consider a "history of the effects" of Bible study when it has been class or gender based. Consider the inaugural sermon of Jesus in Luke 4: "The Spirit of the Lord is on me, because he has anointed me to proclaim good news to the poor. He has sent me to proclaim freedom for the prisoners and recovery." A new religious movement may repeat this admonition from Isaiah over and over, and memorize it like a theme song, so that clears away a lot of the brush that interferes with hearing texts that liberate.

2

The Message of Matthew Then and Now

If new Christian movements are often grounded in and driven by new readings of biblical texts, then total immersion in texts becomes appropriate. Luther found in Galatians and Romans a lifeline for his own spirituality. Paul's gospel "saved" Luther and provided the leverage for reforming the church. Even today, five hundred years later, Lutheranism purports to live by St. Paul.

A movement calling itself Matthew 25 Christians is likely to become totally immersed in the Gospel of Matthew. One can enter into the Gospel of Matthew at home, immersed in devotional reading, perhaps with the assistance of a commentary on Matthew. Or, better, in a desegregated Bible study class with other believers puzzling over this Gospel text and determined to let it speak. Or, if a church has adopted the "common lectionary," then Year A is devoted to Gospel readings from Matthew, and these could generate an entire year of "Matthew immersion." When the pastor conducts a weekly Bible study with members of the congregation to discuss the text(s) to be preached on the following Sunday, preaching on Matthew can become a communal effort. To hear Matthew in the church's liturgy is to hear a living voice in the midst of one's liturgical formation. Shaking meanings from the text happens more readily when studying it as a communal project. Or when it is followed by a sermon on that text. (Keep the preacher honest.) When Christians individually and in groups read biblical texts while troubling over the crises and opportunities of their age, and when they begin to see and hear the same things, they may well turn into, and feel called to become, a *new religious movement*. This is the story of Matthew 25 and social justice Christians. When we are totally immersed in it, Matthew 25 can become a conversion story.

PROVENANCE: EVERY BOOK HAS ITS STORY

It is commonly proposed that Matthew was written as early as 55–60 AD or as late as 80 AD, to a mixed church of Jewish and Gentile Christians, perhaps in an urban community in Antioch, in the Roman provenance of Syria (the northeastern Mediterranean), probably undergoing persecution. A dominant characteristic of Matthew's telling is the very extensive allusions to the Old Testament. Not only that, but some see Matthew exercising the style of *Jewish midrash*, in which students of Scripture embellish and cumulatively add commentary to it, extending the reach of the text along the way. Matthew 25 Christians are doing this too. They embroider and expand Matthew as the answer to the political and economic problems of our age. They draw Matthew out as good news to the poor, as Jesus did when quoting a text from Isaiah in his inaugural sermon in Luke.

IMAGINING JESUS AS KING, SEEING WHAT NEEDS TO BE SEEN

Matthew is all about Jesus as King *and* being able to recognize and acknowledge his kingship becoming visible to believers. Jesus' appearance and visitation is called the parousia. Jesus' self-disclosure and arriving presence, to all who are looking, means seeing this King as one who completed an earthly mission, to which disciples too are called, and who by way of cross and resurrection becomes enthroned with the Father and reigns over all the earth. It's JESUS AS KING we are called to see, and surprisingly, in the least of these. Matthew is obsessed with the kingdom of God (heaven). In the course of Matthew's narrative, the disciples keep stumbling over this challenge to see, as have believers down through time. Modern disciples struggle to take this seriously and let it challenge their imaginations and their ethics as they keep praying in the Lord's Prayer week after week their whole lives, *Thy kingdom come. Give us bread and debt relief.* The challenge is not to spiritualize this kingdom into the sweet by-and-by, but to acknowledge it on present ground. The poor do not just exist in a story long ago. Matthew 25 Christians see it as their calling to see and acknowledge the King and to take up discipleship in the earthly space the kingdom opens up.

APOCALYPTIC WATCH

Apocalypse means revelation, uncovering, unveiling, or disambiguation, and is connected to catastrophic events which, when seen through by prophets, reveal the meanings that underlie a coming course of events in religious history. As a genre, it arose in postexilic Judaism and appears again in New Testament times and is unmistakably connected to the ministry of Jesus. The apocalyptic parable of the ten virgins on duty waiting for the bridegroom to arrive, which immediately precedes Jesus' last judgment story, has five of them running out of oil for their lamps and is about urgency and alertness. These are attitudes and postures, indeed a mindset, the church is called to practice. The apocalyptic dimension, mostly written off in modern times, remains among millennialist evangelicals who fear being "left behind" when Jesus returns and therefore must point their lives towards the final days and the rapture. In the posture of straining toward the heavens and diverting one's eyes from the present, it is easy to forget that Jesus was killed by the state, with the complicity of religious authorities. (Some see this as a disturbing characterization of what is happening today.) It is particularly difficult to keep in mind that Jesus was plotted against and judged by the religious establishment. Matthew 25 Christians hold on to this insight, while judging the intuitions of their age. A supreme irony in this account of Matthew 25 for today is that while alert Christians are called to wake up and see the presence of the King among the least of these, it is precisely many (conservative) Christians whose ideology ignores the least of these and deliberately denies their call for recognition. Matthew 25 attracts enthusiastic detractors among evangelical conservatives!

PREFERENTIAL OPTION FOR THE POOR

A "preferential option for the poor" is a term from Latin American Catholic liberation theology, but it is unmistakably present in the prophets and in the Gospels, perhaps especially Matthew. And among the Matthew 25 movement. It turns out to be the opposite of what small government advocates, or capitalists who see themselves responsible only to their shareholders, do not see and indeed object to seeing. A new religious movement sees that if the moral community that is the Christian church doesn't get it, nobody will. So Matthew 25 Christians keep beating the drum for justice as the "social form of love." A good exercise of the moment is to Google "the poor in the Bible" and then wait for the avalanche of evidence to overwhelm. The poor are everywhere! And God is grieving for them. And the prophets are angry about it. And widows, orphans, and strangers are always objects of God's special attention. No political platform, including that of liberal Democrats under Biden, comes close to espousing a preferential option for the poor. When will presidential speeches regularly conclude with, "God bless the poor"?

MATTHEW AS A MANUAL OF DISCIPLINE FOR NEW DISCIPLES

Think of Lutheran or Catholic confirmation classes, or evangelical churches that prepare young people for "believers' baptism." Imagine Matthew as the church's catechism for discipleship. This is less about *Christian information* or Bible quizzes (my wife used to win them as a teenaged Bible star) than *Christian formation*. Church liturgies and rituals do this too as they form character among worshippers before sending them on their way into a world that lacks spiritual vision. Any new movement with a textual base to it is likely to saturate itself in continuous study of such texts. Think of the *textualism* of American constitutional originalism movements, or liturgical renewal fanatics. None of these can get enough of the texts that ground and inspire them. Matthew 25 Christians may be inviting their fellow Christians to become "originalists" and "textualists." Matthew was training Christians to become the Christian story, to master its vocabulary, to be noticeably different from the world, to be aware of the cost of discipleship.

MATTHEW SEES THE CHURCH AS THE NEW MESSIANIC COMMUNITY

The shape of Matthew's narrative may be pointing towards the emergence of the Christian church at the end of the first century. *Ecclesiology* refers to the doctrine of the church, or to what kind of shape or structure or thrust it should display. Down through the history of Christianity the church has concretized and institutionalized and intentionalized in various ways. There's Catholicism, which is united under its pope and bishops to make a certain kind of cultural and religious mark on the world. There's Calvinism, which seeks to transform society and bring it under God's dominion. There's the Anabaptist vision, which sees the church as a dissenting and nonconforming community that resists the ways of the world and specializes in its adopted biblical story and voice, and deliberately wants to be different. There's Lutheranism, which wants to be shaped and motivated by a specific understanding of the gospel and continually talks about and *appeals to the gospel as normative and decisive* as no other denomination does, often asking the question in difficult times, "Is the gospel at stake here?" Unfortunately, Lutherans have not led the way in asserting that if the least of these are not attended to, then the gospel is at stake. Doing so would make the presence of the poor *a mark of the church*, which Lutheranism does not typically do.

Among the discourses that form the structure of Matthew's narrative, the last is called the eschatological discourse. The Messiah is arriving! The birth pangs of a new age are alluded to. Watchfulness and the ability to anticipate the King's presence are the order of the day. There are also messianic pretenders to watch for, who arise self-appointed and diverting Christian attention. As I write this, a few Christian prophets are announcing that Donald Trump will assume again the presidency after all—soon and very soon. Messianic pretenders, including Trump himself, are abundant, and they embarrass Christianity and distract from its gospel message. And they render their followers delusional.

Alas, the rediscovery of the least of these is not titillating. And would not serve the purposes of Christian nationalism and might require the re-regulation and re-encumbering of a capitalist economy. While some evangelical traditions feel called to point themselves towards the final coming of Christ and the end of the world, and to anticipate those "left behind," Matthew 25 Christians believe Matthew is calling them to see through to Christ's Kingship now, in this world, waiting for transformation. A Messianic community would re-enchant the world. The least of these, after all, live now, in this world, and Jesus says he can and must be seen among them. Why is it so hard to discover the poor when they are everywhere under our noses? In my university town they are readily visible on the outskirts of town and in our city park. Strangely, when the city council boasts a conservative Christian majority, it becomes time to roust the homeless. But Matthew 25 Christians want to see and to shape a new kind of society, a genuine commonwealth. Can the parousia be allowed to occur among the poor and outcast? Dare they expect that good news is on the way, as Jesus promised in his inaugural sermon? Will a Matthew 25 movement make them visible to everyone—sheltering and feeding and clothing and visiting them? Will it invite them into the beloved community, the term Martin Luther King coined to evoke a society based on justice, equal opportunity, and mutual love? Are "corporal works of mercy" lining up to reappear in American cities, reaching a prominent position in the public square?

EXEGESIS OF THE LAST JUDGMENT STORY: MATTHEW 25:31–46

I am following here the preeminent commentary on Matthew by Ulrich Luz (three volumes, in the Hermeneia series). In his third volume he comes to Matthew 25 and begins by noting that this last judgment story is the last before the story of the passion begins and at the same time is Jesus' final instruction to his disciples. It therefore carries great weight in Matthew's narrative for the church in the final decades of Christianity's first century. Luz devotes considerable space to three different interpretation histories of what is intended when the Son of Man comes in glory to judge all peoples. Who are the least of these and who is being judged for how they were treated? The criteria for judging are clear enough: works of mercy shown toward the marginal, the poor, and the suffering of the world, seen as the least of Jesus' brothers and sisters. And as a prominent location of his parousia in the world.

1. *The universal interpretation* sees Jesus judging all peoples, and the "least of these" are all the people of the world who are in need. The story is then seen as a summary of the whole teaching of the Gospel and a restatement of its demands. This interpretation implies an undogmatic and practical Christianity. It seems that what is important is love of neighbor, not confession or belief. In his story "Where Love Is, There God Is Also," Leo Tolstoy concludes that God is the love that resides in people and overcomes all separation. In all epochs of Christian history this is the basic text for the "seven works of mercy" expected of Christians and embedded in Christian culture.

In view of the assertion that even the good do not know whom they are actually serving when they serve the least of these, many conclude that the work of love must be done for its own sake. The German moral philosopher Immanuel Kant, wanting to establish an objective ethic, especially emphasized this point. This view is also central to Latin American/Catholic liberation theology. Gustavo Gutierrez, for example, argues there is no way to God that bypasses the "sacrament of our neighbor." Faith is on the side of the poor. This story is basic not just for ethics, but also for ecclesiology and Christology. The German Protestant Jürgen Moltmann asserts that "the least of Christ's brothers and sisters is where the church belongs."

In his play "The Gold Crowned Christ," the Korean poet Kim Chi Hah suggests that by helping the poor, the gold crown of Jesus will be removed and his lips freed to speak. This is how it happens: In front of a Korean church stands a cement statue of Jesus with a crown of gold. Beggars sit beneath it. A fat priest and a businessman pass by without noticing. A policeman tries to chase the beggars away. One of the beggars complains, "What does this block of cement have to do with me?" He wants to steal the gold crown. The statue begins to weep. It says to the beggar, "You have freed me from my prison, take the golden crown. A crown of thorns is good enough for me. Take the gold and divide it." The play ends when the priest, the businessman, and the policeman return, take the crown from the beggar, and arrest him. Jesus again turns into stone. Conclusion: Christ becomes human in the poor; his incarnation continues as he speaks to them and gives himself to them.

Some moderns see in this universalizing understanding of the story the relationship of Christianity to other religions. Many religions advocate the "corporal works of mercy" depicted in Jesus' story. There is nothing specifically Christian about them. The judgment thus seems universal. (Luther thought that Turkish Muslims were more likely to do the works of mercy than German Christians.) After the European Enlightenment's natural religion of reason and love, some moderns saw in this story a freeing of Jesus from a particularism that would limit him to one particular religion. Thus this story can take on a new theological significance in a post-Christian modern society. The story enables a new encounter with God. This universalizing interpretation is in the modern world, if not earlier than the nineteenth century, the most widespread.

2. *The classic interpretation*, widely accepted up until 1800, saw the "least of these" to be members of the Christian community, and all those

being judged were also Christians. Possibly in Matthew's day the least of these were seen to be the "itinerant radicals," who, following Jesus' command, moved around spreading the good news and were very often in need of sustenance. In the early centuries of Christianity it was sometimes expected that every Christian home should have a "Christ's garret," a spare room where Christ, which is to say the homeless, have a room available to them. A beloved saint in the Middle Ages was Martin of Tours. He was a soldier in fourth-century Christianity who at the city gate gave a poor person half of his assigned garment, the last that he had. The following night Christ appeared to him dressed in this half of his garment and declared to him that he himself had met him in the person of this poor man.

Christologically, many thought that Christ himself was not capable of suffering, but he suffers in his body, the church. True God and true man, Christ is rich with regard to what he is but poor with regard to what he has from human beings. His suffering lasts until the end of the world.

Following John Calvin, the deeds of mercy were designated not as the basis of salvation but as the sign of predestined election. But Catholics insisted the interpretation is causal and not consecutive: salvation is given not merely after one's works but also because of one's works and is therefore based on merit.

3. *The exclusive interpretation* emerged in the eighteenth and nineteenth centuries and reappeared after 1960. The "all nations" appearing for judgment are "all pagans." Only non-Christians appear before the world judge. These non-Christians are judged on their behavior toward Christians. This was especially in reference to how missionaries were treated.

What else can be said? Which interpretation does Luz choose? At first, he thinks Matthew would have meant interpretation number two. For sure, readers should be finding themselves in the text. Surely this cannot be merely a self-serving interpretation, as in number three. All the nations must include all peoples of the earth, including the church. Final judgment must include the church. From the portrayal of future judgment, readers learn something about their own present. The "ignorance motif" is probably a literary device to refer to how drastically disciples can miss the point, as already elsewhere, and repeatedly, in Matthew's Gospel. When the Judge identifies with the "least of these," we are to see the surprising miracle of his identification with them. The overall *standard of judgment will be love*. This story is a concentration of Matthean

Christology. The risen Christ is with his church as Immanuel until the end of time by, among other things, identifying with the poverty and suffering of his followers. This is in continuity with how Jesus himself suffered during his earthly ministry. So this references the entire way the Son of Man has gone, from his time on earth until his presence even to the end of time.

But then Luz makes an unexpected move, as he opens a discussion of "Meaning for Today." Even though Luz chose number two as Matthew's probable meaning, he now moves back to number one and the fascination of the universal interpretation of the text, which seems to be at the heart of the Gospel. Even if Matthew saw the least of these as needy disciples, can we now interpret the text contrary to its origins when the resulting meaning of number one is central to the Gospel and is helpful for modern people who receive it? What are reasons for answering Yes?

What is the basic orientation for deciding possible modern meanings of a text in the entire biblical story to which new interpretations must correspond? Jesus indeed spoke of unconditional love of strangers and even of enemies. If we take the crucified interpreter, Jesus, as the guiding principle, it is possible that today the universal interpretation of Matthew 25 can *break through the limits of love in a way that is congruent with the New Testament proclamation.* And it is congruent with Matthew's story itself that no self-absolutizing of Christianity or the church is allowed. If we go by Luz's "history of effects" in reflecting on Matthew and what it can mean for Matthew to "come true" in the present age, then the question is whether a new interpretation of a text produces an all-encompassing love as witness to God. The universal interpretation does this. It sees Jesus judging all peoples, and the "least of these" are all the people of the world who are in need. It makes possible the discovery anew of the poor of the world. Jesus is the one who gives us new eyes to see this ultimately larger meaning of the text, the poor person and God. The new reading of the text makes possible the judgment of the world.

While continuing to work at setting Matthew 25 in the modern age, we will see how necessary it is to look at the least of these and the way the world ignores them and fails to see the presence of Christ the King among them. The twenty-first century has a tin ear for hearing Matthew 25 and, worse, an entire array of economic, political, and cultural constructs that shut this message out. And directly contradict it. And authorize the reverse.

What about judgmentalism? Medieval Christians entering their cathedrals through the great western doors would look up and see awe-inspiring and threatening last judgment scenes. Among other stories, they reminded churchgoers of the judgment scene in Matthew 25. They got it. Does anyone get it today? Does any modern architect frighten visitors with judgment scenes in the church buildings being designed? For fifty years or more we have been told that judgmentalism and its corresponding guilt are not useful emotions for moderns. Indeed, therapists aim to set their clients free from such outdated religious baggage.

And yet Matthew peppers his Gospel six times with "weeping and gnashing of teeth." The entire Gospel has been pointing towards a conclusive last judgment story. Matthew 25 is not a one-off, not an outlier, not an aberration. All of the several discourses that form the structure of Matthew's narrative end with announcements of judgment for the church. Did you remember that it concludes the beloved Sermon on the Mount? The charming parables? *Judgment* is a key word. Nicely, the Greek word is *krisis*, and the "parables of the kingdom" teach us that the coming of Christ and his eschatological proclamation throw the world, and individual disciples, into crisis. It began already with John the Baptist, who calls onlookers and inquirers to repentance. The message is not benign; it demands a radical response. It ends with Jesus' final warning to the disciples on the Mount of Olives about a threatening judgment to the church. Luz calls this Matthew's cantus firmus (the sturdy tune that structures polyphony) and leitmotif, "a recurrent theme throughout a musical or literary composition, associated with a particular person, idea, or situation." The last judgment is a Matthew imprint, in part derived from Matthew's "sayings source."

So when is the last judgment, the parousia sighting of the reigning King, coming? The New Testament, including Matthew, seems to register uncertainty here. But always in church history, including among the prophets who had anointed President Trump for end-time duty, there are people on tiptoes, peering into the near horizon, often getting it wrong. As we know from the parable of the ten bridesmaids and their calling to celebrate the arrival of the groom, a parable that precedes the last judgment story in Matthew 25, the point is watchfulness and readiness. And not being caught without oil in your lamp—the whole point of their presence at the wedding. Will such a stance of responsible alertness fly in the American church today, amidst so much American self-congratulation (on the right) and guilt-free mellowness (on the left)?

Matthew is far less interested in predicting the future than in present churchly behavior. Are Christians alert for the presence of the risen King, especially in unlikely places and among unlikely people? Luz calls this *eschatology in the service of ethics*. Who knew a swallow of water to the thirsty, hospitality towards the stranger, becoming as lowly as a child would turn out to be telling criteria of the state of the church and of Christianity? Will the costs of discipleship pile up around homely metaphors?

Matthew salts his narratives, especially also in his closing chapters, with parables of judgment. Scholars commonly discuss parables as homely stories that invite hearers into an imaginal edifice unexpectedly. As they are comfortably looking around at familiar settings, the door is closed and the parable closes in. Who saw the climax of the story coming? The people squeezed into what they thought would be the pleasant reality of the parables see suddenly they are being held to new viewpoints and necessary decision and life change.

Of course, Matthew speaks a theological language that seems quite different from Paul's. We will consider in the next chapter how to reconcile, if possible, if necessary, Matthew and Paul and Luther. Did Luther run from Matthew's good works in order to preserve Paul's doctrine of justification, while John Wesley ran toward them in the service of a doctrine of sanctification? Then there is the Lutheran Dietrich Bonhoeffer observing, in his reflections on Matthew and the cost of discipleship and the trap of cheap grace, "Only he who believes is obedient, and only he who is obedient believes."

What shall Christians conclude today about judgment and grace? Does Matthew's judgment motif destroy the gospel proclamation of grace? Do we all face the end of our lives with uncertainty and fear that we will not pass the test—as medieval portrayals of the dying in anguish, as sickbed devils hover, seem to suggest? What is the balance between God's love and the believer's fear? Consider the words of the famous and much quoted *Dies Irae*, a thirteenth-century poem that became part of a Requiem Mass:

> What trembling there will be / When the judge comes / To divide everything rigorously. Give me a place among the sheep / Separate me from the goats / Putting me on your right.
>
> What shall I, wretched one, say then / To what advocate shall I appeal / When even a just man is hardly safe!

The Enlightenment substituted autonomous reason for such a God. The twentieth century simply dethroned him as incompatible with modern psychology.

Given the thrust I have given Matthew in this field guide, given my suggestion that Matthew 25 Christians will succeed to the extent that they exert the eschatological pressure of Matthew's ethic about the least of these to produce a church-propelled move towards social justice across the land, I ask, for myself, what kind of ethic do we now need? It is currently common among Christian progressives to proclaim to a white supremacist society that racism is America's original sin. And that the American founders are entirely complicit in this sin. And that we all, therefore, are compromised. So shall we preach condemnation, compel white shaming, "cancel" much of our tradition? Or is a positive vision, not mostly guilt-giving, the way to inspire both religious and secular progressives to imagine a government, an economic system, a national culture that ambitiously seeks justice for all, starting with a profound concern for the least of these? And that may produce a society whose example we can hold up for the world to consider. (I take this up in the Epilogue, under the theme of "collaborative eschatology.") Is faith active in love more promising than pummeling people with the law? Is clothing Matthew 25 in the entire New Testament proclamation the way to go?

GETTING SOMEWHERE WITH MATTHEW—FROM THEN TO NOW, FROM CHURCH TO SOCIETY AND COUNTRY

How are we to preach Matthew today and from it empower a vigorous social ethic? Scholar-activist Liz Theoharis, co-chair of the Poor People's Campaign, in many articles and in her book *Always with Us? What Jesus Really Said about the Poor,* goes out of her way to assert Matthew's concern for the poor in the face of conservative American evangelicals who comfort themselves with the inevitability of poverty, the supposed pathology and moral inferiority of the poor, and the inappropriateness of letting the gospel become a radical call for social justice in the political realm. She also critiques those who see the economic rights of the poor as a call to charity while avoiding deliberate biblical calls for justice for all or the agency of the poor themselves in attempts for economic justice.

Theoharis goes much further than many American Christians in portraying Jesus as a social movement leader with a revolutionary economic program. She calls Jesus a "new Moses" who wants to be a liberator to the Galilean villages and Syrian towns, one who brings new instruction and a new understanding of law and justice to a people in need of dignity and freedom. Jesus' disciples are called to watch and learn, as Jesus ministers to needy crowds. When John the Baptist's disciples come to see if Jesus is the genuine messenger from God, Jesus offers as one of his bona fides that "the poor have good news brought to them," then adding, "And blessed is anyone who takes no offense at me" (Matthew 11:5–6). When a rich young man appears as a master of the commandments and seeking Jesus' verification of his discipleship, Jesus breaks open his self-praise by saying, "If you wish to be perfect, go sell your possessions and give the money to the poor" (Matthew 19:16–22).

3

Contextualizing Matthew 25 in the Bible and Christian History

THIS STUDY CONSIDERS TEXT *and context* and the role they play in the founding and evolution of a religious movement. If Matthew 25 Christians are going to claim eminence for the text of Matthew 25, some context must be considered if such a claim is to hold up. Does Matthew 25 perhaps sit only on the edge of the overall biblical message? Is its significance overrated? Is a new religious movement calling itself *Matthew 25 Christians* making a single Gospel story carry too much weight? Is it really true that Matthew 25's "corporal works of mercy" are indispensable "marks of the church"? Does biblical Christianity revolve around the poor? Or is Matthew 25 only what the British call a "one-off"? Are we talking John 3:16 here, or just a pithy saying that could come from Proverbs? Could Matthew 25 be a normative "canon within the canon" like Galatians and Romans were for Luther? Or the book of Revelation is for millennialists? Is this a story that illuminates and determines how we interpret all others? Could it be true that if the church doesn't get Matthew 25 it doesn't really get Christianity? And the gospel? Must I lay the groundwork for seeing Matthew 25 as normative and fundamental to understanding the whole Bible? Will Matthew's context in the rest of the Bible, both Old Testament and New Testament, confirm the claims made on behalf of Matthew 25? Will Matthew's "effects" over time provide a confirming context that once did and now again establishes its place in new religious movements?

GOD'S HEART FOR THE POOR IS EVERYWHERE ON DISPLAY

In both the New Testament and the Old, the poor play a starring role. They are to be attended to, and whether or not this happens becomes a test case of biblical religion. In the Sermon on the Mount account in Matthew (5:2–13), Jesus prefigures the judgment story of Matthew 25 regarding the "least of these" with ethical and also eschatological remarks about the poor. "Blessed (Happy? Fortunate?) are the poor (broken) in spirit . . . those who mourn . . . the meek . . ." When I was in eighth grade I had a starring role in our Sunday school Christmas Eve pageant back in Dubuque, Iowa, for which my parents bought me my first suit. Before an admiring congregation I was to have memorized and declaim the song the Virgin Mary sings in Luke (1:46–55), which the church ever since has called the Magnificat from its opening line: "My soul magnifies the Lord." Mary's song became one of the eight most ancient Christian hymns. Down through the history of the church it appears in Catholic and Orthodox worship, especially Catholic vespers, in Anglican and Lutheran evensong, and in some Protestant hymnody and in Bach's great setting, as well as many others.

But how many see it as a radical song of the poor, as much modern scholarship does? How many have noticed the Magnificat as a startling *song of reversals*? Was gentle Mary a radical visionary? How many people have come to see this as a theme of Christmas—abundant presents for the poor? Allow yourself to be astonished by verses such as these: "God has scattered the proud in the thoughts of their hearts. He has brought down the powerful from their thrones and lifted up the lowly; he has filled the hungry with good things and sent the rich away empty." Elsewhere in Luke (14:14) Jesus says to his host: "When you give a banquet, invite the poor, the crippled, the lame, the blind, and you will be blessed, because they cannot repay you, for you will be repaid at the resurrection of the righteous."

Or consider this admonition from 1 John 3:17: "How does God's love abide in anyone who has the world's goods and sees a brother or sister in need and yet refuses to help? Little children, let us love, not in word or speech, but in truth and action." The New Testament can be very specific in the treatment of the poor that is to distinguish the church. Note James 2:2–5: "For if a person with gold rings and in fine clothes comes into your assembly, and if a poor person in dirty clothes also comes in, and if you take notice of the one wearing the fine clothes and say, Have a seat here, please, while to the one who is poor you say, Stand there or Sit at my feet, have you not made distinctions among yourselves, and become judges with evil thoughts?"

To set biblical truth in proportion, consider that homosexuality is possibly mentioned in the Bible seven times and poverty over three hundred times. Yet demands for religious liberty in the United States privilege the church's right to repress homosexuality and exclude it from civil rights obligations. The well-known evangelical pastor Rick Warren counts two thousand verses that mention God's concern with poverty! How hard do you have to work to miss them? How much like Thomas Jefferson are you, in scissoring out verses that cause you discomfort? Where are these emphases among the Christian Right? And the rest of Christianity? Are they featured in pastors' favorite sermon series? Are the poor and hungry sitting among the congregation as well—hearing messages that set them free and mutually rejoicing? Are the poor invited to sit in on Bible studies that consider God's obsession with the poor and their claims on us?

What is especially remarkable, if you are coming upon Old Testament passages for the first time, is that they move *beyond generic concern for charity to very specific programs for social justice*. Consider, for example, Leviticus 19:9–10: "When you reap the harvest of your land, you shall not reap to the very edges of your field, or gather the gleanings of your harvest. You shall not strip your vineyard bare, or gather the fallen grapes of our vineyard; you shall leave them for the poor and the alien: I am the Lord your God." This Old Testament ethic is grounded in the exodus legacy: "You shall not wrong or oppress a resident alien, for you were aliens in the land of Egypt. You shall not abuse any widow or orphan" (Exod 22:21–22). Or this from Zechariah 7:8–10: "The word of the Lord came to Zechariah, saying, Thus says the Lord of hosts, Render true judgments, show kindness and mercy to one another; do not oppress the widow, the orphan, the alien, or the poor." If you and your friends had a starring role in a Lenten pageant, you might want to memorize some of these admonitions and take turns declaiming them. Would your parents be proud? Or would they suspect the youth pastor is a college leftist and move to another church? What next—socialism?

There is much more. Exodus 22:22–23: "You shall not abuse any widow or orphan," God tells the Israelites. "If you do abuse them, when they cry out to me, I will surely heed their cry; my wrath will burn."

Deuteronomy 15:7: "If among you, one of your brothers should become poor, in any of your towns within your land that the Lord your God is giving you, you shall not harden your heart or shut your hand against your poor brother." Isaiah 10:1–3: "Woe to those who make unjust laws, to those who issue oppressive decrees, to deprive the poor of their rights and withhold justice from the oppressed of my people, making widows their prey and robbing the fatherless. What will you do on the day of reckoning, when disaster comes from afar? To whom will you run for help? Where will you leave your riches?" Zechariah 7:8–10: "This is what the Lord Almighty said: 'Administer true justice; show mercy and compassion to one another. Do not oppress the widow or the fatherless, the foreigner or the poor. Do not plot evil against each other.'" Notice that *acts of charity* are not the primary covenantal requirement of the children of Israel. *They are commanded to build a social and economic system that provides for the poor.* I will return to this point in subsequent chapters when I test the policy visions of the Matthew 25/social justice movement—whether it is making alliances with liberals and progressives and the government itself to insure social justice across the land—and giving notice to the government that the poor are out there waiting in line and must be heard.

Choose for your hair shirt still more verses as *tests of a religious stand on the poor.* Psalm 113:5–8: "God raises the poor from the dust and lifts the needy from the ash heap; he seats them with princes, with the princes of his people." Isaiah 25:4: "Lord, you have been a refuge for the poor, a refuge for the needy in their distress, a shelter from the storm and a shade from the heat." Isaiah 58:6–11:

> Is not this the kind of fasting I have chosen: to loose the chains of injustice and untie the cords of the yoke, to set the oppressed free and break every yoke? *Is it not to share your food with the hungry and to provide the poor wanderer with shelter—when you see the naked, to clothe them, and not to turn away from your own flesh and blood?* Then your light will break forth like the dawn, and your healing will quickly appear; then your righteousness will go before you, and the glory of the Lord will be your rear guard. Then you will call, and the Lord will answer; you will cry for help, and he will say: Here am I. If you do away with the yoke of oppression, with the pointing finger and malicious talk, and if you spend yourselves in behalf of the hungry and satisfy the needs of the oppressed, then your light will rise in the darkness, and your night will become like the noonday.

The Lord will guide you always; he will satisfy your needs in a sun-scorched land and will strengthen your frame. You will be like a well-watered garden, like a spring whose waters never fail.

Amos 5:23–24: "Take away from me the noise of your songs; I will not listen to the melody of your harps. But let justice roll down like waters, and righteousness like an ever-flowing stream"—quoted in Jimmy Carter's inaugural address. Do verses like these ever play in July 4 sermons?

Do not imagine that passages like these went down any easier in Old Testament times than they might at your next Bible study. When Amos called for recognition of God's option for the poor, the king's chaplain sent word to the seat of government: "Amos has conspired against you, in the very center of the house of Israel; *the land is not able to bear all his words.*" And so, as we may paraphrase, the president's lackeys said to the prophet: "O seer, go, flee away to the land of Judah, earn your bread there, but never again prophesy in Washington, DC, for it is the king's sanctuary and it is a temple of the kingdom" (Amos 7:10–13). You couldn't make this up; the Bible itself far outdoes any militancy from the Matthew 25 movement.

Did Matthew 25 Christians grow up hearing this entire biblical witness? Did they take courage in telling the needs of the poor in the ear of their congressional representatives, or the mayor and city council? Were they expecting to become a resistance movement? And is this true of all Christianity? At the next Sunday school pageant, act out this scene from Jeremiah 36, a test in speaking truth to power. Jeremiah is writing down in a scroll all the words God was giving him to say. Today's president wants a copy for the Library of Congress, but fancies a private reading from the prophet would be nice. Then it's all downhill. As Jeremiah reads his lines out and the scroll unwinds, the president, increasingly infuriated, takes out his penknife, cuts off the prophet's pages one by one, and throws them into the fireplace. Fox News can't get enough of this story, the president is very pleased with himself, and MSNBC releases a statement: *This is how the powerful regard the justice God demands for the poor.* When every last page from Jeremiah's scroll is burned, he goes back home and writes it all down again. But the peppy new youth leader who thought this would be a dramatic pageant to stage is fired.

Nor can the church get by with a charity drive alone. God wants much more. He takes up the case of the poor and advocates for the oppressed and proposes that his servants become instruments to overcome poverty. Now it really gets wild. No new religious movement today, certainly no political platform, could imagine this: Leviticus 25:8–16 orders a "Jubilee" every fiftieth year, when debts will be cancelled, slaves freed, and land returned to its original owner. Karl Marx never dreamt this big. And every seven years, which is to say every "Sabbath Year," there is a required program of *debt forgiveness*. (As I write this, President Biden is moving with extreme caution to consider student loan forgiveness.)

Now the church's song leader gets involved. He commissions new hymns drawn from the Psalms and insists on teaching them to the congregation. From Psalm 9:9: "The Lord is a refuge for the oppressed, a stronghold in times of trouble." Psalm 12:5: "Because the poor are plundered and the needy groan, I will now arise, says the Lord. I will place them in the safety for which they long." Psalm 35:10: "Who is like you, Lord? You rescue the poor from those too strong for them, the poor and needy from those who rob them." Psalm 109:30–31: "With my mouth I will greatly extol the Lord. God stands at the right hand of the needy, to save their lives from those who would condemn them." Psalm 72:3–4: "May the mountains bring prosperity to the people, the hills the fruit of righteousness. May he defend the afflicted among the people and save the children of the needy; may he crush the oppressor." Psalm 72:12–14: "For God will deliver the needy who cry out, the afflicted who have no one to help. He will take pity on the weak and the needy and save the needy from death. He will rescue them from oppression and violence, for precious is their blood in his sight." Psalm 113:5–8: "Who is like the Lord our God, who is seated on high, who looks far down on the heavens and the earth? He raises the poor from the dust, and lifts the needy from the ash heap, to make them sit with princes."

A new Christian social justice movement, however, is most likely to appeal to the New Testament and to connect all these Old Testament references to Jesus' own ministry—since from the early days of Christianity the Old Testament became part of the Christian canon. Jesus clearly wants to fulfill the Old Testament dreams. He closes his inaugural sermon in Luke 4 quoting Isaiah 61:1: "The Spirit of the Sovereign Lord is on me, because the Lord has anointed me to proclaim good news to the poor. He has sent me to bind up the brokenhearted, to proclaim freedom for the captives and release from darkness to the prisoners."

JOHN COMPLEMENTS MATTHEW: JESUS' FOOT WASHING IS THE POSTURE FOR SERVANT-DISCIPLES

In a *Christian Century* article from March 25, 2020, called "A Strange Humbling Ritual," Amy Frykholm tells a lovely story about foot washing in an Episcopal church in Leadvillle, Colorado. A conspicuously homeless person who had been coming to receive supper for many weeks ended up sitting in church next to the priest's five-year-old daughter, when the time came for foot washing. As was the custom, the little girl knelt down at his feet, as if it were totally natural. She lifted his feet into the basin of warm water, put soap on her hands, and began to wash. The homeless man, whom everyone new as Kenny, began to laugh nervously. And then to cry. Then everyone began to cry, except the little girl Lara, who continued in a businesslike manner. *Imagine President Trump—or any American president—stripping down to robe and towel, kneeling, and washing the feet of immigrants arriving at the Texas border.*

In his book *Washing of the Saints' Feet,* Matthew Pinson explores the tradition of foot washing down through the ages since Jesus first inaugurated it. This would be a "history of the influences" of an original biblical text. Pinson discusses how foot washing came to be called an *ordinance,* rather than a sacrament, and cites hymns that can be sung to accompany it. Foot washing comes with a theology and is not just an act of humble service. It can be a centerpiece of incarnation as well as an act of humility and community among disciples. It is a "two-pronged, full-orbed gospel," and goes together with Communion. Communion goes with justification and God; foot washing with sanctification and loving your neighbor.

With foot washing such a transparent ritual and its holding up obedient service as the mark of disciples, you would not think the church could get it wrong, other than allowing the practice to atrophy over the years. But for a time the Catholic Church got it disastrously wrong. In *A New Commandment: Toward a Renewed Rite for the Washing of Feet,* Peter Jeffrey documents how when Catholics were developing the modern rubrics for renewing this rite in 1956, *they excluded women!* He believes this arose "from an unwise attempt to alter the ceremony into a kind of liturgical drama," which of course was originally exclusively male. That women have participated in foot washing ceremonies for much of Christian history, including in the early church, is well documented. Jesus' own washing of his disciples' feet had a twofold meaning—participation in his death and eternal life and as an example of humble servanthood. Neither meaning justifies excluding women. And so the exclusion of women was eventually corrected, and even Pope Francis, beginning in 2016, now conspicuously washes the feet of women in a great festival service on Maundy Thursday evening, that includes non-Christians as well. At the beginning of Holy Week when Jesus was staying with friends in the village of Bethany, a woman named Mary, in effect, washed Jesus' feet and anointed him with precious oil (John 12). Jesus even says that future ages will preserve "the memory of her." So foot washing is the posture of obedient discipleship, the Christian yoga to keep the servant-body in practice.

RECONCILING MATTHEW AND PAUL AND LUTHER IN CHRISTIAN HISTORY

Luther called James an epistle of straw because it seemed to emphasize "good works" more than grace. Although he didn't denigrate Matthew, John was Luther's favorite Gospel. Are Matthew and Paul reconcilable? Might Matthew's emphasis on being grasped by Christ the King and recognizing the presence of the King be parallel to grace and faith in Paul? And is Matthew's seeing Jesus in "the least of these" parallel to Luther's faith active in love? Yet there is no way Luther was going to make the good works in Matthew 25 one of "the marks of the church," which Luther limited to right preaching and right celebration of the sacraments. But Catholicism and Wesley might well celebrate Matthew's good works done on behalf of the least of these as "marks of the church."

Paul and Luther would have said we are not capable of knowing God on our own terms, it is a gift of grace. Is *seeing Jesus amidst the poor* a gift of grace? Matthew, too, would see the disciples' becoming aware of who and where the King is as a gift from Christ, the master discipler. Augustine, often seen as pre-Lutheran (or Lutherans as post-Augustinian), famously said that *"God created us without us but will not save us without us."* Wesley and others have said that Matthew implies that *good works are a means of grace*, which might make Lutherans shudder. And yet Matthew implied that grace is seeing Christ in the poor, which we too are (Luther said on his deathbed, "We are all beggars. This is true."). And the modern Lutheran Dietrich Bonhoeffer is famous for the somewhat confounding statement: "Only he who believes obeys; only he who obeys believes." Remember that his famous book *The Cost of Discipleship*, from which this quote is taken, was a meditation on Matthew. So church history becomes a history of the influence and effects and difficulties of biblical texts, and also their periodic eclipse, and we may have to wrestle with how to reconcile Matthew and Paul and Luther and Wesley and Bonhoeffer.

Maybe the "results" of famous theologians are not the same as the theologians and their affirmations themselves. German Lutheran feminist Dorothee Soelle proposed a "hermeneutic of consequences." Maybe the difference between law and gospel (Luther's template over all theology) is not the content but the effect. Soelle also said wryly that the religious establishment acts as if they know where God is not located—for example, on the road from Jerusalem to Jericho. But that is precisely where the parable of the good Samaritan locates God's call to be a good neighbor to those in need. In *On the Freedom of a Christian*, Luther, like Soelle, seemed to consider proper effects: "A Christian is lord of all, completely free of everything / A Christian is servant, completely attentive to the needs of all." Just as we are freely bound to God in Christ, we are bound in Christ to the neighbor and, in the history of effects, experience a terrifying vulnerability to the needs of others.

If we fearlessly wrestle with the Bible, including Matthew, and great traditions like Catholicism, Lutheranism, and Wesleyanism, we may reap not contradictions but rich reconciliations. And achieve the complexity of faith.

THE INCARNATIONAL DEPOSITS OF MATTHEW 25: SAINTS AND PROPHETS

In Christian history saints were sometimes seen as reminders that Jesus, who ascended into heaven long ago, had not left the church without witness or his presence. So the saints became incarnational deposits. Someone like the Catholic Dorothy Day might say that if the poor and the homeless are not spotted in the precincts of the church, then the church may be functioning without the witness of the living Christ, who lives among the least of these. When some contemporary Christians call themselves Matthew 25 Christians, they are announcing their commitment to becoming the kind of people called for in Jesus' last judgment story. To illustrate the history of Matthew's effects, how Matthew has "come true" over the ages, consider the likes of Martin Luther King, Francis of Assisi and his namesake Pope Francis (to whom this book is dedicated as the patron of the least of these), Mother Theresa, Sister Simone Campbell, John Lewis, Dorothy Day, Rev. William Barber, Vincent DePaul, William Booth of the Salvation Army, and the Jewish Abraham Heschel. To stimulate your own immersion in the history of Matthew's effects, pick several of these names to Google and see how Matthew has come true in the lives of saints ancient and modern.

ACTING OUT MATTHEW 25 IN CORPORAL AND SPIRITUAL WORKS OF MERCY

Matthew also comes true in the so-called "corporal works of mercy" done to the least of these in Jesus' story, and how they achieved larger meanings and lives of their own, for example from Jesus' mandate to visit the imprisoned, to engaging in prison reform and efforts to abolish capital punishment. Over time works of mercy became attached to the very culture of the church, beginning with monasticism and then medieval Catholicism and after the Reformation to Wesleyan Methodism.

Following the long Catholic tradition of embracing works of mercy, Methodism became a singular Protestant example. Eventually, summaries of John Wesley's theology and practice evolved into what came to be assembled as a "Wesleyan Manifesto." It constitutes remarkable statements of Christian practice on the ground and also a kind of midrash, or meditative expansion, of Jesus' own catalog of works of mercy—expanded into a social program that Christians should strive to adopt and practice in their contemporary personal, parish, and denominational life. Even today the aims of the "Manifesto" constitute a remarkably up-to-date agenda for the church in the modern world:

1. Reduce the gap between rich people and poor people.
2. Help everyone to have a job.
3. Help the poorest, including introducing a living wage.
4. Offer the best possible education.
5. Help everyone feel they can make a difference.
6. Promote tolerance.
7. Promote equal treatment for women.
8. Create a society based on values and not on profits and consumerism.

9. End all forms of slavery.

10. Avoid getting into wars.

11. Share the love of God with everyone.

12. Care for the environment.

Matthew 25 can turn into theological reflection and great poetry. In imaginative piety surrounding the obligation to clothe the naked, some Christians recalled that God clothed Adam and Eve. They also considered the implications of the fact that God, who had clothed humans in the garden of Eden, in Christ disrobed himself for the washing of the disciples' feet at the Last Supper. This inspired the great Puritan John Milton to write:

> Before him naked to the aire, that now
> Must suffer change,
> Disdained not to begin
> Thenceforth the form of
> Servant to assume,
> As when he washed his servants' feet so now
> As Father of his Family he clad
> Their nakedness with Skins
> Of Beasts.

Beginning in the twentieth century, much of the Protestant tradition began to expand the call of Matthew 25 as well. At the macro level, Lutheran World Relief would be one example, but perhaps the most well-known and best financed is the evangelical relief organization World Vision. It calls itself a Christian humanitarian aid, development, and advocacy organization, and prefers to present itself as interdenominational, including non-evangelical Christian denominations as well. It has begun referring to Matthew 25 in its mission statements. It was founded in 1950 as a service organization to meet the emergency needs of missionaries. In 1975 development work was added to World Vision's objectives. It is active in nearly ninety countries with a total revenue in 2017 including grants, product and foreign donations of more than $2 billion. Unlike Oxfam, another relief organization, World Vision has been and remains conspicuously Christian and makes its appeals a response to Jesus' own call in the New Testament. There are always issues, however, over the professionalization of an organization over against its distinctive Christian identity. Twenty years after founding World Vision,

Robert Pierce criticized the organization over that issue and went on to found Samaritan's Purse, a conspicuously evangelical organization that soon after its founding came to be led by the conservative evangelical and eventual Trump supporter, Franklin Graham (Billy Graham's son). This is the Samaritan's Purse mission statement: "After sharing the story of the Good Samaritan, Jesus said 'Go and do likewise.' That is the mission of Samaritan's Purse—to follow the example of Christ by helping those in need and proclaiming the hope of the Gospel." They pride themselves on answering people in the field who ask, "Why did you come?" with always the same response: "We have come to help you in the Name of the Lord Jesus Christ." (I confess that in my own tithing, beyond the parish and denominational level, I choose to support organizations who are "always ready to give an account of the hope that is within them" (1 Peter 3:15).)

Still another Protestant Christian works-of-mercy relief organization is the Salvation Army, a descendant of Methodism in theology and piety. It is both an actual church and an international charitable organization, reporting a worldwide membership of over 1.7 million. Its founders sought to bring salvation to the poor, destitute, and hungry by meeting both their "physical and spiritual needs." It is present in 131 countries, running charity shops, operating shelters for the homeless, disaster relief, and humanitarian aid to developing countries.

There can be, and are, different motivations and actualizations in response to Jesus' call for works of mercy. The Catholic Worker Movement saint, Dorothy Day, worked in direct, on-the-ground ministry to the poor, in contrast to the vast, sophisticated macro, systemic (and often government-lobbying) responses to world poverty by huge church relief organizations. Dorothy Day and her cohort Peter Maurin insisted that what really counts is individual Christians actually meeting the poor, coming among them, eating with them. This is an argument for the works of mercy becoming part of the very fabric of Christian faith at the parish and individual Christian level. But many, including me, while lauding Day's efforts, also call for a structural diagnosis and response to the plight of all those in a social and economic system who desperately need works of mercy—many of them victims of late capitalism and neoliberal governments who shame and marginalize the poor and decline the entitlement funding that would lead to greater social justice. Bread for the World, founded by Lutherans, is an example of an organized response to feeding the hungry whose whole approach is not soup kitchens but lobbying the government. They famously emphasize that one bad vote against food stamps in Congress can be more consequential than all the charitable contributions from American churches in a year.

Consider another category not mentioned in Jesus' story. Not "*corporal* works of mercy" but "*spiritual* works of mercy," which gradually achieved its own status, such as: instruct the ignorant, counsel the doubtful, admonish the sinners, bear patiently those who wrong us, forgive offenses, comfort the afflicted, pray for the living and the dead. These too have appeared in some religious traditions.

LEARNING TO SING MATTHEW 25 TODAY

Another test of how much works of mercy have appeared in the piety and practice of religious communities is whether they show up in the hymns that congregations sing. Most hymns related to Matthew 25 in Christian history were about last judgment themes, as were the sculptures at the entrance to medieval churches meant to admonish (or terrorize) Christians coming in to worship. But specific evocation of corporal works of mercy in congregational song is only a recent phenomenon. Contemporary hymn writers have begun writing new songs on Matthew 25 themes, even if they are typically set to historic tunes. Very recently, even the plight of immigrants is being sung.

Protestant worship is more hymn-based than Catholic worship. New hymns, mostly in Protestant settings, give evidence of the specific recovery of Matthew 25 as Christian markers. It is easy to find new hymns, by topic, by Googling websites that list hymns relating to various lectionary readings in the church year, certainly including relating to Jesus' last judgment story in Matthew 25:31–46—featured on Christ the King Sunday in Year A of the lectionary cycle. Unfortunately, denominations that rely heavily on their own hymnbooks, renewed only every decade or less, are less likely to be pioneering the works of new hymn writers. But the "least of these" have begun to show up in new freelance hymn texts. The following hymns, and more, can be Googled. Consider this particularly striking hymn-dialogue for congregation and soloist (or choir) by the prolific hymn writer Carolyn Winfrey Gillette, to the tune of "O Master, Let Me Walk with Thee" (Maryton).

When Did We See You Hungry, Lord?

(Congregation):	When did we see you hungry, Lord?
(One voice)	"I work two jobs so we can eat …
	I search for food we can afford …
	I am your neighbor down the street!"
(Congregation):	When did we see you thirsty, Lord?
(One voice)	"I carry water miles each day …
	I long for water, close and pure …
	I am your neighbor far away!"
(Congregation):	When were you still a stranger, Lord?
(One voice)	"I moved to your community …
	I wait your hand at your church door …
	I am each stranger that you see!"
(Congregation):	We see the child whose shoes are worn …
	We see the man in hospice care …
	We see the prisoner many scorn …
	A voice cries out; Will we be there?
(Congregation):	Jesus, your presence here is real;
	You came a servant on your knees.
	May we, your church, now humbly kneel
	And serve you in the "least of these."

Another hymn by Carolyn Winfrey Gillette, set to the tune of "Immortal, Invisible, God Only Wise," is the following:

Whatever You Do

"Whatever you do to the least ones of these,
I tell you in truth that you do unto me!"
Lord Jesus, you taught us! May we learn anew
That when we serve others, we also serve you.
When poor, waiting children pray hunger will end,
When those long-forgotten cry out for a friend,
When thirsty ones whisper, "O Lord, where are you?"—
We hear, in their longing, that you're calling, too.

In prisons and jails, Lord, we find a surprise;
We see you in people whom others despise.
At hospital bedsides we offer a prayer
And find, when we visit the sick, you are there.
When we reach to others in flood-stricken lands
And offer our hearts there, and offer our hands—
We notice, Lord Jesus, the gift of your grace:
We see, in the crowds of the suffering, your face.
"Lord, when did we see you?" Your teaching is clear
That when we serve others, we're serving you here.
And when your church heeds you and helps those in pain,
Then out of the chaos, hope rises again.

Still another hymn by Carolyn Winfrey Gillette is this one that evokes Christian responsibility to refugees. It can be sung to the tune of *Aberystwyth* (Jesus, Lover of My Soul):

God, How Can We Comprehend?

God, how can we comprehend—though we've seen them times before—
Lines of people without end fleeing from some senseless war?
They seek safety anywhere, hoping for a welcome hand!
Can we know the pain they bear? Can we ever understand?
You put music in their souls; now they struggle to survive.
You gave each one gifts and goals; now they flee to stay alive.
God of outcasts, may we see how you value everyone,
For each homeless refugee is your daughter or your son.
Lord, your loving knows no bounds; you have conquered death for all.
May we hear beyond our towns to our distant neighbors' call.
Spirit, may our love increase; may we reach to all your earth,
Till each person lives in peace; till your world sees each one's worth.

A hymn now common to very many hymnals is this one by Albert F. Bayly, that can be sung to the tunes *Hyfrydol* and also *In Babylone*. It was written in the mid-twentieth century in response to a Hymn Society of America search for new hymns on social welfare.

Lord Whose Love in Humble Service

Lord, whose love in humble service
Bore the weight of human need,
Who upon the cross, forsaken,
Worked Your mercy's perfect deed:
We, Your servants, bring the worship
Not of voice alone, but heart;
Consecrating to Your purpose
Every gift which You impart.
Still Your children wander homeless;
Still the hungry cry for bread;
Still the captives long for freedom;
Still in grief we mourn our dead.
As you, Lord, in deep compassion
Healed the sick and freed the soul,
By Your Spirit send Your power
To our world to make it whole.
As we worship, grant us vision,
Till your love's revealing light
In its height and depth and greatness
Dawns upon our quickened sight,
Making known the needs and burdens
Your compassion bids us bear,
Stirring us to ardent service,
Your abundant life to share.

4

Can Matthew 25 Be Heard Today?

WHICH "ERRAND INTO THE WILDERNESS": RIVAL TEXTS AND CONTEXTS

IN "ERRAND INTO THE Wilderness," a famous election sermon in 1670, the Puritan preacher Samuel Danforth invited reflection on what exactly his forefathers had been seeking when they came to these shores. He was alluding to the story in Matthew 11 when the beleaguered John the Baptist sent word to Jesus, "Are you the one we are to expect or should we look for another." What had John gone out into the wilderness to see?

In the late twentieth century, as a response to the challenges of modernity and the secular marginalization of religion, a new and militant religious nationalism arose on the Christian Right. Instead of recognizing the call from God to the wilderness, in ancient Israel and again in Jesus and John's ministry, instead of, still today, a call to acknowledge a liberating God and a painstaking social covenant in response, there was substituted instead an idol of self-congratulation. By the time of President Trump, national idolatry had become a red hat with "Make America Great Again" its insignia. But in Facebook posts, Trump was often depicted by critics as a golden calf, the false god Israel had once worshipped instead of the God who had brought them out of Egypt.

Luther would have called Matthew's message a "theology of the cross," but Christian nationalism a "theology of glory." One of the reasons the disciples, and the crowds assembled at judgment day, were not able to *see Jesus among the least of these*, was that they had not understood or accepted that Jesus' parousia was a journey that went through the cross on the way to exaltation as Christ the King. In adopting the term "theology of the cross," Luther wanted to affirm that our knowledge of God and how God saves goes through the cross and does not immediately jump to a theology of glory attached to human self-congratulation.

The function of this field guide is to analyze Matthew's prospects, gauging the possibility of Matthew's text being heard in today's context. Consider the din above which Matthew waits to be heard. Can Matthew 25 Christians, having resolved their own spiritual quest, resolve the problems of their age? Was Matthew setting his narrative amidst a struggle early Christianity faced towards the end of the first century? Was Matthew's context a crisis in understanding discipleship? As Jesus approaches Jerusalem as the culmination of his ministry, he invites the disciples to reconsider the road he is traveling and whether a king's parousia can emerge via a cross. William James proposed that *once born* people conform en masse to the consensus reality of their age, but *twice born* people achieve their direction by resolving *an identity crisis*. In this process, this conversion story, their souls are transformed and fixed into a new direction for their age. Messengers of Matthew 25 to the modern age *appeal for transcending the givens of modernity, not accommodating them, not settling—and certainly not absolutizing them.*

In our age, while self-congratulatory Christian nationalists were erecting their idol, counter stories were being proposed, like Howard Thurman's *Jesus and the Disinherited,* and James Cone's *A Black Theology of Liberation* and *The Cross and the Lynching Tree.* Many Christians then and now were declining to consider the discomforting truths of black oppression and liberation amidst the self-congratulation of white Christianity—whose premise is lately named "whitemanism." One errand fixes on personal behavior and individual salvation; another sets out to acknowledge social sins and construct social justice.

In 2006, the distinguished evangelical historian of American religion, Randal Balmer, published *Thy Kingdom Come: How the Religious Right Distorts the Faith and Threatens America, An Evangelical's Lament.* The cover blurb summarized: "For much of American history, evangelicalism was aligned with progressive political causes. Nineteenth-century evangelicals fought for the abolition of slavery, universal suffrage, and public education. But contemporary conservative activists have defaulted on this majestic legacy, embracing instead an agenda virtually indistinguishable from the Republican Party." Must the magnification of Matthew take place not only against a secular society but Christian conservatism championing national culture as well?

THE TRIUMPH OF THE NATIONAL CULTURE AS LIMITING CONTEXT OVER MATTHEW'S TEXT

Is there any room in the inn for Matthew? Even in the first century Matthew was documenting a continuing struggle between Jesus and his disciples, between Jesus and the religious establishment, between Jesus and contemporary political power. It is the same today. To cover investments in the status quo, many imagine a gospel that is apolitical, scarcely noticing the forces arrayed against the status quo-defying claims of Jesus. The churches and their members hardly notice either, though the Anabaptist traditions are aligned against this sellout. It may be very difficult for Matthew to break through the defenses of the twenty-first century, including both many Christians and the spiritual but not religious. In the early days of Jesus' ministry, followers of the potentially disruptive and nonconforming John the Baptist sent emissaries to Jesus asking, "Are you the One, or shall we keep looking?" Too few are asking these days. Perhaps because they sense that the Jesus who is deeply concerned with the poor is not the religious leader they have been looking for.

At the beginning of the twentieth century, following the Gilded Age, which was perhaps only a shadow of what we now face, there emerged a Protestant social gospel movement that became a monumental contribution to world Christianity. Its time passed soon enough as conservative Christians realized it was rooted in Protestant liberalism. Later, the programs of Franklin Delano Roosevelt and then Lyndon Baines Johnson seemed to draw on such a social gospel in many ways. (It is suggested that LBJ had learned about it in Sunday school.) Now we are a very long way from those days, and a social gospel is said to be a suspicious idea smelling of cultural Marxism. The period from Reagan to Trump championed a *small government ideology* with an opposite pitch: no entitlement programs for the downtrodden, low taxes that shield the wealthy from demands for their fair share towards the good of the commons, capitalism disencumbered from responsibility to societal stakeholders, free market fundamentalism as God's plan. All these together constitute a defensive wall against Matthew's vision. The least of these are squeezed out of the idea of a commonwealth, and even the word seems merely quaint, a relic of a bygone age. The poor have been deleted from the social imaginary. Citizens can be arrested for setting out bread or water for the stranger. As I write, Georgia has just criminalized the offering of water to drink to people waiting in line to vote.

SECULARISM AND MATERIALISM, WITH THE SPIRIT GONE OUT

Though no one frankly admits it, secularism has settled as the official ideology, the native language, of the public square inhabited by the prosperous, while the white lower classes have been persuaded that social programs will disinherit them. Social, cultural, and economic forces have *subtracted religion* from intellectual consideration. Sociology names this process "secularization theory," and Max Weber broke the news of the *disenchantment* of the world. *Matter and spirit* are no longer in balance. They used to be like a teeter-totter in the game of life. Long ago some villages would connect their playground seesaws to a mechanism that pumped water to the community wells. Community play supported the common good and achieved social capital. Now, just one end of the teeter-totter stubbornly anchors reality, while the opposite floats inaccessibly in the air. No balance, no water for the common wells. Materialism is a one-sided departure from a balance between the material and the spiritual. The old moral reasoning that could imagine and fund the virtues of a good society is no longer sustained. No one seems to be looking for the "habits of the heart" that could sustain a godly commonwealth. A self-satisfied post-Enlightenment age pits the full implications of a materialistic worldview against the ghosts of Western Christianity once seen in moral progress, universal values, and human exceptionalism. Even Christian humanism.

LIBERTARIANISM AND INDIVIDUAL AUTONOMY VS. THE CLAIMS OF OTHERS

Ayn Rand, the patron of libertarianism, has her hero Howard Roark declare the meaning of his life: "I do not recognize anyone's right to one minute of my life. Nor to any part of my energy. Nor to any achievement of mine. No matter who makes the claim, how large their number or how great their need." Rand's world is defined as a battle between creators and parasites. The creator is self-sufficient, self-motivated, self-generated. He lives for himself. The parasite lives secondhand and depends on others. When Paul Ryan, whose patron saint is Ayn Rand, was still the Speaker of the House, the Georgetown Jesuit faculty admonished him that his social and economic philosophy had nothing whatever to do with the Catholicism he also claimed. Facebook routinely posts satirical images of people denouncing the arrival of a "socialist snowplow" amidst a severe blizzard. No one, including "small government," owes anybody anything.

MILTON FRIEDMAN'S FREE MARKET CAPITALISM GOES UP AGAINST MATTHEW

The legacy of economic theorist Milton Friedman is to declare the only responsibility of capitalism is to achieve maximum profits for its shareholders and to renounce all claims from so-called stakeholders, which is to say the commons, the victims of gross inequalities (externalities), and the environment. What started as an economic theory became unchallengeable economic science enacted by *rational actors* (posited as any sensible person) and installed as political reality. As in the Gilded Age that preceded the turn of the twentieth-century social gospel, so the Reagan gospel is the simple (and naive?) celebration of a capitalism disencumbered from a responsible role in the life of the commonwealth.

Hedge fund managers acknowledge no connection between their economic capital games and the social capital of the world in which they are played. They stick to takeover targets and job losses. The CEO of the Bank of America once admitted that he could not see any way to separate what's good for the US from what's good for the Bank of America. Wall Street cannot admit that it has designed and profits from a world that privatizes gains when they work and socializes losses when they don't.

At least until recently, St. Milton Friedman and "the Chicago School" had entrenched a free market orthodoxy in much of economic thought in the United States and suggested that this was not a matter of debatable theory but of hard facts, the kind that any rational actor would adopt and exercise. So no religious movement based on Matthew's good news to the poor could achieve "standing," a term the conservative Supreme Court likes. Most Christians could not imagine that they have any right to question the world of bankers or even that they are inhabiting the same world. Almost explicitly, Friedman set business and the economy free from any claims to social justice (that might stem from a reading of Matthew).

AMERICAN EXCEPTIONALISM, CHRISTIAN NATIONALISM, AND THE AMERICAN DREAM HAVE NO ROOM FOR MATTHEW

At the Republican National Convention in August 2020, vice president Mike Pence intoned what sounded like a biblical invocation: "Let's run the race marked out for us. *Let's fix our eyes on Old Glory* and all she represents. Let's fix our eyes on this land of heroes and let their courage inspire. And let's fix our eyes on the author and perfecter of our faith and freedom and never forget that where the spirit of the Lord is there is freedom—and that means freedom always wins."

But here is the actual biblical invocation that Pence appropriated: "Therefore, since we are surrounded by such a great cloud of witnesses, let us throw off every encumbrance and the sin that so easily entangles, and let us run with endurance the race set out for us. *Let us fix our eyes on Jesus*, the author and perfecter of our faith, who for the joy set before Him endured the cross, scorning its shame, and sat down at the right hand of the throne of God" (Hebrews 12:1–2).

In the Sermon on the Mount Jesus evoked "the light of the world, a city on a hill" to describe the Christian calling. In his seventeenth-century shipboard sermon en route to Massachusetts Bay, governor John Winthrop admonished the Puritan colonists to disembark with a very high standard of aspiration to become a city on a hill. President Reagan famously improved on Winthrop's rhetoric by adding *shining* to describe our status on the hill. A transformational aspiration became a boast.

In *As a City on a Hill: The Story of America's Most Famous Lay Sermon,* historian Daniel Rodgers argues that Winthrop's "we" never meant any human kingdom but was aspirational for Christian believers: to purify and enlarge the church itself. Winthrop was calling these Puritans not to become too at home in the world. Even the most devout are prone to stumble, and there is a slight chill of the judgment of God in Winthrop's exhortation. But Americans lost no time in shifting the metaphor. *When all American politicians close every speech with God bless America, they actually seem to mean "May God congratulate America."*

What came to be called "American exceptionalism" morphed into the idol of American nationalism. A frequent icon in the last years of the Trump presidency had people bowing down to a golden calf, while cynics were quoting the lines from Simon and Garfunkel's "Sounds of Silence": "And the people bowed and prayed to a neon god they made." Is America an expression of or a rival to Matthew's frequent appeal to the kingdom of heaven? In *The Myth of the American Dream,* D. L. Mayfield uncovers the dream as affluence, autonomy, safety, and power—the central values of entrenched privilege. This God is not to be found on the road to Jericho.

It is necessary to note, however, that in the week leading up to July 4, 2021, a remarkable number of articles appeared on Christian blogs, even in evangelical magazines, and also in Facebook posts denouncing the appearance of American flags in churches. There was even a liturgy for removing the American flag from the chancels of churches. Patriotic hymns were also called into question, and Christian services that were more about country than God. I have never noticed this before, and it is worth asking what in the national setting occasioned this. There was even a post on how to understand "Onward Christian Soldiers" as a hymn that was not about Christian militarism, or "supporting the troops," but about how biblical themes could suggest the vigorous presence of the church in the world standing up against all the forces arrayed against the kingdom of God. (In view of positions taken in this book, perhaps it could also be appropriated against the forces of capitalism that decimate the least of these.)

DARK MONEY INSURES AGAINST SOCIAL JUSTICE

Social ethicists make the point that creating space in which to do good is an act of moral imagination. Room for action toward the good is cleared. Questions about what sorts of persons we should be and how we should live return to public space. But with assistance from the Supreme Court massive amounts of dark money insure against claims of social justice. The ethics of good citizenship and virtue ethics, whether from natural law or biblical religion, are hemmed.

What was it that conservatism arose to conserve? Its advocacy of corporate and individual liberty is somehow matched by antipathy toward civil rights for all, a rejection of the newfangled Black Lives Matter, and any social equalization that smells like socialism. The icon of nineteenth-century conservatism, Edmund Burke, believed the lower classes should remain in place. His penetrating eye did not notice issues of class domination. So what is being conserved is class domination and oppression? Thomas Paine thought that it was power and not principles that Burke venerated. Interventions abroad were permitted, if they supported the dominant but never the lower classes. Man-on-the-street conservatism cherry-picks arguments that reinforce a well-entrenched status quo. Above all, it affirms a permanent place in the hierarchy of power for those who have historically held power. It defends inherited and acquired social status as a providential gift. The power of government is harnessed to protect historic privilege. White supremacy is a deeply held assumption that offers comfort and status to the dominant class. Such conservatism would seem to function as an *antidote to Matthew 25* or the liberating claims of the kingdom of God or some (unrealized) ideals eloquently invoked by the founding fathers. Jesus' claims to kingship offended the state and religious establishment in Matthew's time, and still does today.

If working-class and middle-class conservatism should stumble, billionaires are standing by as enforcers and provisioners. In her book *Dark Money: The Hidden History of the Billionaires Behind the Rise of the Radical Right,* Jane Mayer documents who is paying for the reign of privileged entrenchment that is modern conservatism. It is a multipronged strategy. At the outset, the ground was prepared in intellectual enterprises, chiefly think tanks and universities. The purpose of these "investments" was to nurture a new generation of "free-market conservatives" who would guarantee the dynamics of public discourse. A second prong of the strategy was to press state and federal legislators and the courts (with carefully screened judges like the recent Amy Coney Barrett) to shift economic policy to their (self-interested) way of thinking. Consider the devastating 2010 Supreme Court decision *Citizens United,* which in a 5–4 vote paved the way for the buying and selling of politics and government by wealthy investors, leaving a vast percentage of the populace, perhaps 98 or 99 percent, with an ever smaller voice. Not to leave the commoners behind, billionaires helped foster the grassroots efforts that eventually produced the Tea Party and its great significance in the Republican Congress.

Most of Mayer's analysis is devoted to the already legendary Koch brothers, Charles and David, who held their noses and went with Trump, procuring everything they dreamed of in a social and political system wedded to their interests. Their extraordinary wealth funds their heavy-handed attempt to dominate American politics. As Warren Buffet has said, "There's class warfare all right. But it's my class, the rich class, that's making war, and we're winning." The brothers are at the very center of the war machine. Though the Koch brothers provide a convenient (and worthy) target, they alone are not responsible for the wrenching changes that have taken place in American politics over the past several decades. The brothers preside over a network of billionaires and centimillionaires who operate in tandem in support of the most virulent right-wing (and late capitalist) causes and candidates in the country's politics. A total of some three hundred individuals constitute the network. As many as two hundred have attended recent annual gatherings hosted by the brothers. The brothers did not invent the tactics that have been used to upend the political order. Mayer credits the late Richard Mellon Scaife, the Pittsburgh-based scion of the Mellon Bank and Gulf Oil fortune. In 1964, Scaife set out to change the terms of political debate by investing heavily in think tanks and academic centers to espouse a radical "free market" ideology and imprint it on a new generation of scholars, lawyers, and activists. Scaife's various family foundations were soon followed by the Bradley, Olin, and Coors Foundations in advancing the right-wing agenda. In addition to Scaife and the Koch Brothers, the "vast right-wing conspiracy" they set in motion includes the recently deceased casino magnate Sheldon Adelson, a pro-Israel donor who has outpaced everyone else in the country in political spending in recent elections, and the DeVos family of Michigan, owners of Amway, as well as other members of the 0.01 percent, a majority whose fortunes were built on oil, gas, coal, and finance. What do they want? The plutocrats in the Kochs' network all profess similar political beliefs, which they characterize as "conservatism," to promote "freedom" and the "free market" in America. Is *conservative* the right word? Or is it radical and reactionary and does it have little to do with historic conservative traditions? Mayer claims that the intellectual agenda that runs throughout this group of supremely privileged individuals is a determination to turn back the clock to the nineteenth century, *repealing every political reform* instituted under Teddy Roosevelt and all his successors—from child labor laws to antitrust legislation to the progressive income tax to Social Security to the minimum wage to government healthcare. They demand the *precious freedom* to pollute, exploit their employees, avoid taxes, drown unions, dictate the terms of political debate, and pass their vast wealth on to their children and grandchildren in dynastic fashion. Whether one calls a certain vision of society the Christian social gospel or FDR's New Deal, this array of wealth is determined to stomp it out. To accomplish their ends, for example, they paid Glenn Beck $1 million to hype the Tea Party, they funded the gerrymandering of congressional districts to insure Republican victories, and they paved the way for Trump's victory by creating an ethos that became his base. They dominated federal elections more successfully than the robber barons of the Gilded Age at the end of the nineteenth century. As needed, they pay for elections.

How does this cartel spend the money at their disposal? They have created hundreds of think tanks, academic institutes, Super PACs, "public welfare" organizations, "charities," and businesses to put their money to work. The Heritage Foundation, the Cato Institute, the Federalist Society (which chose Trump's judges), and the Kochs' most identifiable political venture, Americans for Prosperity (AFP), are well known and substantial. One of these organizations' most distinctive accomplishments is to sow doubt about climate change and beat back all efforts to abate it. They contribute to the "anti-intellectualism in American life" that Richard Hofstadter famously documented, which has come to play nicely with a posture of anti-science and the instinctive distrust of experts, recently pandemic scientists. Towards the end of President Trump's gross mishandling of the COVID-19 epidemic, as respected scientists increasingly challenged it, Trump's new quack scientist arrived from Stanford's Hoover Institute to assure Americans who needed assurance that much of the scientific consensus surrounding how to respond to the corona virus epidemic was—thank God—simply not true.

Legal commentator Jeffrey Toobin has argued that the elevation of the Federalist Society as the arbiter of all judicial appointments and the philosophy of "original intent" and "textualism" were in fact meant above all to insure business interests. All conservative nominations to the Supreme Court (and appellate courts) must be approved by the Federalist Society. Well before he would become a Supreme Court Justice himself, Lewis Powell wrote a now famous memorandum to the United States Chamber of Commerce arguing that businesses needed to take a more aggressive hand in shaping public policy. *He saw the American economic system under broad attack from the consumer, environmental, and labor movements.* The agenda of the Federalist Society would be to transform the Supreme Court into a forum friendly to business interests. Later on, true to such intentions, the *Citizens United* decision would insure a steady flow of dark money on behalf of such interests. Powell's hope was that the "bright young men" of tomorrow would guarantee that the deregulated free enterprise system would come to prevail. Robert Bork and Antonin Scalia signed on as the first faculty advisers to a fledgling organization for conservative law students called the Federalist Society for Law and Public Policy Studies. Its efforts were lavishly funded by the business interests invoked by Powell, and it has trained a generation or two of future leaders. While Trump and Mitch McConnell would accommodate the antiabortion base of the Christian Right, the animating passion of McConnell's career, and that of many conservatives, has been the deregulation of political campaigns, and therefore the championing of business interests. The Federalist Society, in effect, auditions all important judicial appointments that must be relied on to cripple the regulatory state—and, by extension, all calls for government to promote social justice, raise taxes, bend the economy towards equality, or preserve the environment. What looked like a purely academic posture in favor of originalism and textualism was in fact an ingenious method of *guarding against social change*. Who knew the Federalist Society would stand in the way of all attempts to institutionalize the aspirations of Matthew 25 in the social economy! Who could have predicted that the six judges on the Supreme Court who are Catholic would happily jettison a whole century of Catholic social thinking, with its concern for the poor, workers, and unions, in favor of shielding business interests and an unregulated economy!

DOES EVEN THE CHRISTIAN RIGHT STAND AGAINST MATTHEW COMING TRUE TODAY?

An icon of our age could be Albrecht Durer's famous woodcut of the "four horsemen of the apocalypse," with secularism, materialism, libertarian individualism, and pillaging capitalism riding hard over the earth. But the several "Great Awakenings" in early American religious history promised periodic revivals that would stir individual hearts and refresh the commonwealth. By most accounts, these were the distinguished contributions of American evangelicalism, running from Jonathon Edwards' revivalism, to abolitionism, to a hopeful evocation of true religion amidst urban degradation. At their best, these were evocations of John Winthrop's dream of America as a city on the hill. A genuinely godly America would become a beacon for the world.

Surely the answer to looming American greed and materialism and self-dealing and contempt for the downtrodden is *religious revival*. Surely the religious answer to our malaise would be a reborn American evangelicalism with such a distinguished heritage to draw on. The Christian Right offers itself as just such an answer, claiming to be a moral majority that could become a conspicuous alternative to secularism and bound to make America great again. "How's that hopey-changey going?", as Sarah Palin would say.

Many secular progressives and mainstream Christian critics in fact denounce the Christian Right as *the problem not the solution*. Most surprisingly, the highly visible Christian Right religious movement is in fact a highly effective *obstacle* to the new religious movement of Matthew 25 Christians coming true. In the late twentieth century, beginning with the Moral Majority and nationalist religion and captive to the "original sin" of racism and white supremacy, the Christian Right either built up or was co-opted by corporate capitalism as God's economic vision and moral norm. The Christian Right as a new religious movement emerged to contend for the proper shape and piety of the true American Christian tradition. Some argue that it was not political operatives or moneyed interests who turned the South into conservative godly Republicans, but Southern Baptist pastors. (Who infiltrated and co-opted whom?)

Eventually this legacy became a political-religious movement surrounding Donald Trump as God's anointed. As we observed earlier, in spring 2019, a group of evangelical Christians sponsored a large billboard along a Texas freeway. It featured a looming picture of Trump, the slogan "Make America Great Again," and a startling quotation from John 1:14: "The Word became flesh and dwelt among us." To claim the "high Christology" of the prologue to John's Gospel as a fitting metaphor for Trump as God's anointed may instance ultimate blasphemy. Trump would become the fearless leader who would define the American contribution to a postmodern, post-Christendom grand narrative that would shape the dawn of the third millennium and return religion as a public good in a secular age. Consider the carrying capacity of this vision—Trump as God's new incarnation. Then prophecy failed, and Trump lost the election. Even after Trump incited the insurrection that tried to overthrow the vote and pillage the Capitol, the many evangelicals in the mob who had held up crosses and Christian banners insisted when Trump was impeached that indeed he was the fulfillment of "end-time prophecies" and the agent of an apocalyptic wave.

When the God who will save the nation no longer sounds like the one recalled through the prophets and Jesus Christ, and when God's up-to-date voice sounds suspiciously channeled through anti-government, anti-commons, anti-entitlements Wall Street self-regarding corporate interests, we suspect that a popular evangelicalism of self-congratulation, or resentment, or social Darwinist delusion has distanced itself from a biblical theology of the cross. Can Matthew 25 Christians swim in these waters?

The loudest and most media-savvy form of religion proposing to reoccupy the public square and save the country from godlessness is just this movement—lately aided and comforted by Catholic billionaire-supplied economic conservatives who are pleased as well to make abortion the single definition of moral sensitivity. The Christian Right came to represent a *Southern Orthodoxy* of American exceptionalism, white nationalism, anti-immigration, anti-feminism, anti-LGBT, anti-environmentalism, the harsh ethic of free markets, and a peculiar revulsion to kneeling black football players. In this prosperity-promising theology of glory, God's foolish wisdom of grace on the way to the cross and ultimate redemption tarries (just as in Matthew's narrative), and the arrival of the reign of God and the new creation the New Testament proclaimed is usefully *postponed for an end-time dispensation that does not trouble contemporary pursuits.* The Jesus who delivered the Sermon on the Mount is not only not on offer, but would be a moral hazard to the American way of life if he were to come riding into the capital city on a humble beast.

New Testament Christianity produces an excess of grace and gratitude and empathy, but religious nationalists do not demand radical change of the American way—except for cleansing society of gays and persistent women and reducing and confining pro-life ethics to fetuses stored in female bodies under careful observation. The sign outside the church door would have to say to any who show up by mistake or with false hopes of food for the hungry or shelter for the homeless: *Nothing to see here.* We do not preach Matthew 25 here. Jerry Falwell's Liberty University, the largest school of the Christian Right, means to graduate citizens certain of the *smooth continuity between the way ambitious Americans are and the way God is,* the divine hand stimulating the free market. Now Jerry Falwell Jr. has stumbled in the culture wars, for sexual indiscretions that could ruin its evangelical witness to the times, and was forced to resign by an evangelical board that wanted to stand for something. Of course, what brought him down was sexual sin, evangelicalism's favorite kind of sin. Not *social sin*, which makes evangelicals see red because it suggests the necessity of radical social change, which surely would mean ... socialism. Meanwhile, *capitalism (like Trump) has nothing to confess.*

Trump Tower had become a fortified citadel, a pseudo-Christian cathedral—now crashing—where Trump was periodically reanointed as God's just-in-time good news. One in four Americans believes that

God elected Trump to be our contemporary savior. Eighty percent of evangelicals voted for him and were still singing in his choir at the 2020 Republican National Convention. Celebrities like the national chaplains, Paula White, Billy Graham's heir Franklin, the Moral Majority heir Jerry Falwell Jr., and many megachurch pastors had assembled as Trump's "evangelical cabinet," the king's court, *domesticated prophets on retainer*, arisen to proclaim Trump as God's last, best hope. In exchange, they were guaranteed conservative Supreme Court justices and direct access to the White House.

Occasionally truth seeps into Facebook postings, as this one from a 2019 Trump rally-as-worship: "If you want to better understand Trump supporters, we should think of them as his congregation. He is their savior. He preaches to their fears and sense of victimhood. He empowers them. He rallies them. He emboldens them. He tells them whom to blame. He becomes their truth. He is the answer. Any assault on him is an assault on them. Do not deceive yourself into thinking your facts and logic can penetrate that emotional armor." After the massacre on Muslims in New Zealand, for which the white terrorist had seen Trump as his inspiration (as did the synagogue shooter, the mail bomber, and the Coast Guard white supremacist), a columnist for the *New Zealand Herald* wrote: "Trump personifies everything the rest of the world despises about America: casual racism, crass materialism, relentless self-aggrandizement, vulgarity on an epic scale."

No doubt many who look to Trump Tower, evangelical and even Catholic Christians as well as "nones," fear being *left behind* or disinherited in their hopes for well-being and (white nationalist) identity. They do not notice, or cannot name, the self-perpetuating extreme wealth and corporate greed that keep the 99 percent down and gradually lays waste to the earth. Socialism for hedge funds and scarcity for the middle class and the poor is the economic program. The 1 percent are pleased to help fund and cheer on the new religion because it serves their purposes. Wall Street is doing God's work on weekdays, its CEOs like to say. Climate science denial, for example, is not a matter of ignorant yokels, but a well-financed and deliberately conceived corporate plan to protect vested interests. In the Gospels, Jesus regularly condemned the managers of God's vineyards. Countless Americans are losing in a desperately unequal society, but the God-as-liberator and the love-as-justice traditions of the Bible do not loom. That would be socialism. *There will be no welcome mat for Matthew 25 and its partisans.* Trump Tower is the antithesis to a community that feeds the hungry, clothes the naked, heals the sick, houses the homeless, comforts the imprisoned.

We are at a religious impasse. The very social gospel, once regarded as America's distinctive contribution to world Christianity, was derided by American fundamentalists in the early twentieth century as a false delusion that would lead Christians away from the salvation in the hereafter that was their destiny and calling. And relieve the expected behaviors of sanctified selves by displacing them onto government. Christianity is about individualist freedom and individualist redemption, not to mention holding the line on women and gays. One cannot risk this Jesus-in-your-heart plan of salvation just for the sake of the poor. Any New Deal is never to use the word *social,* especially if it is twinned with justice.

So today one hears post-evangelicals and neo-Anabaptists, not to mention mainstream Protestants and Catholics, assert that *the death of Christian Right evangelicalism may have to occur* if the Christian tradition, and American Christianity, is to survive in its historic identity and calling. The wasting of American evangelicalism, together with the denigration of Catholic social thought in a corporate-funded Catholic neoconservatism, began to come in recent years under scrutiny—especially among evangelicals themselves and eventually in the religious press. The apotheosis of an evangelicalism gone dangerously wrong under Trump and already under Reagan and Bush came to be seen and lamented, or denounced, as a great tragedy in American Christianity.

It is not too much, in this time of Trump talk, to speak of a *great collusion* between Catholic and evangelical conservatism on the one hand and capitalist dark money on the other. The 1986 Catholic Bishops' pastoral letter, "Economic Justice for All," had been meant to revive historic Catholic social teaching and severely critique Reaganesque economics. Instead, it made Catholic conservatives crazy. It produced howls of outrage from Catholic neoconservatives. Catholic moral theologian Daniel Maguire compared them to "panicked devils shrinking from God's face in a medieval tapestry." So a Catholic Right arose to oppose this new social gospel, seemingly bent on creating their own counter-magisterium, for example in organizations like the Knights of Columbus. Catholic economic conservatives and libertarians, with funding from right-wing billionaires, seemed bent on a hostile takeover of American Catholicism. Their platform was unrestricted capitalism and small government, often meaning the diminishment of government services on behalf of the poor. A recovered natural law, meaning among other things no modern evolution in human rights, became the magisterial norm and easily overshadowed anything like Matthew 25. Indeed, it became necessary to name it the New Natural Law tradition.

Toward the end of the twentieth century, "post-evangelical" became a meme as the evangelical tradition underwent a division in its ranks. The increasing alignment with rightist politics was denounced by Fuller Seminary president Mark Labberton in a speech at Wheaton College that castigated evangelicals for political dealing, grasping at political power, racism, nationalism, and lack of concern for the poor. The evangelical stalwart InterVarsity Press commissioned a book devoted to the meaning and future of the movement and titled it: *Still Evangelicals? Insiders Reconsider Political, Social, and Theological Meaning*. An anthology by several evangelical heavyweights called itself *The Compromised Church: The Present Evangelical Crisis*. The blogger Michael Spencer aroused many with his essay, "The Coming Evangelical Collapse, and Why It is Going to Happen." Would an American evangelicalism seriously off course bring down much of Christianity with it? Would many Americans and especially young college graduates say "Good riddance!"? Are moderate Catholics and Protestants correct when they intone that it may take an entire generation for Christianity to survive and outlive the scourge of the Christian Right? Would it become a good excuse for millennials who were leaving the church anyway to do so with a clear conscience? Or, would a welcome mat for such as Matthew 25 Christians be put back out?

In her 2020 book *Unholy: Why White Evangelicals Worship at the Altar of Donald Trump*, journalist Sarah Posner examined the relationship among the president, his famously religious base, and the explicitly racist elements that have rallied to his political coalition. In 2008 she also published *God's Profits: Faith, Fraud, and the Republican Crusade for Values Voters*.

While some wanted to excuse the evangelical Right for championing rights of religious freedom they had lost, Christian historians of evangelicalism like Randall Balmer argued that it was more directly responsive to racial issues like the desegregation of public schools, and that it remains invested in distinctly racial politics. It seems clear to many that Trump is an avowed racist and evangelicals continued to support him not *despite* his racism but perhaps because of its permission-giving to their own prejudices. Religious neoconservative fundraiser Paul Weyrich had all along been arguing that the evangelical Right was motivated primarily by public school desegregation and the IRS crackdown on segregated private schools like Bob Jones University or "segregation academies" invented to avoid desegregation mandates.

Still, there can be great moments in religious history, *when the times are right for entertaining forgotten claims*. Matthew 25 Christians believe they are part of such a moment. But during the course of the evangelical Right's triumphs, there emerged the claim that God had chosen and anointed Donald Trump for this moment in American history. God had his hands on the American presidency—as he sometimes had with Old Testament leaders, even non-Israelites. Trump had arisen to beat back the extraordinary perils from globalism, George Soros, secularism, the secular Left, socialism, and other enemies of Christian values. Like King Cyrus in the Old Testament, Trump did not have to be a devout believer to be accomplishing God's plan to restore America. This new bloc of voters delegitimized the news media and science and expertise in general in order to argue the case for Trump. In this they parrot the old hypothesis of Richard Hofstadter regarding the anti-intellectualism and paranoid style in American politics. Amidst the rise of fake news, truth became slippery and alternative facts emerged as a concept of the day. Even amidst the ashes of Trump's election loss, new evangelical prophets have arisen to announce, "He will rise again." Sounds familiar.

Posner's narrative concludes that the Christian Right hopes to transform the United States into a nativist power that accords different rights to different groups of people, based on race, religion, and ethnicity." Trump was merely "a catalyst, not a cause." While Posner sees a long, slow infiltration of Republican politics by the Christian Right, others see the carefully planned takeover of evangelicalism by economic and political conservatives. All along there persisted the view, both among mainstream Christianity and critical non-Trumpian evangelicals, that the Christian Right had, in effect, *made a deal with the devil*. This is the argument of Ben Howe in his *The Immoral Majority: Why Evangelicals Chose Political Power over Christian Values*. The very highly regarded lifelong social-justice evangelical, Ronald Sider, gathered many evangelical leaders to make a similar argument in *The Spiritual Danger of Donald Trump: 30 Evangelical Christians on Justice, Truth, and Moral Integrity*.

In *Trump: Evangelical Plague*, Robert Mamrak makes the now familiar argument that Donald Trump's election in 2016 would not have been possible without the overwhelming support of white evangelical Christians. Trump has rewarded their backing by supporting many of the positions they hold dear, but Mamrak derides the cost to evangelical integrity. He argues that evangelical support of Trump has associated Christianity with cruelty, racism, sexism, corruption, lawlessness, neo-Nazism, name-calling, and mocking the disabled.

While Trump was still seeking the 2016 GOP nomination, twenty-five high-profile Christians, many of them Pentecostal, all of them evangelical, came together to form Trump's Faith Advisory Committee. They helped Trump form policies and develop a message that would resonate with evangelicals. In effect, they provided the candidate with religious cover for a life of immoral decadence. They ignored basic moral and ethical standards for access to power. This (inadvertently?) played into a decades-long campaign, well financed by wealthy right-wing extremists, to co-opt white people by cultivating inroads into the religion many hold so personally. Many critics argue that Trump is not merely morally deficient, but is profoundly unchristian, and so evangelical support for Trump was seen as the great sellout of a lifetime. In *Believe Me: The Evangelical Road to Donald Trump*, the evangelical historian John Fea tried to explain how we have arrived at this unprecedented moment in American politics. Fea argues that the embrace of Donald Trump is the logical outcome of a long-standing evangelical approach to public life defined by the *politics of fear*, the pursuit of worldly power, and a nostalgic longing for an American past. Trying to assess how Trump achieved a huge evangelical vote, Fea addresses the inconsistencies that many conservative religious leaders have demonstrated over time in their responses to different presidents, Clinton and Trump, for example, giving an unlimited pass to one while wanting to burn the other at the stake. Fea quotes a 1998 letter from Focus on the Family leader James Dobson, questioning Clinton's morality: "As it turns out character DOES matter. You can't run a family, let alone a country, without it. How foolish to believe that a person who lacks honesty and moral integrity is qualified to lead a nation and the world!" Fear drives many of the political viewpoints and voting practices among evangelicals who place their hope in compromised earthly powers, especially those who tell us what to be afraid of and how they are the only ones who can fix it. Fea concludes by calling evangelicals to hope, not fear; humility, not power; and history, not nostalgia. Alas, Fea concludes: "The Court Evangelicals have decided that what Donald Trump can give them is more valuable than the damage their Christian witness will suffer because of their association with the president."

In yet another take, Kristin Kobes Du Mez finds that it is toxic masculinity that evangelicals share with Trump. Her 2020 book is titled *Jesus and John Wayne: How White Evangelicals Corrupted a Faith and Fractured a Nation*. In a sweeping account of seventy-five years of white evangelicalism, she seeks to show how American evangelicals have worked for decades to *replace the Jesus of the Gospels with an idol of rugged masculinity* and Christian nationalism, or in the words of one modern chaplain, with "a spiritual badass." In this, evangelicals who are not theologically astute have drunk deeply from one stream of American culture. Evangelical popular culture teems with muscular heroes—mythical warriors and rugged soldiers, men like Oliver North, Ronald Reagan, Mel Gibson, and the Duck Dynasty clan, who assert white masculine power in defense of "Christian America." Chief among these evangelical legends is John Wayne, an icon of a lost time when men were uncowed by political correctness, unafraid to tell it like it was, and did what needed to be done. The heroic male enforcer, always carrying a gun.

Trump is not their first flashy celebrity to capture hearts and minds, nor the first strongman to promise protection and power. The values and viewpoints at the heart of white evangelicalism today—patriarchy, authoritarian rule, aggressive foreign policy, fear of Islam, ambivalence toward #MeToo, and opposition to Black Lives Matter and the LGBTQ community—are likely to outlast Trump. President Biden will not wash them away. While it is common to assume that white evangelicals got duped, bamboozled, and suckered by the candidacy of Donald Trump, Du Mez argues that Donald Trump is not an embarrassing "oops" at all, but the natural outcome of decades of affinity that white evangelicals have had for rugged masculinity, Christian nationalism, and harmful dispositions toward women and "others."

It would be one thing if the evangelical Right got co-opted by big money conservatism and its own white racism, while still holding on to some semblance of biblical Christianity. In that case, this book would not be taking such notice of it. But as it happens, the evangelical right is strongly "defended" against the covenanted justice of the Old Testament and Jesus' vision in the New Testament. *Conspicuously, it stands in the way of a Matthew 25 religious renewal.* Other than through private acts of Christian charity, there is no social and moral vision for the least of these. What could be more opposite than toxic masculinity and loving concern for the least of these? Trump Tower vs. a Jesus Center for the downtrodden?

BUT MR. ROGERS GOT MATTHEW

Is there, then, no public welcome for a movement of Matthew 25 Christians today? No welcome mat in the neighborhood? Only partly with tongue in cheek I nominate Mr. Rogers's legacy. Could he have prepared the way for Matthew's Jesus—like a *Godspell* song infectiously beckoning us to accept and believe? And still be wildly popular and admired, in spite of all I've written above? Was he leading us back to forgotten values, not only to the concept of neighbor but to a sustaining neighborhood? Of course some people eventually discovered that Mr. Rogers was a Presbyterian minister, and so historic Christianity would get the credit for welcoming back one of its own texts. But if you only went by what you and your children saw in his TV neighborhood, there was no Christian church. And no explicit sermons—except for his life, his whole persona. His decency and self-effacement and empathy and integrity are the antithesis of the TV star who came after him, Donald Trump. Mr. Rogers attracted a wide array of people to his way of being in the world, though to some he seemed an unattainable and perhaps unbelievable saint. He recognized the dignity in every person. He demonstrated a remarkable empathy for those who suffered or were vulnerable. You could sense his unyielding trust in common goodness and God's creation—even if he didn't mention it explicitly or you didn't quite have a name for it. To those who know their way around the Gospel of Matthew, and something about Jesus the protagonist of Matthew's story, Mr. Rogers might seem rooted there. Matthew plays in Mr. Rogers's neighborhood. If Jesus constituted a moral argument for the existence of God, Mr. Rogers did too. He drew himself from Matthew's Jesus.

You could almost say that Mr. Rogers constituted a moral universe on American television. Who knew? The reporter Tom Junod wrote a long piece for *Esquire*, "Can You Say . . . Hero?" And he became Mr. Rogers's friend when he went back to see if he was real. Or too good to be true. He eventually wrote the script for the highly regarded film that celebrated Mr. Rogers. The main goal of the film, *Won't You Be My Neighbor?*, is to convince us that while kindness and empathy are in short supply today, it need not be that way. The argument is that Fred Rogers's worldview, a kind of humanism that had roots in Rogers's Christianity but expressed itself as a commitment to everyone's dignity, is what helped many navigate the scariest events of childhood. A leading character in the neighborhood is King Friday, the stern monarch of the Neighborhood of

Make-Believe, who erected a border fence of his own around his castle, and then was convinced to take it down—by messages of goodwill and peace that other characters (both puppet and human) floated over his fence.

What is startling about the movie is the experience of the audience. American viewers experienced the revelation that Mr. Rogers was, as far as anyone seems able to tell, basically the person he presented himself to be onscreen. Is this, then, a life possibility? But that's not what we expected. Watching the film, it's hard to believe it's true. Even *after* seeing the film, it seems a bit suspect. We remain worried that eventually we may be forced to see through it all.

Speaking of neighbors, Jesus told a story to someone who asked, "Who is my neighbor?" It was the story of the good Samaritan, a parable in which the most "righteous" and powerful members of his own society passed by a man lying in a ditch on the side of the road to Jericho. Who finally rescues him and cares for him? A Samaritan—one of the people whom Jesus' listeners considered to be less worthy of dignity and respect than themselves. Of course Mr. Rogers knew this Gospel story when he structured his entire series around the idea of neighborhood. Mr. Rogers, and this story, is radically subversive because we all know life is not like this. But could it be? Does God live on the Jericho road? Could it be a neighborhood with social obligations? Could the message of Matthew pop up in Mr. Rogers's neighborhood? Could text and context come together even today? Is Mr. Rogers our ticket back to Matthew? To Christian humanists like him functioning as earth angels? To Jesus' presence in the least of these? Have we been wrong to be so cynical? Couldn't Mr. Rogers be the real truth, and not Donald Trump? Is Joe Biden the Catholic president trying to get there too?

COULD AMERICAN CIVIL RELIGION PRODUCE A RESONANCE WITH MATTHEW 25 IN AMERICAN CULTURE?

It is not an accident that I brought up Mr. Rogers. Or that I long for a Christian humanism that he exemplified in the national culture. In Part II of this book I will propose that a new religious movement that wants to live by its founding text, that wants to plant and grow it, will have to—as all new social movements must do—institutionalize (plant and nurture) and magnify (embellish and intensify). Successful institutionalization means creating a distinctive social and physical presence in public space, as well as in the life of the church. Institutionalization on behalf of Matthew 25 may well include collaborations between church and other people of good will, between theologians and public intellectuals and critical economists, between religion and government. From all these alliances could grow a broad Christian humanism, or a virtue ethic drawn from premodern moral thought that still grasped grand narratives, that leavens the commonwealth, builds social capital, and evokes social justice across the land. The likes of Mr. Rogers magnified would be a start at a renewed civil religion in an otherwise preoccupied public square. *Civil religion* generally refers to implicit religious values in a nation, exemplified in public rituals, symbols, and ceremonies. Would it be wrong or dangerous to suggest that a renewed *Matthew 25 Christianity* could redeem the church, and society, and the nation? Isn't it Matthew 25 that could render us a true "city on a hill," rather than a slogan for national self-congratulation? Must we fear an incipient theocratic nationalism if its defining essence is concern for the least of these?

I won't linger long with civil religion, lately much critiqued, before returning to the richly biblical, historical, church-based orthodox Christianity we have seen to be the grounding of Matthew 25 Christians. This will be the theme of the next chapters where we ground the church gathered before sending it out. Not everyone in a Matthew 25 movement wants to reach for coalitions beyond biblical Christianity, but those who are not afraid of words like *social* and *structural* may see promise and even necessity in collaborations with government and economic theorists and the social sciences, if social justice is to be achieved and the least of these to become worthy of public attention. Seeing Jesus among the least of these is an exercise in Christian faith; attending to the least of these is also a matter of public policy, truly a New Deal for a social democracy. The intersection of those two is complicated and wins approval from some and rejection from others. We have already seen that some socially conscious Christians want no boundaries crossed between church and state, because of the disasters to country and Christianity occasioned by the Christian Right.

But as a student of Robert Bellah long ago *(Habits of the Heart: Individualism and Commitment in American Life; The Broken Covenant: American Civil Religion in Time of Trial; The Good Society; Beyond Belief: Essays on Religion in a Post-Traditionalist World)*, I do want to pause here to consider the merits and promise of civil religion—even if the Christian Right effectively turned it into national idolatry, even if the "freedom from religion" front think they must abhor it, even if it invites church/state abuses, even if it seems to dumb down historic orthodoxy, even if it remains markedly distinct from biblical Christianity, even if its theology has the odor of sociology.

There is a long tradition of calling the United States a Christian nation (much denied lately for opposing reasons) and of speaking of an American civil religion that brings people together through shared beliefs, experiences, and rituals. Although there is always the danger of an idolatrous nationalism, it may also be fitting to claim America for God, to argue against an assertive secularism that insists on denying such a heritage, that protests the displacement of Christians as an essential part of the country's history. But Calvinist "dominion theology," for example, feels compelled to insist on God's sovereignty in every sphere of human life without necessarily implying theocracy. All this can be an honorable and faith-based assertion of Christianity as a nonconforming resistance movement that wants to lobby for Christian values in the public square, from which secularist ideologies are determined to exclude them while also wanting to reoccupy the public square themselves. In sophisticated Catholic versions it appeals to natural law as a values system built into the universe, claimed by the framers of the Constitution, and in need of reassertion in a post-values public culture where the dignity of humans and human rights need to recover their ontological grounding. In books like Peter Wehner's *The Death of Politics: How to Heal Our Frayed Republic After Trump* and Michael Gerson and Wehner's *City of Man: Religion and Politics in a New Era*, the anti-Trump neoevangelical authors are passionately opposed to those "court evangelicals" who have sold out their heritage in exchange for special recognition of their influence and privilege. But just as fervently, they argue for *religiously motivated involvement in public policy* (just as do Leftist Christians who lobby for a new social gospel in the land). They reject the argument of some secularists that any religiously based idea should be disqualified from public discussion. In this they follow the Lutheran-turned-Catholic Richard John Neuhaus who argued similarly in *The Naked Public Square*. They oppose Christians who want to opt out of political involvement because it is dirty or out of bounds or because they are embarrassed by Christian fanatics who have overplayed their hand. They oppose any neat separation from spiritual and worldly affairs as both illogical and unbiblical. A rich practice of faith cannot renounce involvement in public life. But they also oppose the assumption that Old Testament covenant theology can directly be mapped onto the modern state today—to produce a theocracy. They are very cautious about any movement that sounds like either theocracy or like socialism.

When Christians speak out today, they argue, they should be nonabrasive, culturally sophisticated, and theologically conservative—and in search of common ground rather than delivering monologues of black-and-white statements. Christian academics have similarly argued against prima facie exclusion of religious sensibilities in public universities. But the certainties of the Christian Right must fade away. As also, in their view but not mine, of the religious Left! I myself prize the Left's determination to see in the *social and the structural* the necessary scope of moral analysis. Christians must refuse to be co-opted by either political party, these neoevangelicals insist. They want their readers to focus on these questions: How can religious people exercise influence while maintaining their integrity? What tone should they be known for? How should they think about the role and purpose of government? Which causes and issues, both at home and abroad, ought to be a part of their agenda?

Towards the end of this book I will consider the possibility that the Matthew 25 movement might argue for an explicitly leftist, social-democratic version of the argument these conservative Catholics and evangelicals are making. As a new religious movement that activates the historic meanings of Matthew 25, they are likely to argue for a vigorous return to the public square, from which religion has lately been excluded by many public intellectuals. As neoevangelicals and neo-Anabaptists and progressive politically savvy mainstream Protestants and Catholics, they are likely to argue for Christianity as a vigorous and often dissenting social movement in the body politic, that religious faith is likely to connect God to an economy that has often been self-isolating from moral values, or, as is frequently said today, that a national budget is a moral document. A movement towards a new social gospel will honor and reflect the vision of Old Testament prophets and of Jesus in the Gospels. Their goal is for Matthew to once again come true in the history of its effects!

This would be a commonwealth in which libertarian individualism does not eliminate the possibility of seeing and experiencing one's neighbor. Such a religious movement is likely to heed a call to come together in new ways in order to survive, hold the powerful responsible for their unjust policies and the obfuscations they've promulgated to cover up injustice, and rebuild on foundations of love and justice. This is very likely to mean enacting universal healthcare, living wages, vigorous unions, debt relief, and housing rights for all. It includes holding those in power accountable, demanding that the rich and powerful do not profit from the misery of the least of these. The Matthew 25 movement, through its many activist theologians and ethicists, and in alliances with secular progressives and critics, is likely to argue to abolish systemic racism, end poverty and gross inequalities, turn militarism and our war economy into a peace economy, and protect the earth. They imagine a revolution in moral values that proclaims all life sacred and re-enchants the earth. And never renounces the least of these.

Part II

Taking Matthew 25 Public Today

TAKING MATTHEW PUBLIC IN church and society and country, the theme of Part II of this book, has a Wall Street ring about it. The patron saint of "initial public offerings" (IPO) as a dimension of a new religious movement that takes off is the apostle Paul, who understood his religious conversion to turn him into an instrument of the God of Israel now "going public" across the world and opening Paul's vision and missionary activity beyond the high walls of Judaism to all the Gentiles. Paul turned his personal investment in God's call into a new Christian message to the Roman world, harvesting new "colonies of heaven" and generating ever new religious capital along the way. (In Wall Street practice, an individual investor totally sold on the value of a new venture deliberately seeks the input of many additional investors through an imaginative IPO that attracts sufficient capital for a worldwide effort.) To stay with this metaphor, could an initial public offering describe how the Christian social gospel moves from the church gathered to the church sent, and thereafter attracts a wide array of political, economic, and academic investors and accumulate sufficient social capital to achieve a New Deal for social democracy? *This book wants to be a field guide to such a movement.*

But proposing such a process in an American setting is not an idea out of nowhere. German and Scandinavian social democracies have typically evolved under Christian influence, as reflected in the name of two German political parties, Christian Democratic Union (CDU) and Christian Social Union (CSU). Imagine concern for the least of these as a compelling idea in a social democracy. (Facebook is full of astonishing stories about social welfare states in northern Europe.) It could happen here. Or not—if the cultural and economic forces arrayed against Matthew 25 thinking are simply too overwhelming. In recent decades there have arisen some movements in the United States championing "socially responsible investments." These small movements borrow the metaphor of an initial public offering to attract individual investors. The pitch is to achieve investments that are morally as well as financially rewarding.

I am proposing this public offering metaphor as a way of magnifying Matthew beyond new religious movements in the churches into movements for social justice across the system. As opportune moments for religious values like "good news to the poor" that move from church to government, they propose to bring together religion and society and culture and economics in creating nurturing communities that overcome the polarizations and deficits of a late capitalist age. Martin Luther King was envisioning a moment when the arc of justice would bend down and meet us on the road ahead.

An unexpected contemporary idea lately proposed is that today's progressive left needs to adopt from religion the insistent modeling of new kinds of community that overcome widespread polarization—often manipulated by conservative economic interests—through a common, social-capital-rich society. From religion can come utopian vision that carries progressives and political parties beyond the imagination of can't-do-much-better late capitalism. Around the turn of the nineteenth century, when religious Europe began to attend to the devastations of the Industrial Revolution upon the lower classes, a Catholic moral theology arose to produce worker priests and a churchly imagination that sacramentalized the poor and proposed workers' unions. The worker priests labored full time in factories and dressed just like workers and were part of an effort to reclaim the working poor in the church's imagination. The church went over to the workers so that it could more believably recall the workers to the life of the church. It remains to be seen whether the new Supreme Court justice, Amy Coney Barrett, and her fellow Catholic majority on the court, will rediscover this profound Catholic heritage of social theology or will default to the big business bias of the Federalist Society.

5

Prophets Can Turn New Religious Movements into Church-Wide Reformation

OVERHEARING AN ANCIENT TEXT AND RAISING ITS VOICE IN A NEW CONTEXT

A MAGNIFYING GLASS MAKES something appear bigger. Or hotter! The Greek playwright Aristophanes already knew that a magnifying glass was good for igniting tinder. Is it the sun, or God in the cosmos, that shines through the glass to enlarge or ignite? Prophets hold a glass up to society to magnify what is to be seen but has gone unnoticed. Then they make it burst into flame. The Virgin Mary, newly pregnant with the child to be called Jesus, sang, "My soul *magnifies* the Lord." Ever since, in daily or weekly vesper services, the church has been singing the Magnificat to extol the Lord and God's mercy to the poor by quoting Mary, who first *offered her consent* to a new movement of God. And to remind us to do so. This book is a call to offer our consent to God's initiative, to magnify Matthew.

The thesis of Part I was that Matthew is projected from biblical text into new social contexts when new religious movers turning into new religious movements carry it to new social locations. Matthew is the original, anchoring text now migrating to new situations—transforming individual seekers and possibly resolving the crises of their age. *The thesis of Part II is that the entire church is called to magnify and institutionalize Matthew as a treasure that becomes good news to the poor*—first as Christianity's social gospel and then influencing a new deal for social democracy. Sacred texts become what they can be through the role they play in religious communities. If no one visits "the oracles," they cannot speak. Founders and reformers of religious movements open up the Bible only to find it reading them. Jesus' proclamation of the reign of God requires a response. The dynamic between Jesus and his disciples in Matthew's narrative is intended for modern reader response. The interaction between Jesus and his disciples can come true today, as Matthew becomes a discipleship manual. Periodically, religious movements renew themselves by returning to their sacred sources, as the early Renaissance also did by returning to ancient fountains (*ad fontes*). Sometimes new magnifications in the church catch fire in society.

To magnify is to institutionalize, to establish, to embed. New religious movements, like the current Matthew 25 Christians and social justice activists, are founders and settlers. They give social and cultural shape to religious visions derived from sacred texts. They turn a new movement into a *plausibility structure,* within which people can try out the proposed reality and test the carrying capacity of new revelations and dreams. They lay down cultural deposits in the life of surrounding society. To institutionalize is to move beyond the idiosyncratic, the occasional, the one-off, the individualistic. (Thomas Jefferson introduced his great idea in the Declaration of Independence, but it needed monumentally to institutionalize as a new country or it would have been left in the mists of history.) Successful institutionalization turns movements and cultural ideas into social norms, into regular, established practices. It is one thing to give a handout to a poor person on the sidewalk; it is quite another to create a soup kitchen and then a monastic ministry to the sick and the needy and then a governmental hunger program and then a social security and public health system. Think of monasticism as a vast institutionalization amidst what would become European Christendom. Institutions provide structure and inspiration for recurrent behavior and practice.

Institutions keep evolving too. The federal government is still trying to normalize fair elections in the American South through the Voting Rights Act—just as Southern racists are trying to deinstitutionalize them. Very many Republican conservatives have dedicated their careers and their platforms to undoing the New Deal and even abolishing Social Security and, more recently, Obamacare. In the first weeks of President Biden's term, there was brief consideration by some progressives of renaming and expanding the Department of Agriculture into the Department of Hunger and Food Insecurity and Well-Being. Earlier there had been an argument against appointing a Secretary of Agriculture with close ties to agribusiness, by those who wanted it anchored in small farms and black farms and hunger programs. (Agribusiness won the day, but with promises made by the new secretary.)

As we move through Part II, we focus first on the *church gathered* to celebrate the gospel and then on the *church sent* into the world to proclaim and enact a *social gospel,* to sacramentalize the world, to claim it as the occupied space of Christ's reign. Of course, the church has been around so long one does not readily see it as a "religious movement." As noted above, the church needs to let go of having become "once born," thoroughly adjusted to comfortable cultural norms, and become "twice born" again. It is not called to baptize the status quo but to call its candidates to transformation. There is its challenge. If it is to regain its momentum and the uniqueness of its ethos and the expanse of its vision, it must again become a nonconforming movement in its own self-understanding and a resistance movement among competing moral voices in the public square. In what follows we will watch how new religious movements like Matthew 25 and social justice Christians magnify and institutionalize an abiding presence in the life of Christianity.

CONSIDER HOW NEW RELIGIOUS MOVEMENTS ARISE AND EVOLVE

Very long ago, in fifth-century BC northern India, up near the border with Nepal, a young pathfinder named Siddhārtha Gautama, who would come to be called the Buddha, appeared out of nowhere in this thoroughly Hindu culture. As he began to travel about as a mendicant monk, he was moved by the suffering of life and death, and its endless repetition in the human condition due to endless rebirthing. So he set out on a quest to find liberation from suffering. Eventually he turned to a meditative practice. He famously sat under the Bodhi Tree in the town of Bodh Gaya. (I have a leaf from that tree, picked up on a visit with my wife, a South Asian anthropologist. We returned from India to distribute Bodhi leaves to our friends, as Hindu pilgrims return to their villages to pour out water from the holy Ganges into the public square, and as Mexican Catholics dress their home altars.)

Siddhartha gradually attained *Awakening* or *Enlightenment.* He proposed Four Noble Truths to express the basic orientation of Buddhism: the truth of suffering, the truth of the cause of suffering, the truth of the end of suffering, and the truth of the path that leads to the end of suffering. We crave and cling to impermanent states and things, which are incapable of satisfying and painful. This keeps us caught in saṃsāra, the endless cycle of repeated rebirth. But there is a way to liberation from this endless cycle, to the state of achieving nirvana through a spiritual *Noble Eightfold Path*. As a fully enlightened one, the Buddha attracted followers and founded a *sangha,* or monastic order. He spent the rest of his life teaching the dharma he had discovered, practicing mindfulness and clear comprehension, and then died achieving "final nirvana," at the age of eighty.

Notice that he turned personal discovery and transformation into a disciplined spiritual program and then into an observant community. Matthew 25 wants to be a spiritual program, a kind of monastic discipline, in the life of Christianity.

Over several centuries, germinal *Buddhist oral traditions became canonical writings*—perhaps like the Jewish-Christian Bible. Buddhism achieved a profound influence on various cultures, especially across Asia, and today it is also a significant influence on the "New Age spirituality" appearing throughout the world. The *institutionalization* of Buddhism turned into Buddhist philosophy, Buddhist art, Buddhist architecture, and Buddhist festivals. Buddha's teachings were propagated by his followers, which in the last centuries of the first millennium BC became various Buddhist schools of thought, each with its own basket of texts containing different interpretations and authentic teachings of the Buddha. Over time these evolved into multiple traditions, flourishing variously in different countries

This legacy is now a Buddhism that is the fourth largest religion in the world. Again and again, over succeeding centuries and in changing environments and countries, Buddhism went through continuous evolution, each time newly *magnifying and institutionalizing* some dimension of its origins. So also did Catholic Christianity. So also Protestant reform movements. Not everyone welcomed these movements as they evolved, not everyone cheered them on. At first consideration, the unwelcoming times that greet Matthew 25 Christians, namely the political-economic-nationalistic culture hostile or indifferent to the least of these, would seem to be unmitigated bad news for the new Matthew 25 social justice movements. Still, one can take hope from historic Christian movements that broke through to their times and gained a hearing beyond their times. And produced religious and cultural change.

Could the early twenty-first century become a new spiritual age? Enthusiasts for social justice are not willing to concede that authentic Christian legacies have come to an end in the modern world, that the history of "Matthew's effects" over time is now a dead end, that materialist principalities and powers, the very kind early Christianity struggled against and the apostle Paul named as something Christians must wrestle against (Ephesians 6:12), will now have their final say, that new religious sensibilities can no longer come to prevail.

PROPHETS HOLD UP A MAGNIFYING GLASS TO IGNITE THEIR TIMES

As I write this on Martin Luther King Jr. Day, January 18, 2021, I cannot omit mention again, as in the Preface, of prophetic figures and the role they have played in the Bible itself, from Moses to Elijah to John the Baptist to Jesus to Paul, and in Christian history from Augustine to Francis to Aquinas to Luther and Calvin and Wesley. And to the black Wesleyan-Holiness preacher, William Seymour, who brought a three-year-long Azusa Street Revival to downtown Los Angeles and then birthed the American religious movement called Pentecostalism. *These things do happen.*

Pause to nominate your own great figures of recent centuries. Is the world still evolving? Consider the several *Great Awakenings* in the history of American revivalism. Were they determined by great figures or by the right times? To take a kindred example, did the New Deal come about because of FDR or because the times were right? Think of presidents who failed their times. Or made them worse.

Consider the seeming emergence out of nothing of American Pentecostalism in the early twentieth century, an unlikely movement at the time that not only would come to saturate American Christianity but go on to leave major imprints in the global South, from South America to the African continent. This is Wikipedia's description: "Pentecostalism is a form of Christianity that emphasizes the work of the Holy Spirit and the direct experience of the presence of God by the believer. Pentecostals believe that faith must be powerfully experiential, and not something found merely through ritual or thinking. Pentecostalism is energetic and dynamic." The current social justice movement should be so fortunate! Lutherans like me have often disdained Pentecostalism, but today it is the fastest growing Christian movement, carrying dramatic Christian growth worldwide, as most Christian denominations are losing members.

Matthew 25 Christians are too small and too recent a movement to be looking back on yet. But think about how different interest groups remember different things about Martin Luther King, each taking a piece of his legacy. They create and re-create a great figure they can get behind, one who does not frighten them or break with their entrenched prejudices. Some see a patron saint of racial harmony. Or, more boldly, a prophet of civil rights. Others see a provocateur who connected the black experience to poverty and capitalism and Vietnam. J. Edgar Hoover saw a Communist agent. Or a dupe. King's most well-known protest writing, "Letter from Birmingham Jail," evoked "a great cloud of witnesses" who would become the cheerleaders of promising religious movements. Consider Hebrews 12:1, as perhaps King did: "Wherefore seeing we also are compassed about with so great a cloud of witnesses, let us lay aside every weight, and the sin which doth so easily beset us, and let us run with patience the race that is set before us. Looking unto Jesus the author and finisher of our faith; who for the joy that was set before him endured the cross, despising the shame, and is set down at the right hand of the throne of God."

King said, prophetically, "If today's church does not recapture the sacrificial spirit of such early Christians, it will lose its authenticity, forfeit the loyalty of millions, and be dismissed as an irrelevant social club with no meaning for the twentieth century." If Matthew 25 Christianity were to achieve its full vision coming true, would it include the achievement of a new social gospel, one that cannot coexist with unregulated capitalism or the disinterest in social justice characteristic of President Reagan's "small government" ideology? Consider how radical is Jesus' last judgment story, in which Jesus plays the envisioned King to come having first appeared in the midst of "the least of these." Could the "justice is the social form of love" movement replant New Testament Christianity with its good news to the poor in the life of the American church?

The God of the Old Testament and the New called prophets to speak for him. Those of their times did not always rejoice at their appearance. King Ahab called Elijah the "troubler of Israel." In a classic duel, Elijah hurls thunderbolts against the royal chaplains on retainer at the king's court. Before Elijah can be repudiated or assassinated, he is taken up to heaven in a fiery chariot (2 King 2:11), a scene American blacks have kept alive in communal memory and song: "Swing low, sweet chariot, coming for to carry me home." Some see in their celebration of Elijah's chariot an allusion to the Underground Railroad and the abolitionism meant to echo the exodus from Egypt. But the first Obama campaign threw Jeremiah Wright, the black prophet from Obama's church in Chicago, under the bus—for sounding so un-American.

On Reformation Day Lutherans read Jeremiah 31:31–34: "The days are surely coming, says the Lord, when I will make a new covenant. I will write my law on their hearts and I will be their God and they shall be my people. I will forgive their iniquity, and remember their sin no more." In Jeremiah 22:1–3 we hear a less cheery message: "Go down to the palace of the king and declare. Do what is just and right. Rescue from the hand of the oppressor the one who has been robbed. Do no wrong or violence to the *foreigner, the orphan, or the widow*, and do not shed innocent blood in this place." President Jimmy Carter liked to quote these pithy admonitions: "Let justice roll down like waters, and righteousness like an ever-flowing stream" (Amos 5:24) and "What does the Lord require of you but to do justice, and to love kindness, and to walk humbly with your God?" (Micah 6:8).

The much praised lore around the Old Testament King David may imply that kings and prophets are always on friendly terms. Lyndon Johnson hoped for a sunny relationship with Martin Luther King, but eventually King broke with the president over Vietnam. The relationship between President Trump and the cabinet of evangelicals was much more reliable. They never questioned him, and he always kept them on his speed dial. They assured the president, and themselves, that he was in fact God's anointed, sent to America just in time. But consider this classic prophetic text in 2 Samuel 12. The prophet Nathan came to court one day to tell King David a story that would not be congratulatory or fawning.

> A rich man had many flocks and herds and a poor man had just one little ewe lamb that he raised and treated as his own child. When the rich man had guests to entertain, he did not want to take an animal from his own flock, so he took the poor man's lamb. [Have you seen this story in the papers?] As the king listened attentively, he grew incensed and demanded that that evil rich man be put to death and the poor man compensated fourfold. Then the prophet Nathan denounced the king, *You are that man!"*

The prophet challenges the king; the king repents. Not a typical story, on either side.

Imagine inviting a prophet to speak at a Fourth of July celebration, as a nationalistic religion would do. It happened. Early in his ministry, Amos (chapter 5) presided over a national event. He took his audience on a rhetorical tour of the lands bordering Israel, denouncing each one by one. The crowd went wild. "USA, USA!" they shouted. Suddenly, the tour de force turned homeward and God's judgment was directed to Israel itself, for breaking their social covenant with God and each other. Listen to these words as if delivered at the National Mall today: "You sell the righteous for silver, and the needy for a pair of sandals; you trample the heads of the poor into the dust of the earth, and push the afflicted out of the way." Then on to the betrayal of the national story: "People of Israel whom I brought up out of the land of Egypt, you only have I known of all the families of the earth. Therefore I will punish you for all your iniquities."

Prophets rub against the grain as they say what needs to be said. The Jewish scholar Abraham Heschel said prophets sing one octave too high. They question the national mystique, the ethos of self-congratulation. In the sixties they were called the "hate America first" crowd. In Amos 7:10–17, Amaziah, the king's hired chaplain, accused Amos as a prophet of treason. He admonished God's mouthpiece that the government is "not able to bear the prophet's words." Get out of Dodge, prophets are told: "O seer, go, never again prophesy in the king's sanctuary, which is the religious center of the kingdom." Amos answers back with God's latest message, "This evil country shall surely go into exile." It did. Is it inconceivable that America is in self-exile from its visionary origins, from the Puritan "errand into the wilderness" on a transformative mission, from a prophet's call to be a city on a hill? Old Testament prophets brought "covenant lawsuits" against the nation. Listen to the charges: The 1 percent has devoured the vineyard that is the land God provides for all, the spoils of the needy end up in the mansions of the wealthy, who crush the people and grind the face of the poor.

But at his inauguration President Biden found a prophet who had not lost her voice. Amanda Gorman told the truth in her poem:

The Hill We Climb

When day comes, we ask ourselves:
Where can we find light
In this never-ending shade

The loss we carry, a sea we must wade.
We've braved the belly of the beast
We've learned that quiet isn't always peace.
When day comes, we step out of the shade,
Aflame and unafraid.
The new dawn blooms as we free it,
For there is always light,
If only we're brave enough to see it,
If only we're brave enough to be it.

WHAT ARE PROPHETS' CHANCES TODAY?

I began the Preface to this book with the story of the rediscovery of the book of Deuteronomy in the renovation of Solomon's Temple during the reign of King Josiah. The exodus and the covenant had become, like social justice and good news for the least of these today, *discarded images*. Today they are dismissed as tired leftist slogans with nothing left to say to the contemporary economy and society. *Then* the king ordered national renewal. And *today*?

While the Poor People's Campaign plans for national marches on the capital, preceded by Moral Mondays, members of Congress are likely to stop their ears. University students taking courses in Hebrew Bible typically read stories about ancient prophets, but Religious Studies departments have constructed their syllabi so no student is in danger of conversion. There are brief nods to great literature, but not meant for existential encounters and transformations. No life changes required for the final. Business majors often cannot fit the humanities of the Western tradition into their thick curriculum of economic realism and money-making by rational actors. Indeed, Republicans recently proposed a surcharge on humanities courses because they do not contribute to the needs of the economy. American Bible-believers prefer a spiritualizing Jesus to an angry prophet. Jesus is invited into spiritual hearts but not into the economy. Bay Area spiritual speakers look for renewal through encounters with nature at Big Sur, but quickly return to Silicone Valley realities when the weekend is over.

If prophets *escaped from ancient pages and appeared on the streets today*, or preached political sermons in safe churches, or became mad uncles at Thanksgiving tables, would their messages be self-validating or disturbingly off the wall? If Matthew 25 preachers were to appear in city council chambers, would the mayor ask who let them off the reservation? In the sixties, protesting students were always asked, especially by California's Governor Reagan, "Who let you off campus?" (I am sorry to report that Governor Reagan once said that if he had college-age children, he would certainly send them to Chico State, not Berkeley. Chico was the number one party school in the nation and I was in its Religious Studies department). In mid-2021 the Supreme Court ruled that union organizers trying to communicate with workers would be trespassing on private property. When feisty women were told to leave the chambers of Congress, the complaint went up: "And yet they persisted." The FBI tracked Martin Luther King and tried to shame him into suicide.

True prophets move resolutely "from page to stage" and appear where they're not invited. But keepers of ancient traditions try to lock them in the Old Testament canon and throw the key away. A similar attempt was made to lock up the apostle Paul when he came to town preaching. "Lock her up, lock her up" has a certain ring at political rallies. To strangers asking difficult questions comes the taunt, "Go back where you came from." In a presidential debate, Ronald Reagan said to Jimmy Carter, "There you go again." Still, prophets refuse to ask for official authorization and disdain required passports. The Chinese say: "Better than the assent of the crowd is the dissent of one brave man." Pascal admonished: "Trustworthy witnesses are willing to sacrifice their lives." Martin Luther King and Mahatma Gandhi sealed their legacies with martyrdom.

Who talks with prophetic bravado? Who yells Matthew 25? The public vernacular is materialist and secular and capitalist. America-speak is not prophet-speak. Nothing to see here. Towards the end of this book you will read the phrase "divine economy." Can you force those words to come together without snickering? Who thinks the national budget is a moral document except the Jesuit faculty at Georgetown? Are farm subsidies meant to feed the hungry or enrich agribusiness? Can prophets witness on Wall Street? (Well, there was the "brave girl" sassily staring down the Wall Street bull.)

AUDITIONING TO SPEAK MATTHEW'S LINES TODAY

This is how prophets arise. *Seekers and seers* with good eyes and ears find themselves perplexed by all the things that have gone wrong in this world and look for the handwriting of God in history. In the face of *troubling contexts*, they begin to recall great *historic texts*. They put them together and go out into the streets. A call from God, unexpected and possibly unwelcome (remember Jonah), turns them into converts and witnesses and social critics. They are deputized as voices for God's ambitions. The comedian Jon Stewart prophesied to Congress on behalf of healthcare for the 9/11 first responders, and even broke into tears while doing so. You can't always guess where a prophet might come from. Prophets seem to believe that *history has a plot and they are called to name it and claim it.*

Playing God's dreams on public stages is guerilla theater meant to disturb audiences and enlist them to take it outside. Like Marx, commonly called a secular prophet, they offer an analysis meant to change the world. The *freedom of God to do something new* becomes the prophet's calling card. God told Moses to tell Pharaoh, in case he should ask who's calling, that God's name is "I will be who I will be." American blacks decoded the liberating God of the exodus who stood in the face of the status quo. God is not content to be a household idol kept at the Smithsonian, but an iconoclast on behalf of a new age. Like the well-known garden gnome (or Bernie Sanders with new woolen mittens) he keeps appearing everywhere, from kitchen tables, to church entrances, to public squares. True religion echoes the pain of God and transforms the numbness of history.

Prophets, like poets, are "indicator species." What will happen to the rest of us first happens to them. They sound alarms, concentrate the mind, escape sentimentality, face evil, expose our hiding behaviors. In ages of assured sunshine, prophets retain the ability to see in the dark. Consider this touching poem by Jack Gilbert, who like the ancient prophets, does not speak in Hallmark verses:

Games

Imagine if suffering were real.
Imagine if those old people were afraid of death.
What if the midget or the girl with one arm
really felt pain? Imagine how impossible it would be
To live as if some people were
Alone and afraid all their lives.

So Part II of this book imagines new religious movements, perhaps driven by prophets arising at the right time, arising to *magnify and institutionalize* historic *texts* as what desperate or beckoning *new contexts* may require. Think of how the American colonies wielded the language of the Enlightenment to justify their separation from Britain. Or the French Revolution's thrusting *liberty, equality, fraternity (community)* against the ancient regime. Or Jesus against the self-satisfactions of temple religion. Or Paul against the "other gospel" that offered itself as a false alternative to what the times required. Or Augustine's slogan that communities are defined by what they love, as he tried to find space for the "city of god" in the landscape of a declining Roman Empire and defend the Christian movement against false accusations. Or Martin Luther's incessant evocation of grace and faith and justification, anchored in Scripture alone, as the response to what a decadent late medieval church required. Or the several "Great Awakenings" that attempted to stage the call of God and the response of waking hearts as the American experiment moved westward on its errand into the wilderness. Or historian Sidney Mead's portrait of America, which he titled, following G. K. Chesterton, "a nation with the soul of a church." Curiously Chesterton had called America "a home for the homeless"—a remarkable irony given how enthusiastically contemporary America ignores the homeless and turns them away.

The day after the inauguration of President Biden, as with past transitions of power in the United States, the Washington National Cathedral hosted the National Prayer Service, also called the Presidential Inaugural Prayer Service. The service was primarily virtual due to the pandemic, with many who sang or read Scripture at the cathedral wearing face masks and socially distancing. Bishop William J. Barber II, the co-chair of the Poor People's Campaign and an avid reader of Matthew's lines, warned Joe Biden and others listening in against issuing "simplistic calls for unity." Barber called for people to choose to repent of policy sins and to "repair the breach." He defined a breach as a gap in the nation between what is and how God wants things to be. "Transposed to our time, the breach is when we say 'one nation, under God, indivisible with liberty and justice for all' with our lips, while we see the rich and the poor living in two very different Americas." *Domestic tranquility,* a feel-good aspiration, can only be ensured when we establish social justice. We cannot address the nation's wounds with simplistic calls for unity.

A first-time-ever *repentance for a common prayer* astonished everyone. Christian author Jen Hatmaker, one of a group of interfaith leaders for the National Prayer Service, had prayed an assigned prayer: "Almighty God, You have given us this good land as our heritage." When she thought about her prayer later that day, she apologized for the first line of the prayer that effectively erased Native Americans. She said: "I was proud to offer the final liturgical prayer which was written by the organizers to serve as an anchor. Now I have one regret and thus apology. The very first sentence thanked God for giving us this land as our heritage. He didn't. He didn't give us this land," she said. "We took this land by force and trauma. It wasn't an innocent divine transaction in which God bestowed an empty continent to colonizers who had 'discovered' it. That is a shiny version of our actual history. If God gave this land to anyone, it was to the Native community who always lived here."

6

Focusing Matthew 25 on the Kindling of the *Church Gathered*

MATTHEW MAGNIFIED AND TURNED INTO FLAME

When I was a boy, we used to take a magnifying glass, hold it so the sun would shine directly through it, and focus the sun's rays on a pile of leaves that soon would burst into smoke and flame. Perhaps the life of the church could burst into the flames of the Spirit if Matthew were focused directly on it, which is the point of this chapter. Perhaps a social gospel would burst forth from society if we focus Matthew directly on it—this is the topic of the next and final chapters.

It's not as if nobody has ever heard Matthew 25 read out loud. Or preached. Or worked over in a Bible study. Many churches utilize a "common lectionary" that reads through the Gospel of Matthew in Sunday services every third year. The common lectionary can be surrounded with study and devotion in the life of congregations, though it rarely is. Perhaps some congregations will adopt this book or others mentioned here as guides for the study of Matthew. Or to help pastors think about their sermons, together with congregational members, each week.

Consider books like *Sacred Drama: A Spirituality of Christian Liturgy*, in which Patricia Wilson-Kastner makes the most of liturgy as sacred drama, which evokes a larger story in the unfolding of God's vision and issues casting calls for vigorous indoor training leading to outdoor action. *Liturgy involves spiritual formation and then a ritual procession from church to society.* Take Matthew seriously as a manual for discipleship that can turn the entire Christian community into a resistance movement that practices Jesus' call and makes its presence known in the public square.

In *Radical Discipleship: A Liturgical Politics of the Gospel,* Jennifer McBride wants to *form* readers into people able to grasp the social and political character of the good news proclaimed in the Gospels, to transform faith into a social ethic. She proposes to accomplish this by connecting the shape of the liturgy with activism and theological reflection. True discipleship requires that privileged Christians place their bodies in spaces of social struggle and distress to reduce the distance between themselves and those who suffer injustice, and stand in solidarity with those whom society deems guilty, despises, and rejects. We are not to escape from these texts, or the actual poor, and leave ourselves untouched by them.

But Americans need to be cautioned about "being at ease in Zion." Old Testament scholar Walter Brueggemann has asserted that *faith in a God who doesn't guarantee the present social order is forever an anomaly.* We may have been looking for something quite different to come along. The conservative Christian assumption is that socialism is demonic, and unfettered capitalism is God's way. So, stay the course!

We will have to aim Matthew into the present, inside and outside the church, to make Matthew come true today, to "complete" the history of "Matthew's effects," rather than to declare him an ancient Word of God and go no further than Word-worship. Søren Kierkegaard once observed that the prized "objectivity" of the philosopher is like wandering into an antique shop and discovering a board on which is written the word *laundry*. But as a text only it is irrelevant because you cannot bring any clothes to the antique shop to get them washed. It is one thing to declare first-century Matthew a freeze-dried holy and inerrant Word of God. It is much more obedient to the New Testament text's *gospel proclamation that requires a decision* to follow its influence and legacies down through Christian history and determine today what is required. What might we become through the effects of this text? Where might we go with Matthew in the twenty-first century as Christians call for a new social gospel after its complete lapse in the years from Reagan to Trump?

From observing American churches and the determination to keep the pastor's sermons apolitical, you might assume that one ironic function of preaching is *to protect the hearers from the claims of the text!* Or to steer the congregation away from any obligations implicit in the text that run contrary to prevailing worldviews. But there are over three hundred biblical texts that address matters of social justice and that instruct the faithful on how to think about and to treat the poor, including Proverbs 14:31, whose meaning underlies the Matthew text ("Those who oppress the poor insult their Maker, but those who are kind to the needy honor him."). Social justice, in fact, is what the Messiah's coming is about. We have seen Jesus' inaugural sermon in Luke 4, in which he quotes Isaiah 61: "The Spirit of the Lord is upon me, because he has anointed me *to bring good news to the poor.* He has sent me to proclaim release to the captives and recovery of sight to the blind, to let the oppressed go free, to proclaim the year of the Lord's favor," no doubt a reference to the Jubilee Year in Leviticus 25, a text which would sound like dangerous socialism to most Americans. These normative texts seem outside the range of recognition or memory of very many contemporary Bible-believers.

It would seem it is not off base to speak of a "divine economy" in which matters of money are of divine interest and how the *state* spends its money in care of "the least" will be a matter of God's judgment. It is lately in to insist on seeing *the congressional budget as a moral document.* Following the American fiscal crisis of 2008 and the government's saving the rich while mostly abandoning the poor—under Obama—it is remarkable how so many Christians supported such an approach. Imagine "income replacement" being rejected on biblical grounds! During the COVID-19 epidemic many in Congress who "identify as Christian" were obsessed that assistance to the poor might encourage them to be lazy. They acted out the role of the goats in Jesus' last judgment story. Many who have come across it want to insist that Jesus' little last judgment story is marginal to the whole Bible.

As called for in an earlier chapter, read Matthew in the company of the poor, so it won't require such a strenuous act of imagination to see them. Look up from group Bible study and ask, can we see the poor from here? Can we even imagine them? Is anybody here hungry today? I often recall Victor Hugo's trenchant comment that French upper-class society somehow imagined the poor must live on a planet more distant from the sun than they. Let the presence of the poor require a new hermeneutic that trains Bible students to see Jesus as a stand-in for the poor (and vice versa), and that epistemologically, politically, and morally grants them agency and even leadership in the ways Matthew could come true in the modern age. If biblical texts have been stripped of their organizing power, their resistance power, their nonconforming power, and the obvious presence of the poor in about one-sixteenth of the New Testament, let the reversal of that divestment begin. When engaging in Bible study, avoid "common sense hermeneutics." That means assuming that the Bible probably means what someone of your class, status, gender, or color would naturally think it means. Or what any good American would assume. Or what the common presuppositions of early twenty-first-century culture would indicate.

As a spiritual exercise, stop every time you pray the Lord's Prayer when you get to the petition, "Thy kingdom come." What could that possibly mean? How would you know if it were coming true? Would praying "Thy *empire* come" keep us from spiritualizing the kingdom away from social and political reality? When you get home from church, where you have prayed the Lord's Prayer in common, go over and over it as you go to sleep every Sunday night. Think about bread and debt relief (there they are, right in the middle of the prayer) as the ancient and continuing concerns of the poor.

Consider certain practices like exercising and turn them into what Jesuits call *spiritual exercises*. For example, walk downtown and don't just fling a coin to a beggar. Engage him or her. When feeling good about doing charity work rescuing people in danger of drowning, ask yourself, "Who's throwing them in upstream?" Turn the tables when reading Matthew 25. Ask whether, in your community and even in your Christian community, "Jesus himself is one of the least of these"? Could seeing the parousia, that New Testament Greek word for presence, arrival, or official visit, include this?

In this and the next chapter of this book, I urge two different considerations of Matthew 25. In this chapter, I imagine Matthew 25 Christians *focusing Matthew on the life of the church and radical discipleship* until it sets the pews on fire. In chapter 7, I imagine *focusing Matthew on society, or focusing the church outward, in a way that evokes a new social gospel* and social justice throughout the land.

Some might think that I am evoking two different Christian traditions here. Possibly I am. Calvinist thinkers like Abraham Kuyper assert that our faith should be evident in all parts of our lives, that no sphere should be untouched by the sovereignty of God. Christians are to use their political power to urge state and society to conform to God's will. Catholic Christianity seeks to install Christian institutions in the life of society, in ways that leave an unmistakable residue. *Integralism* is the mostly abandoned but extremely bold idea that the Catholic faith should be the basis of public law and public policy within civil society, wherever the preponderance of Catholics within that society makes this possible.

But the Anabaptist and Pietist and much of the evangelical traditions generally pair faith with the intense spirituality of Christians as individuals and gathered in church, while retaining a strong skepticism of sanctified state power. They are likely to fear the word *social* attached to theology, lest it invite socialism or even "cultural Marxism." Or corrupt the way of salvation to be practiced by pious individuals. They like to connect the word *sin* to the individual, not the social—which leaves capitalism or governments with no accountability. Nothing to declare, as you go through the line at customs. Nothing to repent of!

Luther seemed to keep Christians in church and Christians as citizens of the state separate in his "two kingdoms doctrine." Service to church and state require different, even incompatible ethics and loyalties. Yet Luther's high doctrine of the *Christian calling* applied to Christian citizens in both realms. But is what we can accomplish in the earthly kingdom severely limited? The public theologian Reinhard Niebuhr was making a similar claim in *Moral Man and Immoral Society,* so that not much could be expected of social systems. (Politicians loved him for that.) So neo-Anabaptist thinkers like Stanley Hauerwas doubted that Niebuhr was even a Christian thinker. The Christian's focus is on the unique story the church is called to tell, and in the church's own language. This may suggest that disparate Christians might choose quite different handbooks to Matthew. If so, they should read each other's favorite.

COULD MATTHEW 25 BECOME A NEW CANON WITHIN THE CANON?

Matthew is a comprehensive theological narrative from which emerges one of the Bible's kerygmatic witnesses to the life and significance of Jesus Christ. It does not aim to be quaint little stories (or even inerrant proof texts), but *life-threatening theological proclamation (kerygma)* that turns the world around and sets people free. Christian discipleship and Christianity itself are the heirs of Matthew's radical call to discipleship and what Dietrich Bonhoeffer in his reflections on Matthew calls *costly grace*. Matthew gives his readers a story to shape a life and *become the story they are going with*, that will live and be told in new ages—with a unique language that is a biblical language, a distinctive vocabulary required to get the story right and keep the story straight. Enough text for every context. Anabaptists in particular see that the call of the church is to own its own story, to tell the story faithfully, to *become the story*. Matthew was once nonconforming in its posture, and so the church must be in each age.

Lutheran theology, and Luther in particular, is known for positing a canon within the canon of Biblical testimony. Luther was personally set free by Paul's letters to the Romans and Galatians. Luther's criterion for canons within the canon was *what drives home or inculcates Christ most. What makes Christ necessary.* What illuminates all the rest of the biblical witness. The evangelical devotion to Proverbs would have mystified Luther! Whatever in the Bible makes Christ the indispensable center is the essential *kerygma*, the proclamation that illuminates and clarifies everything else. Luther swept away the favored approaches of analogical, allegorical, and typological meanings he inherited from medieval Christianity in order to embrace the "plain reading" of the Bible, and for him that meant Jesus—and faith and grace—as the interpretive center.

Could Matthew 25 become as crucial as John 3:16 or Paul? This may suggest that postulating a normative canon happens as a product of its times in the history of the church and its witness to society. And varies with the times. Could Matthew be coming true in our times in ways not characteristic of earlier times? (As we saw earlier, this is an example of paying attention to the "history of Matthew's effects" in the life of Christianity.) The Lutheran Reformation appealed to Paul, and to grace/faith/justification, as the antidotes to the problematic practices of late-medieval Catholicism. What times require Matthew's good news to the poor?

The point would be that different times may require different biblical emphases. Might Matthew be coming into his own in an American society imprisoned in gross inequality and rapacious capitalism and completely indifferent to the poor and desperate for a new social gospel? Different times might find that Matthew's testimony is just what those times require. John Wesley already wanted to correct Luther by balancing his seeming exclusive emphasis on justification with a call for sanctification—for which Wesley appealed to Matthew.

It cannot be accidental that early in the twenty-first century some American Christians began calling themselves "Matthew 25 Christians." In view of a late capitalist society that relegated the poor to the ash heap of the social system, "small government" disdained any responsibility for social justice. And the early twentieth-century liberal Protestant social gospel and FDR's New Deal were only distant memories long obliterated by the Reagan revolution. *Matthew 25 Christians name themselves for what the times require,* a recognition of our responsibility to "the least of these." To achieve God's dreams for a covenanted community among all the people, they felt uniquely called by Matthew's New Testament witness. Perhaps all readers of the Bible select, and are convicted by, key passages that uniquely speak to them and to their times. That deliver them from spiritual and moral dilemmas, that seem a promising way out of being locked into the way things are. The Bible is a collection of treasures in the Christian backpack from which believers ransack and shake loose what they require. Old Testament scholar Walter Brueggemann sees in the Old Testament *testimonies and counter-testimonies* in which prophets arise to correct the taming and self-dealing manipulation of earlier traditions. Sometimes the pages of the Bible come loose and flutter across the lives of Bible students reading in the present.

Of course, there is always the alluring danger of narrowing the Bible to what contemporaries want it to say. Defenders of slavery employed a "commonsense exegesis" to get from the Bible what they needed. Thomas Jefferson scissored out from the Gospels the supernatural things that offended his Enlightenment consciousness. Today Bible readers are tempted to overlook class, status, and skin color and the hermeneutical effects they have on how the Bible is read and what it is made to say. On his first day in office, the new President Biden was already attacked for decrying *white supremacy* out loud. This was a no-no to conservative Christians whose Bibles never mentioned "critical race theory." Somebody told Biden that the Bible and the church should always stretch us, jar us, and make us uncomfortable, because God's plan is to remake us and the world into what we are not yet.

MATTHEW AS A COURSE OF CHRISTIAN DISCIPLESHIP

The story of Jesus washing his disciples' feet in the Gospel of John can be seen as an example of the *posture of discipleship*, almost like a daily yoga exercise that shapes the participant and trains for a healthy spiritual life. All four Gospels portray true discipleship, and its costs, through stories about how often the disciples don't "get" Jesus but sometimes do. The Matthew 25 last judgment story is an evocation of the disciplined practice of keeping sight of Jesus, especially in unlikely places, for example among the poor and downtrodden. The technical Greek term *parousia* is usually taken to refer to the ultimate and much awaited return of Christ at the end of the ages, but the insight of Jesus' judgment story allows for no postponement to the afterlife, or the rapture, of the vision of Christ. *True disciples are to practice naming and recognizing Jesus now,* not in the sweet by-and-by. Matthew became a manual for discipleship in early Christianity and there is evidence that the second-century church particularly studied Matthew for guidance to the new church's role in the world. *Discipleship is a churchly word and a post-baptismal aspiration.* The church is the place where discipleship is commissioned and taught and trained and practiced. A Christian life in the world follows baptismal candidacy, in which the newly baptized first renounce the ungodly ways of the world, then move down the aisle to the altar, and then, after the Eucharist, turn back to the world as new people with a new mission.

To catch the full scope of Matthew's manual of discipleship, start at the end of the Gospel where Jesus' "Great Commission" is proclaimed: "All authority in heaven and on earth has been given to me. Go, therefore, and *make disciples* of all nations, baptizing them in the name of the Father, and of the Son, and of the Holy Spirit, and teaching them to *obey everything that I have commanded you*" (Matthew 28:19–20).

Matthew's structure of *Five Discourses* should be understood under Matthew's overall theme: *Jesus of Nazareth is God's chosen king to rule forever on earth so that people from every nation will commit their lives to him*. Here are the five discourses in Matthew's catechism of discipleship:

1. The Matthew 5–7 Sermon on the Mount, including the Beatitudes and the Lord's Prayer. The character and behavior of followers of Jesus is expressed as a set of blessings, of love and humility rather than force, of Jesus' teachings on mercy, spirituality, and compassion, and caution about false prophets.

2. The Matthew 10 missionary discourse, the little commission to the twelve disciples as itinerant followers of Jesus.

3. The Matthew 13 parables of the kingdom of heaven, including the sower, the tares, the mustard Seed, the leaven, hidden treasure, Pearl of great trice, and drawing in the net, which disclose what being caught up in the kingdom and trying to follow Jesus is like.

4. The Matthew 18 discourse on the church and life in community, including the parables of the lost sheep and the unforgiving servant.

It anticipates a future community of followers ("Matthew's Church") and the roles of the apostles in leading it, including such practices as binding and loosing. The importance of humility and self-sacrifice in the anticipated community of the church.

5. The Matthew 24–25 discourse on the end times and their apocalyptic presence and living in hope in the light of fulfilled prophecy, the necessity of vigilance in view of coming judgment and perhaps of cataclysms like the destruction of the Jerusalem temple.

Altogether Matthew's Manual on Discipleship anticipates a full and strenuous and joyous life, in which disciples, and eventually the entire church of the late first century, live out the meaning of Jesus' kingship. And model it for all.

"MATTHEW 25 CHRISTIANS"

We have looked at the history of Matthew's effects across times and cultures. Sometimes Matthew is clearly internalized in the Christian tradition, as in medieval Catholicism and its emphasis on "public works of mercy." Sometimes Matthew is eclipsed by other forces, as when the Lutheran Reformation seemed almost antagonistic to Matthew because of Luther's aversion to the prominence and necessity of "good works." Sometimes Matthew's concern about the public works of mercy becomes one of the "marks" of the church, and other times such good works are precisely *not* numbered among the necessary and validating marks of the church. The Reformation included only the proper preaching of the Word and celebration of the sacraments as the indispensable marks of the church. In this Luther was arguing for the legitimacy of the new Lutheran churches, over against papal condemnations.

Now, strikingly, in the early years of the twenty-first century, some Christians began to call themselves *Matthew 25 Christians*. This is surely a remarkably *new effect of Matthew, a new epoch of Matthew coming true, a new test of Christian legitimacy.* Are there Matthew 25 Christians coming true near you? Will whole Christian movements begin to adopt that title? The neo-evangelical and neo-Anabaptist Sojourners movement, which eventually attracted Catholics and mainline Protestants as well, was one of the early leaders in this appropriation of Matthew 25 as one of the (necessary) marks of the church in a troubled age. But note: this field guide to Matthew does not solely attend to self-identified "Matthew 25

Christians," but to all contemporary Christian efforts on behalf of social justice in the name of Jesus. (Yes, yes, some "social justice warriors" seem mostly obsessed with their own "wokeness.") The prize to keep one's eye on is binding Christian believers and Christian citizens, church and society, theologians and public intellectuals, ethicists and sociologists and economists in efforts toward a new social gospel, and then on to a new deal for social democracy.

Jim Wallis, the influential founder of Sojourners, has cited Matthew 25 as his "conversion text." (Think of Luther's conversion texts, which would be in Romans and Galatians.) Rev. William J. Barber, a leader in the Poor People's Campaign, also frequently references Matthew 25 in his sermons and online statements. "The government is the people coming together to enact our values for how we want to live together and provide for the common good," he says. "Christians throughout American history and over a much broader history have advocated for government policies to reflect their values as Christians." The day after President Biden's inauguration, when Washington was filled with happy talk about unity, Barber poured some cold water on it all as he insisted that prayers of repentance were what the times required. Red-Letter Christians, another activist movement and blog, which appeals to the actual but neglected (red-letter) statements of Jesus, is another prominent voice for the Matthew 25 movement.

Early in the Trump presidency, and over against Trump's self-regarding vision and unjust policies, a new pledge emerged across the country with local organizers and congregations. It arose after a broad spectrum of pastors, heads of churches, grassroots activists, and leaders of national faith-based organizations and networks came together in retreat and prayed and discerned together about the election results, reaching consensus to act in solidarity with those most at risk in the new administration. It produced the very simple but influential Matthew 25 Pledge: "I pledge to protect and defend vulnerable people in the name of Jesus." It has since been widely adopted. Is your congregation involved? Your church body? Is it a sign on your door?

But certain political policies and practices create a direct conflict between church and state. Some of the commands from the Trump White House were directly at odds with the commands of Christ. Its anti-immigrant policies *lost* nearly six hundred children's connection to their parents, from whom they were forcibly separated—even as the country claims a special relation with the Bible, that document whose

Old Testament is obsessed with the plight of migrants and strangers. If the government tells churches that they can't help, assist, harbor, or welcome immigrants and refugees, they will be putting themselves in direct conflict with Christian ministries and preventing our religious liberty to express obedience to Christ—all the while the Christian Right is boasting of the nationalist religion under Trump. Texas citizens who provide water in the desert for migrants who might otherwise die of thirst can be and are arrested. Much more bizarre is a new Georgia election law that forbids offering drinks of water to citizens standing in line to vote. There is so much Christians must stand up for.

Specifically, the Sojourners effort argued this platform:

1. Support undocumented immigrants threatened with mass deportation.
2. Stand with African Americans and other people of color threatened by racial policing.
3. Defend the lives and religious liberty of Muslims, threatened with "banning," monitoring, and even registration.
4. Sign the Matthew 25 Pledge and enact a "circle of protection" around all the vulnerable.

The circle of protection, sometimes in the halls of Congress where perilous votes are taking place, proved a remarkably visible manifestation of Matthew 25 sensibilities in and around Washington. The argument was that instead of just watching, grieving, and feeling sorry for what is happening to the most marginalized, who are named in Matthew 25, Christians could pledge to join together in circles of support in the name of Jesus. In unjust times, justice often starts in the small places and personal decisions that challenge the big places and structural injustice.

Most interestingly, the emphasis on Matthew 25 began to be appropriated by those who wanted to *bring together New Testament values and political platforms*. For example, Michael Wear, founder of Public Square Strategies and a former Obama staffer, saw that progressives were finding Matthew 25:40 appealing because it "seems like and reads like a very practical verse—it's very much about faith and action." And so there emerged the Matthew 25 Network, a political action committee (PAC) geared towards supporting progressive candidates for American public office who possess what the organization considers to be a strong Christian faith. It was founded by Mara Vanderslice, who already in 2004 was director of religious outreach for the Kerry-Edwards campaign. The Matthew 25 Network endorsed Barack Obama in his bid for the White House. Their efforts focused primarily on reaching out to targeted religious communities that the network felt would be key to his success on election day, including "Catholics, moderate evangelicals, Hispanic Catholics and Protestants," as noted in official literature of the Matthew 25 Network. If many readers of this book have never heard of these efforts, that may indicate they have not reached a wide audience, or have not been particularly effective, or that the Democratic Party has been cautious about acknowledging them. Or they have not been paying attention. Championing the poor has always been a dangerous platform. Even liberal Democrats find it much safer to stick to the redemption of the working and middle classes.

The Matthew 25 Network is based primarily around grassroots efforts by mobilizing progressive Christian voters. In the Democratic primary debates of 2020, moderators asked the candidates about their life mottos. Bernie Sanders, never outwardly religious, offered a quote from Mandela. Joe Biden offered folksy wisdom. But Elizabeth Warren seemed most prepared, quoting the words of Jesus from Matthew 25:40, "In as much as ye have done it unto one of the least of my brethren, ye have done it unto me." She added: "It's about how we treat other people and lift them up. That is why I am in this fight." And in a televised commercial, Pete Buttegieg said, "In our White House, you won't have to shake your head and ask yourself: whatever happened to 'I was hungry and you fed me. I was a stranger and you welcomed me.'" Alexandria Ocasio-Cortez certainly seemed to allude to the verse as well during a congressional hearing about LGBT communities, referencing marginalized communities as "the least of these." She said, "I feel as though if Christ himself walked through these doors and said what he said thousands of years ago—that we should love our neighbor and our enemy, that we should welcome the stranger, fight for the least of these—he would be maligned as a radical and rejected from these doors." Guthrie Graves-Fitzsimmons, fellow at The Faith and Progressive Policy Initiative at the Center for American Progress, said (hopefully): "It shows that Democrats are willing to not just talk about faith and their Christian beliefs in a general way but in an 'if you don't agree with us you're going to hell' way." It should be noted that the Democrats have a long history of distancing themselves from religion, out of concern for the size of their secularist base. Except, of course, black religion. As I write this chapter there are Facebook posts every few days arguing that AOC's policy vision represents a Christian socialism.

But Christian conservatives were having none of this. Leader of the Christian Right Jerry Falwell Jr., the recently disgraced and fired president of Liberty University, tweeted at the time: "Matthew 25 is one of my favorites. You should read the passage closely. Note that it instructs us to help the least of these, not to vote for someone who will tax our neighbors based on the false pretense that the government will help the poor and then waste the $ on so many other things!" And another leader of the Christian Right, Franklin Graham (son of Billy Graham), president of Samaritan's Purse, an important Christian charity organization, opposes Christian attempts to marshal the government on behalf of social justice, which remains an objectionable word and a sign of lurking Marxism among conservative evangelicals. Another way out of the implications of Matthew 25 is the insistence by many evangelicals that "the least of these" in Jesus' story refers only to Christian missionaries. (Over the years, many others have also made this argument.)

Consider another renaming as similar to, and congruent with, calling oneself Matthew 25 Christians. In late 2020, months ahead of their planned annual meeting, some Southern Baptist leaders began embracing an unofficial moniker for their gathering and, in some cases, for themselves: *Great Commission Baptists*. The name simultaneously distances them from a regional affiliation that smells of slavery and focuses on the command of Jesus for his followers to spread his message worldwide, some leaders say. But the name change is also being entertained by some at a time when leaders of the denomination—whose origins in 1845 were marked by a defense of slavery—are reflecting on racial tensions in the country. So calling oneself by a new name can be an act of repentance and an act of new intentions.

FOUNDING AND NAMING "MATTHEW 25 CONGREGATIONS"

Could the new religious movement called Matthew 25 Christians start enlisting "Matthew 25 congregations" across the country? Another way of asking this is, *How could churches start sponsoring Matthew!* Consider how Lutheranism has "sponsored" Galatians and Romans for five hundred years. This book calls for magnifying Matthew and it proposes to be a field guide to taking Matthew public. It can specifically be a guide for churches sponsoring Matthew, or Matthew sponsoring churches. This becomes a question about recognizing what the times require, and whether a new move regarding the history of Matthew's effects at the parish level is appropriate. For example, for some years some Catholic parishes have chosen to call themselves "peace and justice churches." In the ELCA (Lutheran) tradition, there is lately a specific process to be followed if an individual parish wishes to designate itself a *Reconciling in Christ* parish, which is to say a congregation making it clear that it is an LGBTQ-welcoming church. There is an elaborate course of study, typically engaged in adult Christian education classes, and then finally an official congregational vote. If the decision is in favor, the congregation then may self-designate on its website, in its Sunday bulletins, and elsewhere, according with national norms in the movement.

I know of no designated bureaucratic procedure for calling oneself a Matthew 25 congregation, but it is easy enough to imagine how this could be done. A church, in its adult Christian education classes, would make Matthew an object of study, particularly during Year A in the lectionary cycle that features Matthew for its Gospel readings. Every three years a congregation could reconsider its relation to Matthew. After a period of study and a determination of what exactly it would mean, a congregation could declare itself a Matthew 25 congregation. Ideally, *this would include study and ministry and outreach programs to the pockets of society that are clearly "the least of these."* The poor should be in on the discussion. A church may have to go out and find them. That is, practicing what one preaches would be indispensable. Or if the denomination wished to so designate, it would instruct its social action or social ministry arms to move in that direction.

But it should not be forgotten that concern for the least of these should not be limited to charity. Individual congregations, as well as the national church body, should be lobbying Congress and becoming politically active on behalf of the hungry and homeless. Individual pastors and laity could be showing up at city council meetings when debates about responding to the homeless are underway. This whole process is reminiscent of situations in the life of Christian groups when the times call for a statement specific to the situation, which is perceived as a *status confessionis moment*, the recognition that perilous times call for a *We believe, teach, and confess* statement. To call it a "Bonhoeffer moment" is especially crisis-recognizing and invoking to all who know of Bonhoeffer's response to Nazi Germany and its incursions on German Protestantism as well as the entire nation.

In the larger context of a church body's self-understanding, calling itself a Matthew 25 church would be an example of the church as a *nonconforming resistance movement*—a continuing strength of the Anabaptist traditions, for example, or the early Puritans. In England especially "nonconformance" has a distinguished history and is a much-used name, even burying its dead in its own (nonconforming) cemeteries. As onlookers in the early centuries of Christianity sometimes said, *You can tell the Christians by what they do*—burying the dead, never practicing infanticide of the unwanted, taking in orphans, nurturing the sick and the hungry. When I was a young pastor, summer youth camps took as their anthem, "They'll know we are Christians by our love." (Then my church body at the time, the Missouri Synod, protested that this was too suggestive of "works-righteousness" and the song went on the forbidden list.)

Red-Letter Christians were saying *What can we do?* in response to the times. Aren't there many particularly significant sayings of Jesus, standing out in red-letter Bibles, that churches should be attuned to? How could we have missed them? "If the politics going on now are indeed beyond our control—we can control what we do with our own faith and with our own actions." And so Matthew 25 was experienced as *rising up* to the occasion of how believers should be responding to the many diverse and unconnected situations across the county. This was seen as a *movement of the Spirit*: I was a stranger and you welcomed me, I was naked and you gave me clothing, I was sick and you took care of me, I was in prison and you visited me. *A Matthew 25 designation is rising up in the face of a political regime that is making many people feel so ignored and afraid.*

Christians, take the pledge! I pledge to protect and defend vulnerable people in the name of Jesus. Note that this could be a pledge of individual Christians. Or of individual congregations. Or of an entire denomination. It could stop there, and be seen as an effective act of Christian charity. Or it could deliberately and self-consciously move into the realm of political action, of lobbying for programs that provide systemic responses, which is to say social justice platforms, to an acute crisis in society.

The Presbyterian Church has a program for becoming a Matthew 25 church: "Matthew 25:31–46 calls all of us to actively engage in the world around us, so our faith comes alive and we wake up to new possibilities. Convicted by this passage, both the 222nd and 223rd General Assemblies

(2016 and 2018) exhorted the PC(USA) to act boldly and compassionately to serve people who are hungry, oppressed, imprisoned or poor."

This is a vision to unite all Presbyterians: "By accepting the Matthew 25 invitation, you can help our denomination become a more relevant presence in the world. We recognize Christ's urgent call to be a church of action, where God's love, justice and mercy shine forth and are contagious. And we rejoice how our re-energized faith can unite all Presbyterians for a common and holy purpose: our common identity to do mission." So far, three initiatives have been identified:

Building congregational vitality resources

Dismantling structural racism resources

Eradicating systemic poverty resource

Note that these are programs to build up the moral fiber of the churches themselves and to tackle systemically issues of racism and poverty in the world outside.

INSTITUTIONALIZING MATTHEW 25: MINISTRIES, PROGRAMS, PROJECTS

For a very long time the Catholic tradition has had a history of and ambition for institutionalizing its theological commitments—both in its own fabric (public works of mercy) and as moral deposits it leaves in social and governmental systems. So in Europe especially one can speak of a Catholic tradition of social theology that has left its imprint on societal institutions. That is, *the church's moral theology takes up physical space in national life,* for example sacramentalizing the working class and unions, connecting theology and philosophy in the life of universities. Many would argue that Lutheranism in Scandinavia and also in Germany has left moral intuitions in the national culture as a permanent legacy, even after the national church generally has lost membership and influence and privilege. It may be that this happens more readily where there has been a history of "state churches." Social welfare and healthcare programs for all citizens are unmistakable.

This has been less likely in the United States, where church/state separation is written into the Constitution, although there can be no doubt about the (vanishing?) Puritan legacy in American life that led to the saying, "a nation with the soul of a church." Certainly, the various social gospel movements have left significant residues in politics and government. This is true of the mostly forgotten (and decimated by Jim Crow culture) black social gospel movement that briefly followed Reconstruction after the Civil War, and which emerged again, through Martin Luther King and others, in the civil rights movements of the 1960s. A well-known example, as a response to the Gilded Age, is the social gospel movement of liberal Protestantism at the beginning of the twentieth century and that left residues in FDR's New Deal and LBJ's Great Society. The magisterial biographer of LBJ, Robert Caro, allows that some of LBJ's moral instincts about society may have been learned in Baptist Sunday school.

Social justice movements like to emphasize the difference between *charity*, which consists in individual Christian good works but which leaves politics and government mostly untouched and does not mount a major critique of the economy, and *social justice*, which uses religious pressure and political lobbying to move the government to the good works the times require and which often results in vigorous critiques and regulation of capitalism. Social justice efforts are meant to build social morality into the structure of society and culture, as in Social Security or unemployment benefits or public works projects. *The next chapter focuses Matthew 25 less on the church gathered than on "the church sent" into government and society and culture, which is to say it turns Matthew 25 into a social gospel for the world—just as in the biblical announcement of "good news to the poor."* But this chapter has focused Matthew 25 on the church, hoping its hot sun through a magnifying glass will cause the church to burst into the flame of the Spirit. So while this section features the institutionalizations that can occur at the individual church and also the denominational level, I am ultimately committed to arguing for the social justice model and its aspirations, as I also did in an earlier book, *After Trump: Achieving a New Social Gospel.*

Institutionalization means to build a value into the structure of a small or large organization. Or, starting from the angle of Matthew 25 itself, it means to take the Matthew 25 pledge and flesh it out in the life of the church and of all Christians—and eventually in society. *Faith-based initiatives* are something of a hybrid, in that they operate at the level of the church but typically apply for and employ government funding. They often fit into the category of NGO or nongovernmental organizations, though those are more often secular.

World Vision is a vast Evangelical Christian humanitarian aid, development, and advocacy organization. It has recently come to invite and sponsor a Matthew 25 Challenge, a weeklong commitment that will help individuals and families step out of their comfort zones and engage in God's love for the least of these brothers and sisters whom Jesus calls us to care for in Matthew 25:35–40. All who go online and sign up will get one email a day over the next week with a daily challenge, impactful stories, and ways to pray and talk about Matthew 25 with their family. Samaritan's Purse broke off from World Vision in the name of a higher profile Christian presence, but its mission is not unlike the latter. Google them.

Lutheran World Relief is an international nongovernmental organization that focuses on sustainable development projects and disaster relief and recovery. This is its vision statement:

> Affirming God's love for all people, we work with Lutherans and partners around the world to end poverty, injustice and human suffering. We work with people based on need, regardless of race, religion or nationality and *we do not evangelize*. We provide aid in emergencies and help families restore their lives. We partner with communities to build and grow rural economies. We break the cycle of poverty, so families and communities can thrive. Our goal is to help people build self-sufficiency and create new community-owned approaches to problem-solving that will last long after our projects end.

Catholic World Relief Services carries out the commitment of the Bishops of the United States to assist the poor and vulnerable overseas. This is their mission statement:

> We are motivated by the Gospel of Jesus Christ to cherish, preserve and uphold the sacredness and dignity of all human life, foster charity and justice, and embody Catholic social and moral teaching as we act to: PROMOTE HUMAN DEVELOPMENT by responding to major emergencies, fighting disease and poverty, and nurturing peaceful and just societies; and, SERVE CATHOLICS IN THE UNITED STATES as they live their faith in solidarity with their brothers and sisters around the world. As part of the universal mission of the Catholic Church, we work with local, national and international Catholic institutions and structures, as well as other organizations, to assist people on the basis of need, not creed, race or nationality. We put our faith into action to help the world's poorest create lasting change.

United Methodist Committee on Relief is the humanitarian relief and development arm of The United Methodist Church, assisting United Methodists to become involved globally in direct ministry to persons in need. Google it.

Bread for the World is a nonpartisan, Christian advocacy organization based in the United States that advocates for policy changes to end hunger. Bread for the World provides resources to help individuals advocate to end hunger, which might include "an offering of letters" sent annually to members of Congress, meeting with their members of Congress, and working in coalition with others. While it may applaud charity, it especially aims at government action. To justify its lobbying approach, it often makes the point that a single "bad vote" in Congress on food stamps can undo an entire year of Christian charity for the hungry.

Habitat for Humanity is an international nongovernmental and nonprofit Christian organization. This is its mission statement: "Seeking to put God's love into action, Habitat for Humanity brings people together to build homes, communities and hope." Homes are built using volunteer labor and Habitat makes no profit on the homes built. President Jimmy Carter has been its conspicuous face for a long time.

The National Association of Evangelicals World Relief is the humanitarian arm of the NAE, offering assistance to victims of poverty, disease, hunger, war, disasters and persecution. It is supported by churches and individual donors, as well as through United States Government grants from USAID and other agencies. World Relief's core programs focus on microfinance, AIDS prevention and care, maternal and child health, child development, agricultural training, disaster response, refugee resettlement, and immigrant services. The majority of World Relief's income comes from government grants.

Consider this local effort: Welcome to the Matthew 25 Farm. "We are a 501(c)(3) not-for-profit public charity, with farm locations in Tully and LaFayette, New York. We work to ensure that no Central New Yorker goes without fresh produce. To accomplish this, we grow, harvest and distribute fresh vegetables and fruit to those in need throughout Central New York. We also advise others on growing and preserving their own fresh produce."

Google the Matthew 25 Ministry, which provides opportunities to every member of parishes who join on to participate in hands-on activities to fulfill the challenge put by the Matthew 25 gospel.

Google how the Matthew 25 Project in the Catholic Diocese of Camden, New Jersey puts faith into action. On Christ the King Sunday at the end of the church year, the Gospel reading is the last judgment story in Matthew 25 when Jesus welcomes the righteous to heaven because of how they cared for Christ himself by responding to the needs of those who are poor and vulnerable. In this famous passage, churchgoers hear a clear message from Christ: the work of charity and justice is at the heart of their faith. In preparation for this special day, Diocese of Camden Life and Justice Ministries partners with faith communities on the Matthew 25 Project, a five-week series of activities. Parishes throughout the diocese will hosting a wide variety of events. All are welcome!

Each week focuses on one of the five conditions Jesus mentions in the passage:

I was hungry and you fed me, thirsty and you gave me drink: October 19–25

I was a stranger and you welcomed me: October 26–November 1

I was naked and you clothed me: November 2–8

I was ill and you cared for me: November 9–15

I was in prison and you visited me: November 16–22

Have you ever heard of *Buy low and let grow STOCKS*? This is the Matthew 25 Fund, a $124 million equity mutual fund. Manager Mark Mulholland is a devout Catholic, and he named his fund for the parable of the talents in Matthew 25:14–30, instructing followers to invest what they have been given.

Matthew 25: Ministries (www.m25m.org) is an international humanitarian aid and disaster relief organization helping over 18.5 million people each year around the world.

ELCA (Lutheran) Pacific Synod Matthew 25 Fund is an example of a single synod, as part of the national church, seeking to honor Christ as he spoke in Matthew 25:35–40.

Matthew 25 House is a local social justice outreach program for men who are now in the Story County Jail, halfway houses, or an Iowa prison. It helps integrate them into a local church and the Ames, Iowa community.

Matthew 25 Movement: Partner with Us declares, "The Matthew 25 pledge invites Christians around the country to commit to protect and defend vulnerable people. We want to give you tangible resources and concrete actions to work with your congregation to stand with immigrants in your community. At the center of this movement are Blessing not Burden Partners."

Consider also the ELCA Matthew 25 Movement Dreamer Sunday. Here Matthew 25 churches throughout Southern California pray with Dreamers and their families on Dreamer Sunday, in March.

Matthew 25: Ministries (M25M) is an international humanitarian aid and disaster relief organization helping the poorest of the poor locally, nationally, and internationally regardless of race, creed, or political persuasion. By rescuing and reusing products from major corporations, manufacturers, hospitals, and individuals, Matthew 25: Ministries provides basic necessities, skill development, and disaster relief across the US and worldwide.

ENJOINING A MATTHEW 25 CHURCH TO A MATTHEW 25 WORLD

A field guide to taking Matthew 25 public would need to transition from Word to world, from church to society, from gospel to social gospel, from faith to politics, from parish to public square. *This would be the agenda of any ambitious new religious movement that strives to magnify and institutionalize a biblical text in new contexts.* This chapter on the *church gathered* must eventually segue to a chapter on the *church sent*. So I conclude this study by projecting Matthew 25 onto government and society rather than just onto the church and individual congregations. There is no doubt that churches preaching Matthew 25 already focus the gospel story onto the concrete world, onto acts on the ground, onto the material space that the church is called to sacramentalize, which is to say *consecrate* or *grant sacred significance to* or *claim for God's image*. How powerful it already is if the church invites its neighbors to its celebrations of the Eucharist, which is a foretaste of the common feast to come, at a table large enough for all. A common Facebook admonition in 2020–2021 was to build a longer table rather than a higher wall, if the numbers of the hungry grow, rather than finding ways to exclude or ignore them. Just the church's and believers' individual acts of charity already evoke a social world, but the next move is to envision and broadcast a covenanted society.

We have seen that evangelical Christianity is wary of the call for *social justice*, even just pronouncing the very phrase, and believes it is fundamentally a leftist slogan that invites and evokes Marxist socialism and other evils, and has no place in Christianity. As we will shortly see, this abstention tends to leave politics and economics undisturbed, and the Christian Right is often seen as complicit in and even championing the status quo of unregulated capitalism and a small government "on leave." Yet, *evangelical Christianity does produce motivated believers* who can hear the call of Matthew 25 at the local level and through outreach from their congregations like Jesus Centers, which feed and house the homeless. It also resounds in the national evangelical effort called Samaritan's Purse. Matthew 25 Christians may encourage them for what they are doing and for the ways their fervent piety sets a pious example for all and gets the church started on the Matthew 25 path.

The church is made up of believing Christians who acknowledge Christ as their redeemer and king. But these church members are also citizens who, most Christian traditions assert, are called to be responsible to and for the society and culture and world they live in. And Matthew calls disciples to see the enthroned king *everywhere and in every needy person or community*.

In my previous book, *After Trump: Achieving a New Social Gospel*, I imagined a Christian humanism across the land that would be populated by *earth angels*. Abraham Lincoln's appeal in his first inaugural address to the *better angels of our nature* is well known. Luther saw that the incarnation of Christ made *earth capable of heaven*. This is both an incarnational reality and a Christian theology of hope, in which a frankly utopian hope draws heaven to earth—a more earth-changing ambition than projecting heaven to the end of time. The jarring patristic use of the concept *theosis* implied that God became human that we might become divine—a stretch few are willing to assert today. But *spirit present in matter seems to be God's big idea*. All of earth is reclaimed by all of God. The human prospect is wide, and Christians are beckoned to exercise civic virtues that model a Christian humanism that becomes a conspicuous leaven in the life of the country.

If human inertia instead wins, if a "Christian realism" prevails that can only caution about excessive ambition and warn against utopian dreams and reduce moral ambition to individuals (as Reinhold Niebuhr did), then the church is admonished to be safe and inward. When the German Peasants' War turned Luther's gospel into utopian dreams for society, Luther accused them of acting like they had "swallowed the Holy Ghost, feathers and all." But in another mood, Luther encouraged Christians to "sin boldly." When Christians hold back from visions for a new social order, their pessimism may be grounded in a view of God who does everything and leaves no ambitious roles for humans themselves. *Pessimism about changing the world is then God's fault, if an overwhelming theology of grace sucks all the oxygen from the human stage.* But if in the Old Testament God is "enthroned on the praises of Israel," surely the divine zeppelin is launched by human breath—as pre-electric organs once were by the boys who pumped the bellows. Maybe God wills the universe to get somewhere, and Christian humanists are the first to enlist. The boys at the bellows need to keep pumping.

Almost all Christians are willing to see the church as a "field hospital," but they hold back if the goal is to inquire about what in our society or economic system keeps inflicting the downtrodden with post-traumatic stress disorder. And their ambitions do not include transforming people into empowered agents of radical change. What if the churches were preparing landing strips for God's imminent arrival amidst earthly striving? I have mentioned Martin Luther King's dream of the arc of justice bending down to meet us on the road ahead.

Of course, this takes prayer and preparation and what are usefully called retreats—that precede action. *What if American Christianity were flooded with Matthew 25 retreats?* At the time of John the Baptist there was a Jewish Essene community that went out into the desert determined to live lives of such purity that God could not but consent to come down and evoke Israel's return from exile to rebuild the promised land. Radical Matthew 25 Christians are those who retreat for theological reflection and then reengage both the church and society. They see the metamorphosis of gospel to social gospel. They might affiliate with secular progressives who produced the United Nations' "Millennial Development Goals" at the end of the last century, people who wanted to move the world *from not yet to already happening* and aspired to such earthly goals of eradicating extreme poverty and hunger, achieving universal primary education, empowering women everywhere, reducing child mortality, improving maternal health, healing the sick and eradicating prominent diseases, ensuring environmental sustainability, and developing global partnerships for development.

BEYOND CHARITY

These esteemed United Nations millennial goals envision far more than charity. *The insidious side of charity is that it can become a substitute for justice.* Conservatives love charity because it gives evidence of how generous Americans are, it hints that it is much more admirable than wasteful government programs, it seems to excuse the ideology of "small government" from responsibilities to the human wreck created by unregulated capitalism, it detracts from scrutiny of the American economy, gives capitalism a free pass, and comfortably imagines that the invisible hand of the market is in fact God's own. But if God himself is turned into a free-market fundamentalist, then who was Jesus and where is his reign?

The Hebrew Bible is far more aggressive in its long tradition of prophetic protest in the king's face and calling down the mighty from their comfortable seats. The Old Testament tradition, carrying over into the New Testament and certainly into Matthew's portrait of Jesus as its long-awaited fulfillment, dares to imagine redistribution of resources and singles out those who are "grinding the faces of the poor." This posture sends shudders down the spines of all conservatives, including well-meaning Christians, who can only see in it atheistic socialism rather than biblical religion. But many theologians insist that any time "gospel" is used it must also imply "social gospel." They exhort Christians to surrender the pretense that they are two different things, and one of them is optional—or even objectionable.

The American Constitution, with its First Amendment right of freedom of religion, must certainly include the right to have a Christian presence in the public realm, even as it also maintains the separation of church and state. It should be noted that the argument for this does not require special pleading for religion, but only the assertion that in a postmodern age there are "multiple discourse communities" claiming the right to a public presence in the life of society, and these include people of color and women and LGBTQ folk—and religion. Which may also take up the cause of the least of these who are so often excluded from public influence.

As the church recovers or rediscovers the expanse of a *social* gospel, and learns to follow Matthew 25 in representing and pleading the case for the least of these, it will have to ask itself questions like: Can we really see the poor from where we're sitting? Can we imagine ourselves as a social justice movement in the economy of God? Can we reimagine the public sphere as a commonwealth to which we bring our "habits of the heart" and our own moral voice? Can we let go of our libertarian proclivities enough to see ourselves as responsible tenders of community who acknowledge the claim others have on us? Can we expand the scope of our responsibilities to the "care of the earth," a designation both evangelical Christians and the pope have lately adopted? Can we experiment with translating the word *social* in "social gospel" to designating the church as, among other callings, *a "social movement" in the life of society*? Can we imagine that if Christianity is going to become a social movement it is going to have to experiment with *resistance and nonconformity*? Can we come to see that as Christian citizens we must work for a politics and economics and government that pursues social justice throughout the land?

7

Focusing Matthew 25 on the *Church Sent*: Text to Context, Word to World, Gospel to Social Gospel, *Christian* Social Gospel to *Societal* New Deal

A WHIMSICAL INTRODUCTION

IN HER DELIGHTFUL AUTOBIOGRAPHY *Pastrix: The Cranky, Beautiful Faith of a Sinner and Saint,* Nadia Bolz-Weber turns the famous story in Acts about Philip and the eunuch upside down. Philip, a missionary-in-training, is sent by God to an accidental encounter with an Ethiopian eunuch riding by in his chariot. He just might be ripe for conversion and Philip ends up baptizing him. But who really got converted? Perhaps Philip was thinking, "I'll just beat that queer with my Scripture stick until he becomes what I think he should be." But maybe the Holy Spirit was prompting the eunuch, "Invite this new Jewish boy in. He's a representative of those who cling to the law and reject you from God's house (Deuteronomy 23:1 says, No eunuchs!). Invite him in to sit with you. Go, join, invite, ask questions, let him learn from someone who has only faced rejection." So the eunuch converts Philip to God's intention to take the gospel public, and Philip in turn baptizes the eunuch into the religious community!

Now I'm imagining that the church one day joins the academy on its chariot ride. The leftists and the anti-capitalists and the secular intellectuals propose a chat. The Christians decide, perhaps patronizingly, to consent to a mutual conversation. During the course of it, God transforms the missionaries. Out of the conversation comes a social gospel collaboratively converting to a New Deal. The missionaries then baptize the professors!

CONSECRATING THE WORLD BEYOND THE CHURCH

We have considered children focusing the sun's energy through a magnifying glass until it sets kindling on fire. This book purports to be a field guide for sponsoring Matthew 25 as a new public offering, focusing on how Matthew could sponsor a new religious movement in contemporary society. I propose to let God focus Matthew onto society through the lens of the church. This would evoke the process of how the Christian church comes to sacramentalize or consecrate the world, during which the gospel becomes a social gospel. The symbols and needs of the world are gradually inculturated into the life and liturgy of the church. Word to world, world to Word.

Social gospel is of course a fraught term. To progressive or leftist Christians it evokes a promising and God-ordained opportunity to apply the gospel to the world, to give it legs on earth and not just a warm presence in believers' hearts or within the gathered church. To those conscious of Christian history, it evokes memories of the early twentieth-century social gospel movement that distinguished American Protestantism. Or it reminds some of the "black social gospel," which became an experiment in Reconstruction after the Civil War until denounced by Southern white Christians. Or it might evoke the 1960s black civil rights movement emerging from the black church, as led by Martin Luther King. It is easy enough to define it phenomenologically. (I know it when I see it.) But conservative Christians in the past and the present seem to *see red* when they consider it. The very phrase has been banished from conservative evangelical discourse. Even the adjective *social* was banished from evangelical discourse.

Here is how historical theology might describe or justify it: Christian faith calls Christians not only to personal conversion but to social transformation. A social gospel would apply Christian understanding to social problems, especially issues of social justice such as economic inequality, poverty, crime, race, slums, environment, unionization, poor schools—all these and more taken up in the early twentieth-century

Protestant response to the Gilded Age of the late nineteenth century, which was merciless to all but the wealthy.

In millennial terms, a social gospel is *postmillennial*—it expects the second coming of Christ will be a culmination of religious forces that rid the world of social evils and prepare for the return of Christ in a Christian golden age. Yikes.

A social gospel would be an evolutionary state and permanent addition to a Christian outlook on Christianity's role in the world, a kind of cosmological view of the incarnation.

A social gospel moves from diagnosing and mending individual sinfulness to institutionalized sinfulness. With grounding in the Hebrew Bible, Jewish thought sponsors the very nice idea of "mending or repairing the world"—tikkun olam.

A social gospel takes the New Testament concept of the kingdom of God as a larger and more comprehensive category than the church. It sees the earth as territory to be occupied by the sovereign King, Christ.

A social gospel comes to reside all over the occupied space of the reign of God. A social gospel is a gospel that takes up social space.

In terms of this book's focus on Matthew 25, a social gospel is determined to find Christ as King persistently (and annoyingly?) present among the poor, and to perform this insight. Defining is the easy task. There are more difficult tasks: To awaken and energize the church to a social gospel calls for revival. To turn the social gospel into a new religious movement is a text-to-context task, rooted in biblical studies, preached and practiced by the church, traced through historical theology, worked out in Christian ethics, and chronicled in the sociology of religion. All of these disciplines are incorporated in this field guide.

But the surprising task is to understand why many Christians would deliberately and self-consciously oppose and reject the very idea of a social gospel. The Christian Right, but also very many other American evangelicals, reject the call for a social gospel. (Mainline churches believe in it, but only half-heartedly practice it.) Conservatives are instinctively averse to the very adjective *social*, whether used to describe sin, or theology, or justice, or gospel. They reject any role for the church in stimulating governmental activism on behalf of the poor. They fear that social justice or a social gospel would displace individual Christian charity and replace it with wasteful government. Or that it might short-circuit the Christian plan of salvation, which is to say God approaches individuals and beckons them to invite Jesus into their heart—in an individualist transaction. They do not reject Christian charity, or acts of individual Christians or even the charity of Christian organizations or the church reaching out to the homeless or the hungry or the poor—as long as there is no attempt to work via government agencies or collaborate with the academy and progressive economists. Even that is not a pure objection, since many church-based relief organizations seek a "faith-based initiative" status and regularly request federal funds.

For example, Samaritan's Purse, headed by Franklin Graham, a committed follower of President Trump, understands itself as follows: "After sharing the story of the Good Samaritan, Jesus said 'Go and do likewise.' That is the mission of Samaritan's Purse—to follow the example of Christ by helping those in need and proclaiming the hope of the Gospel. Samaritan's Purse receives and channels some funding from USAID." Is this a contradiction?

More importantly for the implementation of a social gospel, very many evangelicals resolutely refuse to mount a critique against a deregulated capitalism that accepts no social responsibility for the poor or the environment. Nor do they accept the lobbying of Congress (except against abortion or homosexuality, for example) to create a "big government" that accepts responsibility for expending tax dollars on behalf of social justice and entitlements for the poor.

RADICAL DISCIPLESHIP FOLLOWS A RADICAL KING WITH A SOCIAL GOSPEL AS HIS DOMAIN

Visiting prisoners can turn into prison reform that takes their circumstances, and the entire social reality of crime and punishment, seriously and tries to change them. Feeding the hungry can turn into Bread for the World, which is a Christian lobbying group trying to move Congress in the direction of resolving hunger issues. The church's worship and liturgy can shape Christians and train them in the posture and the virtues that will reshape society through the power of the gospel. It is like foot washing, the yoga that produces the necessary posture of servant-disciples. A year's worth of Gospel readings from Matthew can move an attentive church from being "at ease in Zion" toward becoming the vanguard of social justice across the land. Catholic moral theology since the late nineteenth century has laid down the foundation for a social Christianity, paying special attention to workers' movements—until neoconservative billionaires aligned with the Federalist Society and big business called for lowered taxes and no significant government efforts on behalf of justice for all. A neoconservative counter-magisterium arose to contest Catholic social theology and took on the pope as well. Matthew places Jesus' last judgment story in the last week of his earthly ministry, climaxed when the religious establishment and government turn against him as too dangerous for social order, and crucify him. It should not, then, be a shock when modern religious institutions and governments turn on the social gospel associated with Jesus' kingship.

THE CHURCH AS A NONCONFORMING RESISTANCE MOVEMENT

Talk of a social gospel requires an appropriate ecclesiology. What kind of institution does the church need to be? The Anabaptist movement that arose during the Protestant Reformation declined to identify with European Christendom and to baptize babies into national citizenships. Instead they saw themselves resisting the existing order and becoming a nonconforming alternative to it, indeed a community of resistance. The Puritan movement that arose in England in the seventeenth century officially identified with "nonconformity" to Anglicanism and indeed buried its dead in nonconformist cemeteries. Today using words like *nonconformist* and *resisting* to describe the American church are unsettling and jarring. And unlikely! Already Paul was warning against "principalities and powers" arraigned against the young church. They needed to be unmasked and resisted. The modern public square in the American commonwealth could become a contested space in which the moral voice of the church is one of those demanding a hearing and contesting for space. I like to subtitle my sociology of religion class as "contesting for public space."

Will there be prophets to lead the way? Will they be sidelined or trivialized or simply ignored by the media as quaint voices in a modern age? Will the academy dismiss them as outliers and certainly not qualifying as "public intellectuals"? Will leftist progressives decline to align with them because they seem embarrassing and a threat to their own secularity? Will the Christian Right so damage the reputation of Christianity that it will not be taken seriously? And make millennials happy to be leaving? Will Republicans acknowledge only Christians who do not disrupt a capitalist system? Will President Biden's devout Catholicism persuade Democrats to form some alliances with the church even at the risk of offending their secular base?

This is *not about theocracy* or even special pleading for the presence of religion in the public square over against the separation of church and state. The church must claim to be one of the voices, one of many "discourse communities" striving for public presence, like Black Lives Matter and Me Too and Friends of the Earth. Wall Street may feel uniquely entitled to *occupy the public square* (as the *Charging Bull* sculpture refused to yield space to the newly arrived and rival *Fearless Girl*). Indeed, it may be that the public square is *preoccupied* by an ideology of secularism and materialism and rational-actor economic man, defined and supported by corporate interests and unchallenged and privileged by the Supreme Court. Then religion must emerge as a rival or competing moral voice, arguing that multiple voices are needed and not a single voice flying under the radar of the First Amendment's prohibition of an established religion—while functioning in precisely that way. In fact, as Catholicism in Europe has long argued, government can and should contribute to the *flourishing of religion* in public commonwealths without straying into theocracy. The American First Amendment surely guarantees, under the "free exercise clause," the right to a public voice. Must the church echo Marlon Brando in *On the Waterfront*, "I coulda been a contender"?

LUTHERAN REFORMATION INITIATIVES ONCE URGED A SOCIAL WELFARE AGENDA ON THE STATE

It is well-known that Luther cautioned his followers about heady ideas of "bringing in the kingdom," by which he meant getting carried away with absolutizing current political solutions and making them into a gospel-defined Christian state. Partly, he was responding to the enthusiastic ambitions of the German Peasants' Revolt, which sought to combine the new ideas of the Reformation with the hopes of the poor for an ideal social order. Luther was sure this would lead to tragic excesses in which the peasants confused their own hopes and the radical movement they founded with God's own kingdom arriving. Fair enough. And maybe Luther worried that the Reformation movement would be ruined in the process. Luther famously tagged such Christians with the epithet "enthusiasts," and suggested they believed they had "swallowed the Holy

Ghost, feathers and all." But the legacy of Luther's caution was centuries of Lutheran "quietism," in which Lutherans, unlike Calvinists, held back from large ambitions for transforming society. Luther kept separate the kingdom of God and the kingdom of the state.

But there is little common knowledge today of how much Luther did enter the realm of the state with strong advice about its responsibility to provide for the welfare of the poor. Long before the onset of Marxism, Luther was tackling the question whether poverty was the result of defects in personal character or the social and economic structure of society. In *Beyond Charity: Reformation Initiatives for the Poor,* Carter Lindberg documents the surprising record of Luther's role as a vigorous advisor to the German princes and to town councils.

The Middle Ages had provided their own answer to how the church should respond to the poor, which Luther came to reject completely in the service of Pauline grace and justification. The poor and the monastic movement together shared in the image of the humiliated Christ. They were following the New Testament legacy in which the rich, not the poor, were the key theological focus. The rich could be saved only by giving alms to the poor. This became the moral map of the medieval universe. Augustine had argued that love is to be directed at God through the neighbor, especially the poor. Monasticism interiorized and projected upon society the human condition of pilgrim and wayfarer. Every pilgrim at a monastic door is Christ himself. This ideology of poverty provided a place in society for the involuntary poor and *made charity a condition of salvation.* Faith is formed by charity. The presupposition of canon law that the merchant is rarely able to please God was a long way from the Calvinist-tinged view at the birth of capitalism that wealth was a sign of divine election. In the medieval view, by giving charity to the poor the rich atone for their sins and receive the intercessory prayers of the grateful poor. It almost seemed that God willed poverty to give the rich an opportunity to atone for their sins. As charity and ecclesiology came together, poor relief passed through the church. Charity became an avenue of penance. Did this sanctification of poverty justify the status quo?

Lindberg insists that the Reformation carried Christian responses to the poor *beyond charity.* Social welfare shifted from church to government. Luther played a key role in the evolution of social theory regarding the poor from the Middle Ages to Reformation times. Faith became active in the development of political, economic, and social structures to serve the neighbor. Luther also advised churches to sponsor a communal chest to provide relief to the poor. Church was now a community of believers, and out of that community came a "common chest." Seeing the gospel in this-worldly terms as prophetic protest against the rich and powerful became a mandate for structural social changes. Lindberg argues that the Reformers came to see that welfare was of little use without changing the institutional structures that create poverty. Renaissance humanism and the Reformation became a sixteenth-century watershed for changes of poor relief. Social control by the state was also an issue. And the outlawing of begging. The beginning of Luther's ideas on the state's responsibility for social justice is registered in Luther's well-known tract, *Address to the Christian Nobility of the German Nation*, already appearing in 1520 amidst the very early days of the Lutheran Reformation. In it the church is appealing to the government—and to the Christian citizenry.

Luther's rejection of the salvatory merit of good works cut the nerve of indiscriminate medieval almsgiving and rejected the valorization of poverty as a Christian virtue. Luther's universal priesthood of all the baptized and his championing of every Christian's (secular) calling led to increased participation in urban governance. Gottesdienst, the German word for Sunday worship, viewed a gracious God as serving the people. And the people serving God, in a great exchange. This freed the congregation for a *second liturgy*, the service to neighbor and commonwealth. The Eucharist could be seen as connecting worship and welfare.

The transition to the Reformation period led to the secularization of charity, whereas the medieval ecclesiastical system of charity had not led to a new social ethic regarding poverty and society. Charity aimed at the salvation of the donor did not lead to the resolution of poverty as a social issue. Poverty as a virtue was challenged by a new urban society, and early capitalism aspired to wealth. Along with changes in economic views, the new Reformation doctrine made major contributions to social welfare and legislation. Citizens who gratefully accepted Luther's assurance that their status with God was a matter of grace found themselves liberated to expend civil energy for social change. Contrary to later Enlightenment, not to mention Marxist, theory, a *religious event could lead to social and structural change*. The Reformation was an urban event. Poverty not tied to the means of salvation and emancipation from churchly control of charity led to the "rationalization" of poor relief and social welfare. Along with this, early capitalism came to flourish, but a Christian obsession with opposing usury as a system that lives off the bodies of the poor was also an implicit critique of the new capitalism. Some Reformers saw this as a *status confessionis*, a social situation that called for Christian protest and government regulation. It is possible, however, to suggest that Calvinism reconnected economics to salvation, though in a different manner than under medieval Catholicism. In *The Protestant Ethic and the Spirit of Capitalism*, Max Weber suggested that the aims of Calvinist theologies shifted towards rational means of economic gain as a way of dealing with "salvation anxiety." Accumulation of wealth seems to be seen as confirmation of salvation—not a Lutheran emphasis.

But it remained true that Luther insisted the world cannot be ruled by the gospel and Christian love—hence the kingdom of God's left hand. Grace cannot be turned into social legislation and there is not a new gospel-defined science of economics. The German Peasants' War remained in the back of Luther's mind. The gospel empowered Christians, and then sent them back into the world with a calling of good work and service to neighbor. There was a transition from charity to social assistance. The civil community and the church community are coextensive and religion is *not* merely a private matter. The new capitalism would threaten this view of the common good. But radical reformers like Thomas Muntzer and the various Anabaptist movements seemed to move in the direction of communalism and socialism.

Lindberg's scholarship redeems much of Lutheranism from the charge of quietism. And it suggests to me, a Lutheran, that one could today call for a Christian social gospel that in turn evokes a governmental New Deal—each mirroring the other but in separate spheres.

SHOULD A CONTEMPORARY SOCIAL GOSPEL MOVEMENT THEN PARTNER WITH POLITICS?

The gospel is the title for the first four books of the New Testament that tell the story of the life and message of Jesus Christ and which intend to challenge the reader to decisions. These books are part of the canonical New Testament, as defined in the early centuries of Christianity, but they also have independent standing as religious literature. The gospel is also a religious category or event or theological type within Christianity. Christian theologians and clergy have always studied the Gospels and the gospel, down through the ages, commenting on them theologically and devotionally. In recent centuries, both church-based and university-based scholars have studied the Gospels and the gospel in the entire Bible.

Typically, they often work cooperatively, and it is not always clear whether the secular-based scholars are also Christian believers and indeed church members. But sometimes, and in some centuries or decades, the two types of scholars may diverge in various ways. This may be in nuance or general approach, or also in significant disagreement. Divergences may occur regarding historicity, provenance, or theological meaning and claims. Christian scholars especially pay attention to the gospel as a theological claim regarding God's action in the world or the meaning of salvation.

In the United States, both kinds of scholars come together in the Society of Biblical Literature (SBL) and the American Academy of Religion (AAR), occasionally uneasily. Some people believe that biblical scholars who self-identify as "theologians" should be teaching in seminaries or religious institutions, rather than in departments of religious studies in public universities, but not everyone holds to this. (I identify as a Lutheran theologian and pastor, but have spent my entire career in the religious studies department of a public university. Everyone knew I was a Lutheran minister, and no one thought I was an illegitimate proselytizer. That I was also a social justice leftist left some people confused but intrigued.) Perhaps it goes without saying that religion scholars in public universities are expected not to proselytize their students, though that is not always a clear distinction in style and effects. (An old joke is that many religious studies professors would not be caught within ten feet of lived religion.) Both kinds of scholars publish in the same journals. I mention this to demonstrate that self-professing Christians and possibly secular scholars are accustomed to working cooperatively when the subject is the Gospel as a book or the gospel as a theological construct.

Should it be a surprise, then, to claim that Christians working with the *social gospel* might seek cooperative alignments with university-based or government-based thinkers and activists? With economists and politicians? So, Christians committed to a social gospel, including social justice issues, not only may but should be partners with nonreligious, or non-church-based, theorists who provide structural critique and analyses of how societies succeed or fail in responding to the total needs of the commonwealth. Such experts may come from economics and the social sciences. While the church is called to be true to its own story and its own language, as Anabaptists especially see, it is not above consulting those who analyze the problems of late capitalism and offer encompassing solutions. The church itself is not necessarily expert on economics or social systems and can profit from consultation as it imagines the contours of a social gospel that wants to move beyond individual acts on behalf of the least of these to large-scale solutions to achieving a just society. (And economists and sociologists are not necessarily expert in social ethics. Or the role of humanism and "habits of the heart" and "virtue ethics" in a social system that may also include an element of civil religion.) I mentioned above that Luther rejected the idea of a Christian politics or a Christian economics—probably to keep theology uncompromised. But this could all the more lead to the conclusion of the above paragraphs that Christian ethicists and non-Christian economists *should indeed be working together* as the occasion demands. Or it must have meant, in a time when nearly everyone in Europe was Christian, that a Christian who is also an economist is *not* doing Christian economics. The Catholic tradition, which means to leave religious and moral deposits in social systems, does not follow this path.

In short, it may be the chief occupation of Christian theologians and pastors to study Matthew 25 and advocate on behalf of its religious vision. But it may, equally, be the calling of secular scholars to develop approaches to social justice, to define and manage government programs, and to examine the failures and possibilities of economic systems—precisely in consultation with religion. Together they may work to achieve a commonwealth that is good for all people and for the earth as well. Together they may aspire to re-enchant the world. And contribute to its evolutionary course. Together they may join in a common vision for the good of all, including the least of these.

IS THE CHRISTIAN CHURCH ACTUALLY INDISPENSABLE TO POLITICAL EFFORTS AT SOCIAL JUSTICE?

In 2015, Pope Francis published his encyclical *Laudato si'* ("Praise be to you: On care for our common home"), decrying reckless consumerism, ecological degradation, and global warming. To exercise *dominion over* should mean not ruthless domination but moral responsibility. Because of his moral care for the earth, Francis will come to be known by the enemies this makes for him. Fox News labeled Pope Francis the most dangerous man on the planet! So: moral vision is the greatest threat to capitalist degradation of the planet.

In 2011 Rabbi Michael Feinberg marched shoulder to shoulder with Protestants, Catholics, and Muslims on behalf of a living wage campaign. This would be an example of religious citizenship, and it was bitterly opposed by Mayor Bloomberg and the New York establishment. *It required religion and unions coming together.* The rabbi never aspired to be a "pulpit rabbi," but an organizer for social justice movements. He is too sophisticated to imagine that the Hebrew Bible (Old Testament) is a simple blueprint for socialism or that a simple transfer from then to now is all that is possible. But the Hebrew prophets' legacy of communalism, concern for the marginalized, obsession with the widow/orphan/stranger, and the need to cancel debt are still powerful moral evocations waiting to be attended to in the modern age. Especially in the modern age. The rabbi understands the shared foundations of Judaism and socialism. Religious socialism straddles church and state, religion and government. For the rabbi, *Bund* (federation of citizens and government) is a resonant word with connotations both religious and secular.

But what kind of federation? We have seen how the Christian Right is completely aligned with the Republican Party and political conservatism, including an unwillingness to critique capitalism, or commit to efforts at social justice, or align itself with almost any movement that includes the word *social*. Alternately, we considered how progressive Christianity, appealing to such witness as Matthew's, might be in the forefront of efforts to see that the gospel becomes a social gospel, that identifying with the least of these would require social programs aimed to benefit the poor and install social justice across the land. Here, then, are two bitterly rival federations of citizens and government.

A field guide to taking Matthew 25 public, such as this, suggests how Matthew 25 Christians might open themselves, and the church, to alliances with the secular world, with public intellectuals critical of late capitalism, with efforts to enlist government on behalf of the poor and, for example, workers' unions. Will Matthew 25 Christians become the paradigms for theologians and pastors working together with social scientists and economists and government to create a new kind of society where social justice prevails and the poor are raised up?

It is one thing to convince the church to engage in such alliances with the secular world. But vice versa? It is still another to convince university-based experts or politicians to seek out or even consent to alliances with the church. Many of them, deeply committed to secularism, wary of breaches of church/state demarcations, critical or even disdainful of religion in general and the church in particular, may be unwilling to swallow hard and team up with religious movements. Or, they may be willing to compromise their instincts and work somewhat with the church, as long as they remain in charge and define the initiatives.

This is extremely shortsighted. *Secular progressives cannot succeed without alliances with the church.* They are not merely doing religion a favor by playing on the same team. Consider many decades of Republican efforts, especially since Reagan, to undo and reverse the New Deal, with its Social Security and unemployment benefits and common healthcare and tending to the commons. A full and determined return to the mood of the New Deal will not happen without religion and politics coming together. This remains to be seen in the Biden administration.

It is widely noted that from Republican president Eisenhower's term on the tax on the very wealthy was around 70 percent. Under President Reagan that plunged to 28 percent. (Part of the tax shortage was made up by taxing Social Security benefits!) It remains there, and even liberal Democrats cannot seem to rise beyond it as a fixed and unquestioned status quo, although there are inklings at the beginning of the Biden administration. Whether pandemic relief, or the forgiveness of education loans, or universal healthcare, or entitlements for the downtrodden, or significant subsidies for higher education as provided everywhere in Europe, or environmental relief, or subsidized housing—the response is always and inevitably "we can't afford it." Crying over the national debt is a chronic response—unless the issue is tax cuts for the wealthy, a regular occurrence in recent decades. Even when Democrats are in the majority, they cannot imagine their way back to, or forward to, a federal budget that insures social justice and requires very significant tax expenditures—not unlike those in Europe. The answer of course is vast pressure from the church, in collaboration with workers' unions and a progressive government. Secular progressives need the church and cannot get along without it if their best ambitions are to be accomplished. This suggests the indispensable contributions of *the church as moral broker*—another subtlety in the church's alliance with the secular world, and vice versa. Will Matthew 25 Christians take the lead?

Consider the argument of Henry Louis Gates's new book and TV series, *The Black Church: This Is Our Story, This Is Our Song*. Gates considers four hundred years of history to analyze how black Christianity helped create a culture to subvert centuries of oppression. (Yes, Christianity has plenty to repent of.) Gates writes: "We need only look at the brilliant use of the church in all its forms—from WEB Du Bois's triptych of 'the Preacher, the Music, and the Frenzy' to the use of the building itself—to see the revolutionary potential and practice of Black Christianity in forging social change." Of course, the black church is one of the parents of the civil rights movement and Martin Luther King its outstanding icon. Black Lives Matter is also one of its heirs.

SEEING WHAT IS TO BE SEEN ABOUT THE SOCIAL-ECONOMIC SETTING OF THE LEAST OF THESE

When we have isolated or distanced the poor, or insulated our social imaginations, it is nearly impossible to *see them*. The version of this dilemma in Matthew 25 is that we cannot imagine Christ's presence among the poor, or the kingdom of God including them. In Jesus' last judgment story, it seems that those judged are singularly obtuse and cannot see Jesus among the least of these. Today it seems more convincing to imagine this inability to see not as obtuseness but as deliberate and willful obfuscation. We've built a social system so they cannot be seen.

As I write this, two California Highway Patrolmen, one Park Ranger, a couple of Chico police, and some heavy equipment operators are clearing out a twenty-five-tent homeless encampment on the edge of our public park and abutting the freeway. Where will these outcasts go now? But last week a Christian realtor donated five acres of land for the sake of homeless shelters. And the Jesus Center in Chico is cooperating with the University Farm to provide shelter and agricultural training for those with no work. We now know that Amazon, whose CEO Jeff Bezos can buy anything and has immensely profited during the pandemic, succeeded in winning the vote against the union in a Southern state. Some critics have charged that many Southern churches were insufficiently involved.

Christians who have staffed soup kitchens or provided bedding for the homeless who come to a local Jesus Center and who launch further inquiries about their dilemma, or take a university course or read a book by critics of capitalism, may come to learn that a very few billionaires in the world have accumulated more wealth than half of all humanity. Those who work on behalf of the poor may have their eyes lifted to see how impoverishment and inequality can be written into the way social systems function. They may be astonished to consider that the immiseration of the poor is even part of the economic plan and indeed a function of corporate capitalism. To minister to the working class, churches do not have to become unions, but they can teach themselves how unions work and why they are necessary, as the French Catholic Worker movement and the American Dorothy Day did. At the end of the nineteenth century in Europe, Catholic moral theologians saw clearly that there was no resistance to, or amelioration of, rampant industrialization without unions. And so they set about to sacrilize or consecrate workers' movements. In the United States the reverse happened: unions were broken, policed, and legislated against. Informed by economists and social scientists, progressive Christians came to understand how unions function to balance corporate interests with that of workers in the growth of an economy. And insure the good of workers. Nearly every European country understands this. Churches, and Christian and other charity workers, can discover how their yearly charitable offerings are regularly undone by economic forces far more powerful than they could have imagined.

Social progressives with abundant dreams for the working classes are lately dismayed to discover that this very class has come to believe that it is liberal progressives whose programs have left them behind. Could Christians who imagine a social gospel help to overcome these divisions and unite the helpers and the helped? Could Christians working among "hillbillies" learn to enlist their progressive partners in government, while also listening to those whose lives have become elegies, and bring both together? Could the churches negotiate useful partnerships?

The metaphor of seeing, and the Christian obligation to see what others do not see or even deny, must also attend to groups among the least of these who particularly go unseen. That would be people of color, and particularly American blacks. Black Lives Matter could be a banner carried in liturgical processions, but would it be? Critical race theory could become a topic in Christian education classes, but would it? Evangelical parachurch organizations who practice a vigorous Christian presence, like InterVarsity Christian Fellowship or Cru (formerly Campus Crusade for Christ) could challenge the consciences of college students, but will they?

And yet—an evangelical publisher, Zondervan, has sold 100,000 copies of a 2020 book written by Jemar Tisby, a black Christian, *The Color of Compromise: The Truth about the American Church's Complicity in Racism*. It not only claims that white Christians have been missing in action, but that they have often worked against racial justice. It is a call for vigorous Christian activism by white Christians. The book is a stunning and unrelenting denunciation of white supremacy from the colonial period to the present. Tisby writes: "When faced with the choice between racism and equality, the American church has tended to practice a complicit Christianity rather than a courageous Christianity. They chose comfort over constructive conflict and in so doing created and maintained a status quo of injustice."

This is scarcely one man's opinion, or the denunciation of a past now corrected. The current storm over "critical race theory" is unrelenting and coming from the churches as well as from conservative Republicans. Emerging in the latter decades of the twentieth century and now a vigorous presence in the academy, law, politics, and public discussion, this movement argues the point that racism and disparate racial outcomes across society are the result of complex, changing, and often subtle social and institutional dynamics rather than explicit and intentional prejudices on the part of individuals. Racism, and white supremacy, is deeply sedimented into social and cultural systems in ways easy to miss, especially if one does not wish to see. The crucial insight and claim is that race and white supremacy are an *intersectional social construction* that serves to uphold the interests of white people. That however does not make the whole debate simple. It may well be true that the critical race theorists often speak with the "woke" arrogance that makes everyone else feel ignorant, or that they appear to denigrate all of American history as unworthy of honor or celebration. And so those opposed to paint with such a large brush argue back, or even reject the entire movement out of hand. Will Christians become the *seers* the times require? Or will the churches participate in the cover-up?

THE POOR PEOPLES' CAMPAIGN, A FORMAT FOR MATTHEW 25 CHRISTIANS

Not every Christian outreach program to, and on behalf of, the least of these calls itself by the "Matthew 25 Christians" title, and yet their entire mission and self-understanding is built around the same theological sensibility. For the third time now I emphasize that a field guide for taking Matthew 25 public is not limited to the small new religious movement explicitly calling itself Matthew 25 Christians, but envisions all recent efforts to achieve a new social gospel or to achieve social justice through ambitious new efforts. It is particularly important to notice that poor peoples' campaigns in the 1960s and again now specifically devoted themselves to appealing to/putting pressure on/developing cooperative ties with the government on behalf of the poor—precisely the approach described in this chapter.

LBJ's War on Poverty in 1964 had raised poverty to national consciousness and there followed new self-identifications by the poor of their need for a national movement. But Johnson then moved on to other causes, especially the Vietnam War. And the Great Society turned the South Republican.

Martin Luther King became the undisputed leader of the "Poor People's Campaign" or the "Poor People's March on Washington," whose goal was economic justice for the poor. Just before his death by assassination on April 4, 1968, he notably was fearing for his life and said that it would be an honor if he became a martyr on behalf of a living wage for garbage workers. Then Ralph Abernathy became the new leader, and the movement featured encampments, marches, and massive pressure on the government across the country. This emerged after it became obvious that the civil rights movement, as effective as it had been, was not significantly focusing attention and winning results for the material conditions of the lives of the poor.

And yet movements come and go, as Matthew 25 Christians will also discover. After campaigns for the poor had had their day, and were beaten back especially by Republican administrations, a new movement arose in 2018, as previously noted. Named the Poor People's Campaign: A National Call for Moral Revival, it is led by William Barber II and Liz Theoharis, both of them pastors, theologians, and activists. There were marches on the National Mall and sit-ins in every state house. "Fight poverty not the poor" became a national motto, after legislatures increasingly turned on demonstrators—just as would be the case with the Black Lives Matter movement. Barber also emphasized that the civil rights movement by no means had resolved all the issues, and that continuous moral activism would be necessary. A "Poor People's Moral Budget" was an example of how movement activists were insisting that concern for the poor needed to be written into the national budget and remain a continuing dimension of legislation. This is an example of Christian activists insisting on working with and exerting pressure on government to resolve national issues surrounding the least of these. The goal was to keep Congress and the country mindful of the plight of 140 million poor and low-income people. The Poor People's campaigners kept showing up in Congress.

A particularly trenchant self-designation is Repairers of the Breach, which sees itself, in partnership with the Kairos Center for Religions, Rights, and Social Justice, the Popular Education Project, and hundreds of local and national partners, as uplifting our deepest moral and constitutional values and redeeming the heart and soul of our country. This multistate movement has emerged from more than a decade of work by grassroots community and religious leaders, organizations, and movements fighting to end systemic racism, poverty, the war economy, environmental destruction, and other injustices.

Among their statements of purpose were:

> We rise to change the moral narrative and demand that the interlocking injustices of systemic racism, poverty, ecological devastation, the war economy/militarism and the distorted moral narrative of religious nationalism all be ended. We rise to challenge the lie of scarcity in the midst of abundance. We rise to lift the voices and faces of poor and low-income Americans and their moral allies with a new vision of love, justice, and truth for America that says poverty can be abolished and change can come.

There is no doubt that this movement, alongside others such as Sojourners, brings concern about the least of these to a new level of organization, statements of purpose, and plans of action. It is appropriate to see such movements as ancillary to all expressions of commitment to Matthew 25 sensibilities and obligations. All are examples of Matthew 25 coming true in new contexts.

CALLING A SPADE A SPADE: DISENCUMBERED AMERICAN CAPITALISM IS A SOCIAL PROBLEM—NOT SEEING THE POOR AND NOT SEEING CAUSES

Fully seeing the least of these and then developing responses that meet their needs cannot successfully occur without also seeing other things—the economic system that envelops and immiserates the poor. Everyone knows Ronald Reagan's famous derogatorily ironic punch line, "I'm from the government and I'm here to help." Reagan wanted to convince Americans that big government is always the problem, never the solution—so that nothing would be expected of government for the welfare of all. Government must keep its hands off capitalism and any attempts to regulate it for higher purpose. While conservative evangelicals may insist that charity is the only appropriate Christian approach—and one that deliberately keeps its hands off our economic system—most analysis would insist on governmental programs, including regulation of capitalism, aimed towards achieving social justice. Matthew 25 Christians and other progressive Christians would insist that Christian citizens/Christian churches/government services/social and economic analysis must come together in mutual partnerships—that spur each other on through mutual lobbying and encouragement.

Without this approach, modern Americans, including Christians, will find it difficult to *see the poor* and do something about their plight. Capitalism throws up a smoke screen around the poor, obfuscating genuine understanding of their plight and its causes. Is it possible to identify the causes of the immiseration of the poor? If certain dimensions of "late capitalism" are the probable cause, why is it that so many of the working class reject the solutions of progressive social thinkers and choose instead to identify immigrants and people of color as the real crisis to be solved? A politics of resentment of "the other," designed and manipulated by monied interests, substitutes for a politics of resolution. Is this carefully crafted and handsomely funded obfuscation? Christian theologians and ethicists and pastors and congregants who take Matthew 25 seriously must allow the vision of Jesus in their midst to reawaken them to new efforts on behalf of a social gospel that goes far beyond charity for the homeless. Christians and others must call corporations to change their ways and say to their faces, "Inasmuch as you are doing this to the least of these, you are doing it to Christ himself." The setting of Matthew 25 during "Holy Week" makes it clear that Jesus was crucified because the political and religious establishment turned against him. Matthew 25 Christians are determined to keep this in the face of government and economic systems.

Should Christians not be trying to imagine and work toward a social system in which justice reigns and create a government that takes the side of the severely disadvantaged and oppressed and commits to achieve social justice across the country? Surely they should be joining in efforts to foster a "social imaginary" where the rich and the poor, politicians and economists, Christians and secularists come together to participate in an economic culture that is also a moral culture. A recovered sense of *commonwealth* would be a necessary construct of such a social imaginary. (So strong is an individualist ideology in this country that some couples' therapists insist that they can respond to individuals only, and not to two people who belong to that abstraction called marriage—an anti-libertarian construct!)

Jesus' story of the last judgment in which Christians will be tested on whether they have been able to envision the presence of their King amidst the least of these and whether they have actually seen and responded to the poor and the homeless and the sick and the hungry and the imprisoned is the wake-up call to the modern church. As we saw in an earlier chapter, God's heart for the poor, as also evidenced in the Matthew 25 story, is a common theme throughout the Bible. Matthew 25 comes heavily contextualized and weighed down with divine pathos. Once awakened to this theme and to God's vision that far exceeds our own, Matthew 25 Christians and their cohorts must surely consider wisely and inventively what to do about it. I have argued in this book that the Christian gospel offers us a redemption grounded in God's love for humans on earth *and also* evokes a *faith active in love*—as everyone from Augustine to Luther to Wesley has seen. While the God-in-Christ of the Bible may be partnering with us in the evolution of the kingdom of God on earth, as mystical cosmologists propose, I am now proposing that the church must devote itself to consideration of moral remedies for a fallen society *and also* seek partnerships in understanding the structural, and not just personal, dilemmas that afflict us and also create economic and political, as well as theological, responses to them.

Here is where Christianity divides in its response to the call of the least of these, as we have been seeing. Evangelicals, including but not limited to the Christian Right, may insist on an individualistic response to human misery, ranging from bringing the gospel to everyone who is then challenged to invite Jesus into their heart and also to offer charitable help to all those suffering. They want to limit their response to their understanding of God's personal plan of salvation, so that its religious uniqueness is not jeopardized by solutions that go beyond theology to include secular responses. But unless religion is enlarged and expanded to include God's plan for a re-enchanted earth, unless the full scope of Christ's kingdom and the public space it occupies is imagined, Christians may be so limited that while imagining ways to "save" Africa, for example, they cannot also imagine this might include worldwide agribusiness as part of the problem, and not yet a solution. So only charity is recommended. Any evangelical would freely acknowledge how modern medicine is a distinct blessing from God to be embraced and celebrated, but might decline to imagine or think well of and partner with all the expertise, including medical science and climate science and economic analysis of gross inequality and the oppressive systems that drive it—as important dimensions of the church's response to the needs of the world. It is not that the church must master all the disciplines that can produce human well-being, but that it should partner with and together become a moral voice that takes its place in the public square and influences the course of the wider culture—as Catholics have always been much more ready to acknowledge than many Protestants.

And so in this section I expand and detail the partnerships and the issues around which Christians and other people of good will might come together. The "collaborative eschatology" in the Epilogue will refer to the partnership with God in redeeming the earth and expanding (and "magnifying and institutionalizing) God's vision for the universe—surely instanced in Jesus' Matthew 25 vision. Mimicking the church's relation with God is its collaboration with all people of good will, including people who may join in God's plan, whether they do so knowingly or instinctively.

I am arguing in this field guide that the envisioning and building of a just society in America, at this point in our history, may and must include critical analyses "from above" of a capitalist economic system that immiserates many people and the environment and "from below" of how working classes have been fed ideologies that do not "save" them but the system that profits elites.

To take a simple example, a pastor making a house call on an indigent congregant who cannot come close to affording the extremely expensive insulin she requires and so must slip further and further into the degradation of her body—such a pastor must wonder what is wrong with such a healthcare and medical-economics system and what, if anything, concerned Christians could do about it. Such a pastor, if broadly educated, may also be aware that the same parishioner in nearly every comparable developed country would not be suffering from such a system in which "big pharma" or for-profit medical systems have been built to profit the extreme wealthy. A pastor who visits people who are distinctly "hunger insecure" will champion food stamps and school lunch programs—even as Congress is very often active in reducing them, lest they make people dependent. (It is never lost on me each month when I pick up from the pharmacy three different kinds of insulin that this would be costing me thousands if it were not for a handsome medical plan from the faculty union that complements my Social Security.)

One commonly reads that a few people have accumulated more wealth than half of humanity. I am calling attention here to a number of economists who have just recently made an enormous impression on contemporary intellectual life and whose very clear ambition is to analyze and solve the problem of gross inequality, the profound and continuing oppression of the poor, the celebration of wealth and the "greed is good" creed of the wealthy.

It is an outworn myth that only Marxism critiques capitalism and therefore that any criticism of capitalism must go light since Marxism, or at least some kind of big-government socialism, is going to be the only alternative. American Christians are remarkably uninformed about the long tradition of Christian socialism, or democratic socialism, characteristic of many European countries. European countries with a history of "state churches" often have a legacy built into their governmental structures of social programs that reach everyone in the country—above all with proper healthcare.

Polls sometimes show that many Americans who learn something about such programs in Scandinavia, for example, would *not* vote for them. Note, then, this is not just a problem of the wealthy refusing to contribute a proper tax share to the whole, but that middle- or even working-class people have instilled in them a false consciousness about the whole human project. Especially white working-class Americans who see incessant Facebook posts about the unimaginable social benefits Denmark offers know they would never consent to that level of taxation, because they assume the American model in which the wealthy do not even come close to paying their share, or are concerned that people of color would inordinately benefit, or because they have taught not to "think the state" in imagining how a society works, or because a vision for the whole commonwealth is not part of their social imaginary, or they have been taught that significant taxation systems are inappropriate and inefficient, or because they believe the elevation of all to minimum standards would contradict their libertarian ideologies.

An innocent American Christian assigned to think through the problems with "late capitalism" as the prevailing economic system in the United States may be shocked to find Wikipedia's matter-of-factly reporting: "Prominent among critiques of capitalism are accusations that capitalism is inherently exploitative, alienating, unstable, unsustainable, and creates massive economic inequality, commodifies people, and is anti-democratic and leads to an erosion of human rights while it incentivizes imperialist expansion and war."

Capitalism has been under criticism since Marx, and also from anarchists, socialists, nationalists, and religion, but I will primarily consider here contemporary capitalist critics, the very kind of public intellectuals Christian theologians and social ethicists may partner with as they attempt to diagnose the prevailing American economic system and whether it is responsible for the profound inequalities that characterize our society, the impoverishment of the poor, the destruction of the environment as one of capitalism's "externalities" that tax dollars must then be spent to mitigate, the great difficulty in finding sufficient government funding for universal healthcare, education, housing, and many other measures that could improve the lives of the working class. Or, in short, why is social justice so difficult to achieve, or to pass in Congress, in the United States—compared to European social democracies (influenced by Christian values)? And isn't *political reform*, assisted by Christians who vote and pay attention and exert moral pressure, the road to structural change of the economy? A common direction for political reform, though difficult to sustain in the United States, is not the abolition of capitalism but the regulation of capitalism, as in a *mixed economy*. The Republican platform, from Reagan through Trump, has developed and adhered to the panacea of *deregulation* (which Eisenhower denounced), in which government keeps its hands off the economy, market fundamentalism reigns, and corporate capitalism, including in its latest and most rapacious forms, goes free from social responsibility. Disencumbered capitalism is not a natural law of the market, but the choice of the wealthy. It is not true that every "rational actor" would of course choose deregulated capitalism, as if it were a law of gravity.

The record is long and ample. Since the Industrial Revolution and the factory system arose in Europe, capitalism has been blamed for unfair working conditions, including fourteen-hour days, child labor, and shanty towns. "Wage slavery" is a term applied to economic exploitation and social stratification, including unequal bargaining power between labor and capital and the evolution of slavery (owning workers) into the renting of workers.

In *Capitalism, Alone: The Future of the System that Rules the World*, Branko Milanovic analyzes how democracy and the market were turned into the handmaidens of modern capitalism. Where capitalism steadily ascends and becomes all-encompassing, liberal democracy gets in trouble. Instead of a new golden age, autocrats and oligarchs align. Where is the church? Ordinary people cannot see their way to social democracy and instead choose bogus nationalisms in which autocrats pose as populists who champion a mystical People. Once, "strong trade unions, mass education, high taxes, and large government transactions" were essential components of a *mixed economy*, but these have lost traction as capital has gained ever more power over messaging, while globalization has spawned competition to cut taxes, slash wages, and reduce regulation. Instead of a prevailing upward mobility, the affluent pass their status along to their children. An upper class becomes self-perpetuating. Louis Brandeis has said that we can have concentrated wealth or democracy, but not both. In *The Globalization Paradox*, the economist Dani Rodrik has written: "Democracies have the right to protect their social arrangements, and when this right clashes with the requirements of the global economy, it is the latter that should give way." Consider this mantra: *Citizenship is the domain of equality, the market is the domain of inequality*. Ideally, all Americans enjoy equality before the law; in fact, wealth, assisted by the Federalist Society and its Supreme Court picks, skews the law. The Supreme Court decision *Citizens United* determined that corporations are people and that they may therefore spend unlimited wealth on behalf of their political agendas—as a species of free speech. Social democracy lost its political power when all-powerful capitalism reclaimed power. (For this analysis, I am indebted to the review "Can We Fix Capitalism?" by Robert Kuttner in *The New York Review of Books*, September 24, 2020.)

In August 2020, *The New York Times Book Review*, under the title "The Plutocrats: Examining the Impact of Economic Inequality on American Society," reviewed Robert Reich's *The System: Who Rigged It, How We Fix It* and Zephyr Teachout's *Recovering Our Freedom from Big Ag, Big Tech, and Big Money*. As we saw in an earlier chapter, Milton Friedman and the Chicago school of economics convinced workers to turn to the Republican Party—what any rational actor would do and what they were promised would serve workers' interests. Instead of through unions, minimum wages, unemployment insurance, Medicare, and generous Social Security, salvation would come through free markets and the maximization of profit. But workers kept voting Republican, in part to reject LBJ's Great Society and its generosity to the wrong kind of people. Thomas Frank had tried to analyze this in his famous book

What's the Matter with Kansas? Why do they keep voting against their own interests?

But the self-interested policies of the super-wealthy go unnoticed by most voters. Christians don't see Jesus in the least of these; voters don't see capitalism oppressing the least of these. The oligarchy comes with its own smoke screen. Another name for the oligarchy is corporate monopoly. Look and see: Centralized, authoritarian government comes under the guise of Amazon, Google, Facebook, Monsanto, AT&T, Verizon, Walmart, Pfizer, Comcast, Apple, and CVS. So the rise of wealth among the 0.1 percent means it now has 20 percent of the nation's wealth, compared to 10 percent forty years ago. Wages, of course, have stagnated. Meanwhile, the oligarchy spends some of its wealth achieving tax cuts and defeating financial and environmental regulation. Both authors believe Ronald Reagan led the charge, but Clinton and Obama did little to reverse course. So it has become commonplace, by no means limited to liberals, to date the present economic impasse to the Republican devastation begun under Reagan and continued through Trump. It will take new miracles imposed on Biden to move beyond implacable sluggishness concerning social welfare. The boldest Democratic proposals would have seemed anemic, not to mention shameful, to Eisenhower.

Increasingly, both leftist and centrist commentators like David Brooks have lately been describing Republican economic theories as bankrupt and beyond redemption. As recently as March 2021 in his *New York Times* column, Brooks, hitherto a conservative centrist, expresses his hope for the "Biden Revolution." He says Biden must move beyond the inflation obsession that has kept Republicans from responding to gross inequality and, more important, imagines a major role for big government in serving the populace. Redistribution is not a sin. This could move beyond the American way of low taxes and low social insurance—what the least of these desperately need. By comparison to American 1998 spending of 11 percent of the GDP on poverty relief, retirement benefits, disability, unemployment, healthcare, and family care, France spent 22 percent. Today, America spends 19 percent on social benefits, while France spends 31 percent.

How could this have come about? Brooks thinks it's because America emerged by contesting against centralized power and has had a high suspicion of the state ever since. As an immigrant nation we believe in hard work and not in safety nets. And we are diverse, with the white working class suspicious of all others. We tolerate far greater inequality than all European countries. Then Brooks's conversion narrative: ten years ago he would have been aghast at a leftward shift; now he celebrates it. Brooks calls out the failure of "trickle-down" economics that imagines everyone profits the more taxes are cut on the wealthy. So government intervention on behalf of social justice, government support for labor unions, government regulation of capitalism, government entitlements for the downtrodden and the middle class—all have been deemed illegitimate. But are now called for. But conservatives, including very many Christians, are sure that Biden is not God-sent (as they thought of Trump) but an heir to voter fraud and election theft. How could this be, Brooks wonders. He sings the praises of an "epistemic regime" in which a decentralized ecosystem of academics, clergy, teachers, journalists, and others who disagree about a lot but agree on a shared system of rules for weighing evidence and building knowledge. Instead, we have come to conspiracy theorists—cynicism and distrust, alienation and anomie. Charges of fake news predominate so no one believes in solutions. The airways are filled with people who say, "I possess important information most people do not have." I have the power to reject experts and expose hidden cabals. If I imagine my foes are completely malevolent, then I can use any tactic I want. And so the new Republican mindset is paranoia. Brooks calls for people of all stripes to come together, reduce distrust and enmity. *Could the churches take the lead in building such community?* It will take a generation, Brooks thinks. Churches will first have to overcome divisions between mainstream and evangelicals, and divisions in their own denominations and congregations. Catholics will have to expose the hypocrisies and self-dealing of billionaires intent on creating a counter-magisterium unique to American conservatism.

More radically, influential economic historians and theorists like Thomas Piketty and many other economic progressives are proposing that we make it almost impossible to maintain fortunes more than $38 million (which is still one hundred times the average wealth of citizens). Jeff Bezos would get a tax bill of $109 billion the first year. Senator Warren proposed a 6 percent wealth tax, while referencing Matthew 25 as the motivation. Senator Sanders proposed an 8 percent wealth tax to fund universal healthcare. Elizabeth Warren proposed a similar tax early in Biden's presidency. Far more ambitiously, Piketty proposed an American tax rate sufficient to raise 50 percent of all income, paying not only for universal healthcare and education, but offering every citizen at age twenty-five a cash payout of $231K!

When analyzing an economic system with reference to social justice across a commonwealth, from gross income inequality to the degradation of the environment, the most common approach is to begin with a *critique at the top*, analyzing the injustices that proceed from deregulated American capitalism and the extraordinary privileges guaranteed to the most wealthy. Could the churches become an important moral voice in the public square? Could theologians and social ethicists partner with notable critics of American capitalism like Thomas Piketty and his influential book *Capital and Ideology*? How soon could such dialogue lead to social gospel strategies for the church and secular progressives? Following a one hundred-year tradition in economics, Piketty is again sounding the alarm regarding the great peril of gross inequality and the bitter struggle over the distribution of wealth. One hundred years ago the richest 10 percent took home 41 percent of all domestic income. Now it is 48 percent. In his 2014 work *Capital in the 21st Century,* Piketty led the modern scholarly discussions of inequality, and this became part of the new Occupy Wall Street ethos.

It is remarkable that many economists now compare the present degradation of the poor and the celebration of wealth and the indifference of government with that of the late-nineteenth-century Gilded Age. Patrimonial wealth has returned! It was this era that contributed greatly to the rise of the liberal Protestant social gospel movement of the early twentieth century. Hence, the continuous argument in this book is for a new social gospel that would remedy and undo the "gilded age" reigning from Reagan to Trump. Incidentally, a gilded age is not required by all Republican thinking. The period from Eisenhower up to Reagan was one of very high taxes on the wealthy, of extensive government intervention on behalf of social welfare, and some significant continuation of FDR's New Deal. To propose today the Eisenhower tax system and the role of government in the economy would today be considered astonishingly liberal, if not impossibly radical. Revolutionary! Indeed, the Republican platform from Reagan on has been to undo high tax structures and government intervention on behalf of social justice. Even Social Security has been targeted, which Reagan began taxing to ameliorate his tax cuts on the wealthy. Nor does contemporary Republican theory have any tolerance for universal healthcare. And anything resembling free education. All of these are commonalities in most European countries.

Piketty goes beyond critiquing capitalism to laying out the way of transcending it. He proposes taxation on income and wealth reaching 90 percent. "Every human society must *justify its inequalities*: unless reasons for them are found, the whole political and social edifice stands in danger of collapse." In discussing "why things fell apart," Piketty discusses how the ideology of the self-regulated market in the nineteenth century led to the destruction of European societies through two wars and then the death spiral of economic liberalism. While Piketty proposes social democracy (not communism), the worship of private-property rights that cannot be questioned becomes the revenge of the ownership society. The conservative majority on the Supreme Court finds union organizers to be trespassers. (For which the Lord's Prayer seeks forgiveness!)

There are other moves to be made that speak to a grossly unjust economic system, both by Christians and secular progressives. There has accumulated a steady literature on the plight of the poor, what exactly life is like for them. It is social science, a necessary discipline for a field guide to taking Matthew 25 public, that has made poverty a much studied topic, and the churches and theologians have lately been learning from them. No doubt a church with the weight of actually seeing the poor laid on its imagination and experience by Jesus himself will want to study and engage in the ethnographies of poverty that are simply stunning and outrageous. Reformers like Dorothy Day would of course insist that the church simply cannot avoid such knowledge if it is directly ministering to the poor and living among them.

Another approach to the good of the whole, not well-known, is the *communitarian movement*, led by such social theorists as Amitai Etzioni. This is a philosophy that emphasizes the living and healthy connection between the individual and the community and the accumulation of *social capital*, the key sociological construct in Robert Putnam's *Bowling Alone: The Collapse and Revival of American Community*. Social identity and social personality and habits of the heart arise from and are largely molded by community relationships, with a much smaller degree of development placed on individualism. One might think that Christianity would be at the very heart of such aspirations, whether derived from the covenant theology of the Old Testament or the "love one another" mandate of the New Testament. And from the patterning of liturgical worship—that shapes us inside and then sends us more fully formed outside. The celebration of community seems more common to Catholicism than to Protestantism, which for various reasons, some indebted to Calvinism, has often celebrated individualism instead. Salvation itself, for many Protestants, is a transaction between God and individuals who have invited Jesus into their hearts—rather than a community where God dwells, an outpost of the kingdom of God, a coming together as a whole among whom the presence of God is celebrated.

This may be the time to celebrate Catholic social theology, well-developed since the late nineteenth century when it arose to champion—and sacramentalize—the European poor who were increasingly victimized by aggressive capitalism and the Industrial Revolution. It is much more in the nature of Catholicism than of Protestantism to mantle all people as made in the image of God, to mark individuals holy, to institutionalize Christianity and its values in the life of society, to consecrate the earth and its goodness as available to all peoples. While "social gospel" is primarily a term used by progressive Protestants, Catholic social theology certainly epitomizes it.

Consider the recent history of social theology in American Catholicism. The Latin American Catholic archbishop Dom Helder Camara once wrote: "I used to think when I was a child, that Christ might have been exaggerating when he warned about the dangers of wealth. Today I know better. I know how very hard it is to be rich and still keep the milk of human kindness. Money has a dangerous way of putting scales on one's eyes, a dangerous way of freezing people's hands, eyes, lips and hearts." He was epitomizing liberation theology's (and the New Testament's) "preferential option for the poor." It is easy to accuse Catholic social theology of being open to socialism, but Max Weber, one of the originators of sociology and present at the birth of capitalism, famously invented the term *iron cage* to refer to how the ideology and inner working of capitalism forces its participants to idolize profit above all else, and to subject all its participants to irreversible teleological efficiency, rational calculation and control, from which there is no escape. He did not decline to mention that Calvinism may have baptized early capitalism with the good news that the accumulation of wealth might be a way to give proof of God's election.

Towards the close of the nineteenth century, European Catholic social thought had begun to side with the working class and to argue the case for workers organizing themselves into unions as indispensable for achieving a social justice that reached down to every class of society. This tradition continued through much of the twentieth century as new encyclicals developed these themes and made them essential to Catholic social ethics—especially in Europe.

Dorothy Day's Catholic Worker Movement achieved the charisma of living "in accordance with the justice and charity of Jesus Christ." Catholicism was uniquely capable of doing more than simply advocating for unions as a strategy for seeking social justice. Catholic liturgical sensibility is capable of hallowing, of sacramentalizing, workers as people specially blessed in God's view of humanity. Think of the famous Mass in the vineyards of California to identify with Cesar Chavez' grape strike, with Bobby Kennedy a prominent guest and workers processing through the fields carrying liturgical banners. Unions are more than a necessary check on the extremes of corporate capitalism and multinational corporations. They can be a liturgical procession—if the Protestant churches would help them see what comes naturally to Catholics. But instead, southern Protestants have helped to create "right to work" states, which is to say making it impossible for unions to flourish as worker-collectives. More than just a calculated economic balance, Catholicism uniquely blesses workers as among "the least of these," as a people of God often forgotten and mostly oppressed amidst the thrust of an economic system bent on delivering shareholder value with no social responsibility. Workers are unique candidates for a long denied social justice that must be part of Christianity's moral theology. To confer unique spiritual value on workers is to attempt mightily to pull back together the ruthlessly separating forces that produce economic inequalities. Alas, little of this shows up so far in the Catholic sensibilities of the new Supreme Court judge, Amy Coney Barrett.

The Latin American liberation theologies that arose in the 1960s were notable for their structural analysis in diagnosing what the problems are and what needs to happen to set people, especially the poor, free. Their approach worried anti-Communist conservatives, not least Pope John Paul II, whose life in Communist-occupied Poland had left a lifelong suspicion of any partnership with left-wing social science. Evangelicals too, like that pope, were deeply suspicious of *social definitions of sin* and wanted to keep it personal. For Catholics the personal is what gets dealt with in the confessional, like sex. But capitalism, like Trump, has nothing to confess and so is given a free pass. Corporations are persons, the Supreme Court has ruled, with the unlimited free speech rights of campaign finance. Meanwhile, evangelicals are convinced that the entire New Testament gospel is about individuals coming to a Christ in their hearts, not in the rough neighborhoods of social systems. Evangelicals are good at confessing, even boasting of, their personal sins and receiving personal grace and forgiveness. To shift the focus to social analysis, it seems to many evangelicals, is to endanger the entire biblical narrative of salvation.

There was already a long moral tradition from the encyclical *Rerum Novarum,* issued by Pope Leo XIII at the end of the nineteenth century. Subtitled "On the Conditions of Labor," it is a major document in Catholic social theology, responding directly to the social conflict that had risen in the wake of European capitalism and industrialization and that had led to the rise of socialism and communism as rival ideologies. To be sure, one of its purposes was to reject Marxism and to reassert the idea of private property derived from the natural law tradition, at least since Thomas Aquinas. But it moves quickly to insist that the primary purpose of a state is to provide for the common good, for social justice—an obvious assertion rejected by many American conservatives. All people have equal dignity regardless of social class, and a good government protects the rights and cares for the needs of all its members, both rich and poor.

This document became a primer of the Catholic response to the increasing exploitation of workers. The pope proposed a balance in which the church speaks out on social issues and the state is charged with responding by promoting justice through the protection of workers' rights. The market must be tempered by moral considerations. And the poor have a special status. A primary concern of *Rerum Novarum* (which means "concerning new things" or "concerning revolutionary change") is the amelioration of "the misery and wretchedness pressing so unjustly on the majority of the working class." So this became a foundational text of modern Catholic social teaching, supplemented over time by later encyclicals such as Pius XI's *Quadragesimo anno* (1931) on the fortieth anniversary of *Rerum Novarum,* Pope John XXIII's *Mater et magistra* (1961), and Pope John Paul II's *Centesimus annus* (1991).

By 2011, during the papal reign of the conservative Benedict XVI, the Pontifical Council on Justice and Peace was speaking decisively against *free-market fundamentalism.* Pope Benedict XVI declared in his encyclical "Charity in Truth": "The conviction that the economy must be autonomous, that it must be shielded from 'influences' of a moral character, has led man to abuse the economic process in a thoroughly destructive way. In the long term, these convictions have led to economic, social and political systems that trample upon personal and social freedom, and are therefore unable to deliver the justice that they promise." And so some Catholic parishes began to identify themselves as "peace and justice" communities.

But the real bomb in America was the 1986 pastoral letter promulgated by the United States Conference of Catholic Bishops, "Economic Justice for All." Dealing specifically with the US economy, it was meant to revive historic Catholic social teaching and severely critique Reagan-esque economics. It did not, however, bring American Catholics together in moral vision. Indeed, it made Catholic conservatives crazy.

Unfortunately, an American Catholic Right, seemingly bent on creating their own *counter-magisterium*, arose to oppose this newly recovered social gospel. Catholic economic conservatives with funding from right-wing billionaires seemed bent on a *hostile takeover of American Catholicism*—as American evangelicalism had earlier been taken over. Their platform was unrestricted capitalism and small government, often meaning diminishment of government services on behalf of the poor. This was a denigration of Catholic social thought in a corporate-funded Catholic neoconservatism. Catholic billionaires made common cause with the evangelical Christian Right and saw it as their calling to cleanse Catholicism of left-leaning traditions. Meanwhile, conservative Catholic bishops had begun to do their best to limit the Catholic social imagination to one issue—abortion.

The strong pull of American economic nationalism tugged American Catholicism in its direction. The Jesuit faculty of Georgetown University once, and unsuccessfully, tried to convince then Speaker of the House Paul Ryan that his enchantment with Ayn Rand was completely incompatible with a Catholic moral imagination. They had little success arguing before Congress that the national budget must be seen as a *moral document* that must not betray and indeed must support the good of the commonwealth. In 2013, Pope Francis said that more restrictions on the free market were required because the "dictatorship" of the global financial system and the "cult of money" were making people miserable. In his encyclical *Laudato si'*, Pope Francis denounced the role of capitalism in furthering climate destruction.

Throughout this entire debate, from Reagan through Trump, and deeply embedded in conservative economic thought, is the unchallengeable doctrine of the *free market* as foundational to economic debate and analysis. And now along comes Mike Konczal's new book, *Freedom from the Market*. Astonishingly he lays out five key reasons why "freedom requires the *suppression* of the market: 1) Markets allocate even essential and life-sustaining goods on the basis of ability to pay, rather than need. 2) They are less effective and efficient than the state at providing certain goods and services, such as health insurance, because of the logic of what economists would refer to as market failures. 3) Market interactions, and in particular the employment relationship, can often be occasions of domination by the will of others. 4) The creeping commodification of everything leaves no reward for things that don't function as commodities, such as the unpaid labor of those who raise children or care for elderly or disabled family members. 5) Markets themselves cannot function without state action, like that required to enforce contracts, protect property rights, or maintain a stable currency." Matthew 25 Christianity and social thought could flourish under such a new orthodoxy!

DEMYTHOLOGIZING DEBT

> We do not have a money problem in America. We have a values and priorities problem.
> —Marian Wright Edelman

Social science analyses of the American underclass sometimes allude to the *permanent handcuffs of debt*. Debt forgiveness is the most radical idea in the Old Testament, says biblical scholar Walter Brueggemann. What does debt mean, anyway? Is it a fixed concept or one subject to cultural evolution and changing definitions? Economics is a social science, not a law like gravity, but debt is typically seen as, like gravity, a natural and objective fact. Yet societies may mythologize debt, in the interests of the debt-holder class vs. the debt-ridden class, so that it is accepted as an unchangeable given, not part of a system that could be changed.

This raises the question of how the Lord's Prayer should be translated. Its presence in Luke and Matthew is surely rooted in the heritage of the Old Testament known as the "seven-year debt forgiveness" laws of Deuteronomy. Is the Old Testament fifty-year Jubilee in the imaginal background of the Lord's Prayer? The Bible's general concern for the poor and the context of Old Testament covenant prescriptions make it impossible to spiritualize the Lord's Prayer into sin forgiveness and avoid any connection to debt forgiveness or trespassing as land reappropriation by displaced peasants. After all, *debt and bread are primary survival issues in peasant life*. Is one praying for bread for all, or just for ourselves? If one does not spiritualize bread, perhaps neither should one spiritualize debt. Theologian Jürgen Moltmann suggests that watching and praying are sort of synonyms. Praying is good, watching is better, he says. Praying is to live attentively. Those who watch have a world in common. Imagine the Lord's Prayer spread through prayer stations, as in the stations of the cross. When one gets to bread and debt, what kind of alertness, watchfulness, is called for? What kind of images from material culture will be set out?

Early and medieval Christianity also understood this petition of the Lord's Prayer in terms of real-life debt or land trespassing—if also the moral dimension of sin forgiveness. Bible translations by the time of the Reformation also understood the Lord's Prayer in such an earthly context. Many might assume that the King James Bible translation "forgive us our trespasses" alludes to the forgiveness of sins and deliberately escapes actual debt, but this is almost certainly false. In the sixteenth century trespassing is set in the context of the upper classes gradually appropriating most land, while peasants were trying to reappropriate their ancient property rights. And Luther's translation of *Schuld* carried monetary and nonmonetary implications. The early Reformed traditions, typically associated with the trading and poor classes, also maintained the financial dimensions of debt forgiveness. For Calvin the poorer classes needed to rely on some kind of debt forgiveness and he refused Communion to those who practiced usury. Catholicism also forbade usury. (Can anyone imagine that the practice of usury would be included in today's Catholic "wafer watch" that determines who must be denied Communion?) We've come a long way since then with the triumph of capitalism! Debt is not a moral issue, usury is indispensable, and the vision of the Lord's Prayer is high off the ground, up in the sky somewhere. No banker or debt collector sitting in church when the Lord's Prayer is said gets nervous. It is probably the case that the great majority of English speakers who pray the Lord's Prayer today imagine they are dealing with sin forgiveness, but *not* a debt or trespassing that has both monetary and nonmonetary overtones. How did this sanitizing and spiritualizing of the Lord's Prayer come to be in the modern world? And especially in the United States, which has the greatest economic inequality of any developed nation? In whose interest have the poor been removed from the social imaginary? (For an analysis of these issues, Google various statements on debt/trespass/sin in the Lord's Prayer, especially "Forgive us our debts: The economics of the Lord's Prayer," written by Marcia Pally.)

As I write, there are debates about whether President Biden and the Democrats in general and certainly independent thinkers like Bernie Sanders or Elizabeth Warren should propose the forgiveness of education loan debt—or whether such an idea is simply too utopian. Never mind that all of northern Europe funds all college debt with taxes on the wealthy. The reason this is even thinkable in Europe is that college loans are most often thought of as owed to the government, rather than to private lenders. So government becomes a benefactor for public education.

At the time of the 2008 Great Recession and the banking crisis and its rootedness in home mortgages, President Obama and his treasury secretary Timothy Geithner "just knew" that they must bail out the banking industry. But they did nothing for homeowner debt relief, while still making it possible to preserve handsome bonuses for bankers. *This came to be called generous socialism for corporate America and ruthless capitalism for homeowners.* If big government politicians were praying the Lord's Prayer, they knew it had to mean actual debt forgiveness for banks but only sin forgiveness for the middle class who had allowed themselves to be talked into loans they couldn't afford.

BLESSING WORKER UNIONS

Both Catholic moral theology and later Protestant theology blessed workers' unions because of the devastations loaded onto the working class by the Industrial Revolution and then of corporate capitalism. As we saw above, Catholicism seemed almost to *sacramentalize* workers, that is to reaffirm *their share in the image of God and to bless their status and dignity as of great concern to God.* Sixteenth-century Reformation theology had championed a doctrine of "the Christian's calling" for everyone, including the lower classes, and this had elevated the idea of secular labor as a call from God no less than monasticism. But by the twentieth century, Protestant individualism, and of course the Christian Right's bondage to the Republican platform, had little enthusiasm for championing workers, even though Protestantism had long since achieved significant evangelization of workers. So in the United States, "right to work" legislation gained increasing ground and by 2020 the percentage of workers who were unionized had dropped to 11 percent. Right to work, of course, really meant anti-union, the right of corporate capitalism to be free of unions, and such legislation grew under corporate lobbying and later on through the power of "dark money." Unions interfered with corporate private property. The irony of this is the amazing capability of big business to construct a national ethos so that the white working class votes against its own interest. Typically, except during the grape workers' strikes and boycotts that Catholic priests turned into liturgical processions, the churches generally are nowhere to be seen during unionization efforts. In my first year in the ministry in the Bay Area, I joined a picket line at Safeway on behalf of farmworkers. One of my parishioners, walking by and thinking she must be seeing things, called out, "Pastor?"

In the 2020 election, even liberal California voters were talked into denying regular labor rights to Uber and Lyft drivers, as a result of $200 million spent on lobbying by those corporations and very little spent on behalf of workers. One has to ask why everywhere in Europe workers have far better rights than in America, not only in wages and benefits but in worker representation on corporate boards, while Americans have let themselves be convinced that unions are dangerous and workers have no rights independent of capitalism's dictates. Perhaps workers don't deserve any better? Perhaps rampant unionism would bring socialism on? What if all Christian churches stood with workers as part of their social gospel duties? What if every political speech ended with "May God bless America and may God bless the working class"? The working class is demythologized, while "our troops" are regularly mythologized as a special class worthy of admiration and embrace.

In *Deaths of Despair and the Future of Capitalism,* Anne Case and Angus Deaton, Princeton economists, argue that working-class life in the US is more difficult than in any other high-income country. Inequality is far worse here than in France, Germany, Japan, and elsewhere. Large corporations have increased market share while labor unions have shriveled. Low-wage *workers are not colleagues but expenses.* We have by far the world's most expensive healthcare system, which amounts to a severe tax on workers—while taxes on the wealthy go steadily down. Whites without college degrees see their circumstances steadily "coming apart." Devastating social indicators track the misery.

PANDEMICS ARE REVELATORY: THE EMPEROR HAS NO CLOTHES

An amazing study well into the COVID-19 epidemic demonstrated that the top 25 percent of Americans actually profited during the outbreak. Jeff Bezos and Amazon turned the pandemic into a huge financial success, with better profit margins than ever before—even while Amazon steadily and successfully resisted unionization as out of the question. Disasters often reveal, in case anyone had missed it, the devastating shortcomings and contradictions built into economic and social systems. It is one thing for churches to respond with charity, as they have been doing. It is quite another for churches, as a vibrant (or lonely?) moral voice in the community, to insist on asking how such a system got built, and why the emperor has no clothes.

Large-scale disasters "surface" variables that otherwise are less visible. Milton Friedman's legacy was to deny that corporate capitalism has any social responsibility to "stakeholders" across the entire commons. He insisted that CEOs owe nothing but to grow profits for shareholders. The "shock doctrine of disaster capitalism" demonstrates how capitalism actually may keep growing when nearly everyone suffers.

In early 2021, Pope Francis urged a gathering of 183 ambassadors accredited to the Holy See to seize the pandemic as a motivation for taking interlocking global crises as an opportune moment for reforming the world by setting out on a new path. He called for universal access to basic healthcare, equitable distribution of coronavirus vaccines, rethinking the relationship between individuals and the economy, and addressing the escalating dangers of climate change. So, not only do pandemics painfully reveal for all to see what cannot be denied—the injustice that pervades almost all economies, and especially the immiseration of the poor—they also provide a wake-up call and an impetus for long delayed action on behalf of social justice across the earth. Who is listening? Have you noticed the churches taking the lead? Is it clear to all that the emperor has no clothes?

RICH CHRISTIANS IN AN AGE OF HUNGER: MOVING FROM AFFLUENCE TO GENEROSITY

I have deliberately chosen a huge bestseller with this title, because it was written by a highly esteemed and unimpeachable evangelical, Ronald

Sider. Sider ingeniously suggests to those evangelicals who are certain that the church is not responsible to further social justice in society that they surely must recognize that at least *in the life of the church itself* they must reflect and practice the exodus, covenant, Jubilee, sabbath, and prophetic traditions of the Old Testament and their adoption into early Christianity itself. This short-circuits the comfortable argument that we simply cannot map the justice and jubilee traditions of ancient Israel onto modern societies.

We can and must map the biblical witness onto the life of the church itself. This does not mean theocracy or literally copying the Old Testament into modern societies. For Sider, it also does not mean that the church becomes a leftist movement producing democratic socialism as the vehicle for social justice—as I am arguing in this book. Sider is not afraid to raise the question of Christian wealth and how it dims one's notice of the poor. He nearly admits, with Catholic liberation theology, that God may be biased towards the poor. Sider is willing to entertain the notion that sin can become embedded in social systems, which is to imply a structural analysis of a late capitalist economy.

Conservative Christians like to restrict their moral imaginations to tithing, while giving capitalism a free pass. But Sider demonstrates how Christians generally do not come close to tithing 10 percent. However, he suggests not only tithing, but, upon reaching a certain income level, Christians should consider practicing *graduated tithing*, perhaps up to 15 percent. Most importantly, Sider, the gold standard in evangelical thinking, does not get caught in a salvation-individualism that relieves believers of all worries about social justice for the poor while they are getting saved.

There are three levels of analysis in Sider's evangelical appeal. *First*, there is the voice of the prophets, and of Jesus, and of early Christianity, who call for Christian generosity in the church's own life. *Second*, if Adam Smith or Milton Friedman are wrong in their market fundamentalism, and if even secular progressivism and structural analysis supports a regulated capitalism, then Christian activism must join in and partner with those seeking social justice. *Third*, even if the biblical story cannot or will not become the modern secular economic story, the Anabaptist view, for example, would be that the church, at least, can be the modern *believer* and *follower* of and *witness to an example of* that story. Given our social and economic and political system, *the Christian vision then becomes a resistance story, a nonconformist story that continuously exerts its own pressure on behalf of the commons and in opposition to capitalist pretensions.* Against all the "realists" out there who patiently and enthusiastically explain why things cannot be done, Christianity espouses a *godly utopianism* that weds the heaven meeting us on the road ahead with the earthly hope the Bible teaches us. In our times, women have called out "mansplainers," men who presume to comment on or explain something to a woman in a condescending, overconfident, and often inaccurate or oversimplified manner. An equally loud and overconfident voice in the marketplace might be called "capitalist-splainers," who presume to explain to the downtrodden why things must be as they are. Surely the churches, custodians of the least of these, should be calling out such hypocrisy. Do they?

I would go beyond Sider myself in calling for alliances between the church and analysts of economic and social systems who have developed devastating critiques of late capitalism, as we saw just above. A field guide such as this must call for the church to be a rare and insistent and unmistakable moral voice in the public debates about social justice—which are almost completely missing from Congress and from the public square and political campaigns. Christians should seek regular collaborations between the churches and all people of good will who seek justice across the land and especially social and economic nurture for the poor. Together the church and secular policy makers could proceed in putting flesh and reality on visions for social justice and letting Matthew 25 come true today in the long history of its "effects."

Even if Christians all became tithers, and even if some Christians began the remarkable practice of graduated tithing up to 15 percent, this will not and cannot be the solution to the structural economic problems that beset us on every side. In other words, charity is admirable but it avoids and evades structural solutions. Charity is not all religion has to offer. Consider Toby Ord, the author of *The Precipice: Existential Risk and the Future of Humanity*. He has documented the perilous futures that beset the human race. He is a model of the engaged thinker, and founded the "effective altruism" movement and an organization called Giving What We Can, whose members have pledged more than $2 billion to effective charities. Remarkable for academics, they have pledged to dedicate at least a tenth of what they earn to the relief of human suffering. He then made a further pledge to limit his personal spending to $25,000 a year and give away the rest—not unlike the examples set by Ron Sider and some other evangelicals. But this is not even close to being adequate. And it still provides a pass to rapacious capitalism.

Another famous example of contributing to the good of humankind is Bill Gates. Guided by the belief that every life has equal value, the Bill and Melinda Gates Foundation works to help all people lead healthy and productive lives. In developing countries, it focuses on improving people's health and giving them the chance to lift themselves out of hunger and extreme poverty. So far they have given over $50 billion. Gates and other billionaires have famously signed The Giving Pledge through which they promise to give away at least half (and in some cases 95 percent) of their vast wealth to philanthropic causes. It began in 2010 with Bill Gates and Warren Buffett, and its causes include poverty alleviation, refugee aid, disaster relief, global health, education, women and girls' empowerment, medical research, arts and culture, criminal justice reform, and environmental sustainability. Now that Bill and Melinda have divorced, one wonders about the future of their philanthropy. But the ex-wife of Jeff Bezos, MacKensie Scott, began immediately after their divorce to give away each year astonishing amounts, drawn from the Amazon stock that came to her in the divorce and far exceeding anything that Jeff Bezos has ever given away (including to his workforce).

Not everyone applauds the charity of the rich. One claim is they themselves pick and choose the recipients. But the chief criticism is that such generosity is partly or chiefly the result of government taxation systems that notoriously favor the extremely wealthy and ignore everyone else. It is pointed out again and again that from FDR's New Deal through the Eisenhower years and continuing up to just before Reagan, Congress dictated a high tax rate that would be unimaginable today. Then the bottom fell out. The era of small government gave high privilege and exemption to the wealthy and offered little to the middle and lower classes. In other words, structural solutions to social justice and the "correction" of capitalist excess were abandoned. And still are.

INVITING EVANGELICALS TOO

Would evangelicals uncompromised by the Christian Right make their own appropriation of Matthew 25? Perhaps, but this would likely be a Matthew with more individual than social effects. Consider the individualist approach of this statement signed a few years ago by thousands of pastors, "Baptist Faith and Message 2000": "Means and methods used for the improvement of society and the establishment of righteousness among men can be truly and permanently helpful only when they are rooted in the regeneration of the individual by the saving grace of God in Jesus Christ." In her book, *When God Talks Back: Understanding the American Evangelical Relationship with God,* Stanford anthropologist T. M. Luhrman, building on a year of participant-observation, shows how evangelicals and Pentecostals are prone to believe that Christian liberals slight individual Christian piety and love of the neighbor and displace it onto government responsibility. At the time of the first social gospel, wedded to Protestant modernism, evangelicals who had a long tradition of civic influence, including abolitionism and the temperance movement, suspected that Christian modernists appealed not to the sanctified lives of individual Christians *but shifted the sanctifying life to government programs*—and compromised much of historic Christianity in the process. No doubt there could be serious debates about how to effect a social democracy by embodying Christian vision, with liberals insisting on structural approaches to social sin and evangelicals looking to Christian charity from individual Christians. And yet, essential to early Puritan self-understanding, the early settlers of America had a twofold sense of calling: *an inward call to redemption* and *a social vocation to the common good.* Yet modern evangelicals unaffiliated with the Christian Right still remain suspicious of the call for social justice, which in their view still comes to light with too much godless socialism clinging to it. And Franklin Graham is worried that big government would waste tax money.

In a recent book, *A House United: How the Church Can Save the World,* Allen Hilton calls for competing groups within Christian churches and competing Christian traditions like evangelical versus the mainline, and the pastors and theologians who lead them, to come together in the "divided states of America" to move toward a deliberate and *open-minded mingling through common mission,* practicing courageous conversations, and saving the world. In other words, Christians of quite different viewpoints and persuasions can still come together on some united fronts, even while continuing in their own spheres as well.

For those committed to structural solutions for the good of the commons and for those whose first instinct is for individual sanctified lives of virtue and witness, it is entirely possible to imagine, if not quite unite, a Christian humanism and an ethos of social justice all fed from historic Christian sources. Both together are driven by a religious vision of humans created and redeemed by God (as even the founding fathers nearly imagined) on a re-enchanted earth. This would require a recovery and reinvigoration of biblical proclamation and historic theological, moral, and life-in-community deposits of historic Christianity displaying faith active in love.

A current, but not well-known, example is the attempt by some evangelicals in business to recover the Old Testament practice of *gleaning*, God's command that the edge of every field's bounty be reserved for the poor and the stranger. This is not merely a personal charity but a reimagination of how to think of one's business and the transformation of private enterprise into shared space and shared community. Always, this exemplary individual or communal practice is meant to evoke similar but perhaps more consequential practice in government and nonprofit programs for the common good—as also in contemporary Christian attempts to mix public, private, and church-based efforts to provide all the hungry with enough food. Such efforts evoke both typical evangelical approaches that emerge from personal piety and practice and mainstream Protestant or Catholic lobbying for social justice as evocations of government policy congruent with their own historic traditions of moral theology.

But what will well-meaning secular proponents of social democracy say? How will "social justice warriors" who have written off religion and lie awake worrying about theocracy and the Christian Right respond? Consider David Bentley Hart's affirmation to *The New York Times* in 2019: "Democratic socialism is a noble tradition of civic conscientiousness that was historically—to a far greater degree than either its champions or detractors today often care to acknowledge—grounded in deep Christian convictions." Consider the prodigious scholarship of Union Seminary's Gary Dorrien, one of whose books, *Social Democracy in the Making: Political and Religious Roots of European Socialism,* traces the roots of social democracy in European Christian public theology. Closer to home is Dorrien's *Reconstructing the Common Good: Theology and the Social Order.* This work draws on some of the most distinguished Christian theologians of the twentieth century who imagined a modern, non-Marxian, Christian socialism, like American Walter Rauschenbusch, German-American Paul Tillich, German Jürgen Moltmann, Peruvian Gustavo Gutierrez, and Argentinian Jose Miguez Bonino. They provide a unique context for addressing all the questions that need to be asked, both by secular idealists and public theologians—freedom and totalitarianism, sacralization and democratization, individual autonomy and the common good. Dorrien focuses on the differing conceptions of the common good that these major theorists have propounded, and explicates as well their theological arguments on the relationship between the kingdom of God and projects of historical praxis.

BUT WAIT: IS CHRISTIAN REALISM THE FINAL TEST OF A SOCIAL JUSTICE PROGRAM AND DOES IT REALLY COME FROM JESUS?

Given how powerful are the principalities and powers that govern our political and economic systems, and given how determined this book has been to move Christians from gospel to social gospel, from inside worship to outside activism, and given how far-fetched it will appear to many Christians today that the rituals of worship will automatically shape them for an activist political theology out in the public square, worrying that the church of the early twenty-first century *might go overboard* in imagining their best ventures will be identified as God's own moves and hence to require great caution—seems hardly something to be preoccupied with. Matthew 25 evokes a bold and radical religion that can see the presence of Jesus in the least of these. Whether they saw a reign of God that takes up social space is the test Jesus gives in his last judgment story. Whether Christians erred by becoming too utopian is not one of Jesus' tests!

So I would argue that pessimistic *realism* about the human condition and human sinfulness are not what the times require at the beginning of the twenty-first century. This is no time for recalling the so-called Christian realism movement of the 1940s and 1950s, mostly associated with the public intellectual and Christian theologian Reinhold Niebuhr. Christian realism was a political theology built on three biblical presumptions: the sinfulness of humanity, the freedom to be human actors, and the seriousness of the commandment to love God and one's neighbor. Niebuhr argued that the kingdom of God cannot be realized on earth because of the innately corrupt tendencies of society. Moral individuals versus immoral society became Niebuhr's watchword. Due to the injustices that arise among people, we must be willing to compromise the ideal of kingdom of heaven on earth. Otherwise we end up with dangerous delusions. Human perfectibility is an illusion and of course the perfectibility of society is impossible, Niebuhr argued. His legacy lives on among many politicians who have read him, including Obama. Politicians love to show off by quoting Niebuhr—perhaps because he lets them off easily?

The Christian realism movement threw cold water on the utopian hopes that remained as the aftermath of the Protestant social gospel movement. Niebuhr cautioned against identifying a naïve idealism with the arrival of the kingdom of God, for example in complete identification with anti-war movements. Gary Dorrien, who is the Reinhold Niebuhr Professor of Social Ethics at Union Seminary (!), has acidly compared the social gospel movement to that of Christian realism: "Christian realism inspired no hymns and built no lasting institutions. It was not even a movement, but rather, a reaction to the Social Gospel centered on one person, Reinhold Niebuhr. The Social Gospel, by contrast, was a half-century movement and an enduring perspective that paved the way for modern ecumenism, social Christianity, the Civil Rights Movement, and the field of social ethics." Neo-Anabaptist theologian and social ethicist Stanley Hauerwas has even suggested that Niebuhr's realism constitutes an abandonment of the church's call to tell its own story in its own language and to be a nonconforming movement of resistance to the world. He wondered where the is Christianity in Niebuhr's vision.

And yet, given what may seem to be the utopian conclusion to this book, it may be worth noting the much milder realism statement of John Bennett, a colleague of Niebuhr and president at Union, and after his retirement there my Christian ethics professor at the Graduate Theological Union. In 1945 Bennett commented on the relation between Christianity and politics. At a time when evangelicals worry that Christian "social justice warriors" may be inviting socialism or even Marxism into the tent, it is worth noting Bennett's point that the kingdom of God cannot absolutely be identified with any human program. Fair enough. And certainly even a progressive Democrat platform does not remotely rise to the level of a society that recognizes and nurtures the least of these as Matthew 25 imagines it. But Bennett argues, as I have in this book, that Christians should serve God's kingdom by working through human institutions, including political ones. Even if none of these is equal to the kingdom of God. So I yield on this point: Even at its most expansive, a church propelled out the door and into society by the ritual pressure of true worship should recognize that its ambitions and alliances never amount to a full vision of the parousia. Curiously, it is the Christian Right, not social justice Christians, who vouch for Trump absolutely as God's anointed and indeed a new "word made flesh," as the Gospel of John says of the incarnate Christ. Progressive Christians never allow themselves the uncritical gushes so characteristic of the Christian Right.

Here is a sample of Bennett's program for America after 1945. He looks for Christians, together with political partners, to work to prevent World War III, control the use of atomic energy, prevent mass unemployment, raise races to equal citizenship, and abolish segregation. He acknowledges that Christians may make differing choices to pursue these goals. And that their achievements will not by themselves constitute the kingdom of God.

Having entered these caveats while also cautioning against quietism and an obsession with human sinful limitation, I press on to conclude this book with audacious imagination. *Seeing Jesus as King*, and not taking our eyes off the parousia, is meant to provoke a crisis of decision and opportunity and an epic response to God's new age. Salvation comes to every disciple, to a new community, to the church—and certainly to the poor. St. Paul would call this an eschatological harvest—reaping the abundance of Christ's legacy *as Paul takes it public. Every country could become a promised land, every soul a friend of God, earth a new Eden. Christians would be an advanced colony of heaven, appearing on the road ahead that reaches down from the future into the present, as earth becomes capable of heaven. Christians collaborate with God in the ultimate destination of earth and the universe.*

Take a deep breath now. Is it possible that an ever more encompassing social gospel that brings good news to the poor and social justice across the land could result in the reimagination of society? That Christians could lead the way, but together with secular alliances, in rethinking the commonwealth? That a different kind of government would become necessary, a redistributive tax structure re-created, an evolving capitalism achieved that produces bounty across the world not the immiseration of the poor, the despoiling of the earth, and shameful inequalities?

8

There and Back Again
A short meditation on a long pilgrimage

We keep a troubled vigil at the bedside of the world.
—*Howard Thurman*

The church cannot have an inner life without having at the same time
a life which expresses itself outwardly as well.
She cannot hear her Lord and not hear the groaning of the Creation.
—*Karl Barth*

When we go before Him, God will ask, Where are your wounds?
—*Allan Boesak*

Go and make defectors of all nations.
—*Matthew 28:19*

There is not a square inch over which Christ does not intervene to say *Mine*.
—*Abraham Kuyper*

The church does not have a social ethic; the church is a social ethic.
—*Stanley Hauerwas*

THE HOBBIT, OR THERE *and Back Again* is J. R. R. Tolkien's classic prelude to his *Lord of the Rings* trilogy. In it, Bilbo Baggins is a hobbit who enjoys a comfortable, unambitious life, rarely traveling any farther than his pantry or cellar. But his contentment is disturbed when the wizard Gandalf and a company of dwarves arrive on his doorstep one day to whisk him away on an adventure. Bilbo reluctantly joins their quest, unaware that on his journey to the Lonely Mountain he will encounter both a magic ring and a frightening creature known as Gollum. This journey can be paired with John Bunyan's *The Pilgrim's Progress from This World, to That Which Is to Come*, a late-seventeenth-century Christian allegory regarded as one of the most significant works of religion in English literature. I have imagined the second half of this book as a performative liturgy that begins in God's house, where God is lifted up by our praises while we are being shaped with the proper habits for a long journey through the world. But such a liturgy must indeed carry us out the door, from gospel to social gospel, from Word to world, from text to context. But again and again, indeed every Sunday, we are returned, *there and back again*, for liturgical renewal and replenishment. We have participated expectantly and enthusiastically with all those seeking a just society. But we must regularly return for renewal and replenishment to God's house, where we meet him without compromise. All this falls under the rubric of the Christian life as a pilgrimage towards God's future for us, not to heavenly, spiritualizing escapes but to the cosmos God ordained gradually coming true for us on the road ahead.

LITURGICAL INCULTURATION

Liturgical inculturation is a term of art in the Roman Catholic tradition, reasserted during and after Vatican II. The default position for liturgy was that it had been permanently fixed, by revelation, in the practice of worship—as if it had dropped from heaven. Similarly, conservative Christians see the icon of social justice as a new secular idolatry dropped into the church, where it does not belong, from the world outside. But this fails to see the world, through all its material symbols, as waiting for God's redemption and destined for God's friending.

Imagine how inculturation would come to work over the life of the church and society and in the history of Matthew's effects over time. Envision how liturgy, including its performative function, could go out and take up the pain of the world, consecrate it, and return to embody it in the church's worship. Think of the stations of the cross during Holy Week or the exodus *movement* out of Egypt and into the promised land.

A common admonition to those considering the ancient pilgrimage route to Compostela in western Spain is, "The way is made by walking." First steps must be taken for the pilgrimage to begin. New liturgies would be called to appear in the vicinities of the least of these, with a view to import the suffering of the poor and their cries for redemption back into the worship of the church. Liturgical renewal wants to insert the church's consecrating power and presence into the culture surrounding the life of the church in such a way that the liturgy absorbs that culture and is thus able to speak from within it. Simultaneously, those cultures outside the church might absorb the church's performative presence and thus the Christian faith upon which it rests. The church and its liturgical worship would become deeply integrated into the social fabric of a troubled world—and vice versa. All this continuously occurs, there and back again, as liturgy performs us, and we it, in the church gathered and the church sent. But ultimately the long journey towards God, the Christian pilgrimage, happens through the world, where we also recognize along the way the presence of God among the least of these. Go out from church into the world, look and see, and return to worship inside with the Christ you also encountered outside—among the least of these, and perhaps among systems that oppress them.

HOLDING TOGETHER GATHERING AND SENDING, WORD AND WORLD, GOSPEL AND SOCIAL GOSPEL

After holding a magnifying glass over the gathered church and letting incarnational light shine through and ignite spiritual fire in chapter 6, I moved in chapter 7 to the outside world and again held the magnifying glass up to let the divine sunshine through to warm the church's presence on the ground in the world. Now in this final chapter I want to hold together the gospel and the social gospel, the church sent and the church gathered, the liturgy inside the church's worship and the liturgy that reveals its embeddedness in the outside world. Some call this political theology.

Matthew set Jesus' story of the last judgment and the trials that accompany it into Matthew 25 and its position in Jesus' closing ministry, during what we have come to call Holy Week. Jesus is warning the disciples, and Matthew is warning the early church, that they will be judged by their ability to see him where he is unexpected—amidst the suffering of the world, amidst the least of these whose condition cries out to God for sustenance, amidst the opportunities to join in God's efforts to redeem the world. The question for Holy Week, as there is set in motion Jesus' *via dolorosa* from suffering to the cross and then to exaltation at God's right hand, is whether the church can keep its *focus on God's redemptive path through the world*. Will the church, also today, be able to keep its eye on the parousia, the presence of the King—or will it be diverted to other concerns that lure the church away from the world waiting to be saved? The way to enter the world without losing one's way, or one's churchly identity, is to set one's attention on finding the biblical Christ in the world.

Imagine how the world could become absorbed into the church's worship so it cannot be forgotten or neglected. And how the church could leave its incarnational deposits, its institutionalizing traces, embedded in the life of the world. Ultimately, they come together, Word and world, text and context, the church's worship and the life of the world, Christ at the altar and Christ amidst the least of these. Are the homeless showing up in our liturgies? Do our performative liturgies carry us into the midst of the homeless? Imagine liturgy staging us at the edge of the Red Sea, the exodus about to begin, liberation to the promised land as our immediate future. Do we require visionaries urging us to get our toes wet, to enter the water, to cross over?

I keep using the word *performative* to characterize worship because liturgical scholars often lament that liturgy, especially Protestant liturgy, is all words and no movement. A common critique is that liturgy most often fails *gesturally*. Liturgy enacted requires worshippers to get up out of their pews and move. Towards each other in the passing of the peace. To the baptismal font. To the eucharistic table. Then out the door and into the world. In my book *After Trump: Achieving a New Social Gospel*, I characterized Christian life as a parade through the world, staging Christianity before bystanders, moving through difficult neighborhoods, attracting crowds to join the parade, discovering while marching and moving that the Christian life itself is a march, a pilgrimage. Words are not enough, but they are important scripts, as the church moves "from page to stage."

What we call the gospel and what political theology calls the social gospel must not be allowed to drift apart. Nor church and society, worship and world. These binaries, the church gathered and the church sent, cannot and must not become separate. It is not a matter of picking one, while leaving the other up in the air. *It is not true to the Christian tradition to keep alive the option of a disencumbered gospel only; nor would it be true to simply leave a hearty theology behind and become social workers or activists in the world free from Christian faith and the divine presence in the world.*

The long Christian tradition, in the history of its effects, moves sometimes confidently and sometimes haltingly back and forth over the thresholds of church and world. It is a back-and-forth life, a pilgrim's uncertain journey, which ultimately in eschatological embrace meets God on the road ahead where heaven touches down and connects with the church's aspiration to meet its King—on the ground, in the world—in transformational moments just ahead. The gathering church and sending church, as identified—sometimes thoughtlessly—in the liturgy itself, are to be enacted each Sunday. Orders of service printed in hymnals and bulletins label the *gathering* and the *sending*, and the rich life of song and sermon and prayers for the world and Eucharist in between. We arrive for church and opening worship mindful of where we came from. And we conclude our worship, if we are attentive, with sending hymns reminding us where we are returning to.

NO CHRIST WITHOUT A KINGDOM

Mark Labberton's book on this theme has the sturdy and surprising title *The Dangerous Act of Worship: Living God's Call to Justice*. Consider this summary:

> What's at stake in our worship? Everything. Worship is the dangerous act of waking up to God and God's purposes in the world. But something has gone wrong with our worship. Too often worship has become a place of safety and complacency, a narrowly private experience in which solitary individuals only express their personal adoration. Even when we gather corporately, we often close our eyes to those around us, focusing on God but ignoring our neighbor. But true biblical worship does not merely point us upward—it should turn us outward as well.

A reviewer praises the book: "Pastor Labberton has become a prophet calling 'Wake up!' Reconnect Christian worship with biblical justice. From beginning to end, worship must pursue justice and seek righteousness, translating into transformed lives that care for the poor and the oppressed."

Ritual movement involves transcending safe worship and awakening to the needs of the world. Have we convincingly begun this movement? Can we say that it is demonstrably connecting every Sunday to every Monday? Do we return the following Sunday exhausted and badly in need of replenishment?

Consider this shrewd observation from German theologian Jürgen Moltmann: *"An other-worldly piety, which wants God without his kingdom and the blessedness of the new soul without the new earth, is really just as atheistic as the this-worldliness which wants its kingdom without God, and the earth without the horizon of salvation. God without the world and the world without God, faith without hope and hope without faith are merely a mutual corroboration of one another."*

Epilogue

COLLABORATIVE ESCHATOLOGY

I CANNOT LET READERS go away wondering if I have dumbed down Christianity to a better social security system. So before reading on, let readers consider their own definition and mission of Christianity. How would you sum up its essence and intentions? And your own?

Compounding your own effort, briefly consider what historic Christian thinkers have said. Early Christians sometimes drew the figure of a fish in the sand, to identify their movement to passing seekers. The letters in the Greek word for fish (*ixthus*) form an acronym for *Jesus Christ God's Son Savior*, considered an early summary of Christianity, practically a disclosive code. A clearer statement of intention is the earliest Christian confession, *Kyrios Christos*, "Christ is Lord," which is to say that Jesus Christ is confessed and affirmed as Lord of all, including lord above that other *kyrios* in the first century, the Roman emperor. So this is a brief but all-encompassing affirmation of who Jesus Christ is and the priorities that stem from that. A much more extensive early Christian confession is the Apostles' Creed, in the Trinitarian form of statements on Father/Creator of all that is, Son/God incarnate on a redemptive mission to the world, and Holy Spirit/initiator of the Christian church.

These confessions stipulate the human relationship to God, the divine creator, redeemer, and sanctifier. But what are Christians who make these confessions to do with their lives? What is their mission in this world? This book alludes again and again to Matthew as a manual for discipleship, which is to say following Jesus and embracing his intentions as our own. In fifteenth-century Europe, Thomas à Kempis called for the *Imitation of Christ*. Matthew 25 Christians hear Matthew as a call for more than individualistic, personal piety. Discipleship must involve a Christian citizenship on earth and collaboration with God's plan for the world. Wondering how I could say all this in a single sentence, I went out and walked the dog and came back with this: *Having created humans for an everlasting partnership, God came down to earth that earth might rise up to God.* Can you do better? Consider clarifications such as that of Thomas Aquinas: Grace does not destroy nature, but perfects it. Or Martin Luther: Human salvation involves grace alone, faith alone, and Christ alone and then acts itself out in love. It should be said that Christianity, with 2.1 billion adherents, is both a living tradition of faith and the material culture that the faith leaves on the ground.

But why allude in this epilogue to *collaborative eschatology*? I closed my recent book, *After Trump: Achieving a New Social Gospel,* with this statement:

> Jesus' announcement of the reign of God was meant to provoke a crisis of decision and an epic response to God's new age. Salvation would come to every disciple and to a new community, the church, called out as God's witness. Paul understood himself to be working towards an eschatological harvest that would reap the abundance of Christ's legacy going public. Every country could become a promised land, every human soul a friend of God, every land a new Eden. Christians constituted as a colony of heaven would be faced with God on the road ahead reaching back from the future into their present. The high Christian calling is to collaborate with God in the ultimate destination of earth and the universe.

Thus, this epilogue brings the essence of Christianity together with radical discipleship and Christians reforming the world. Lately, some theologians, especially Catholics, have imagined a cosmic Christology playing out in the evolution of the universe—a very large vision. Matthew 25, then, evokes a better society that transcends a narrow Christianity. In this view, sin can be construed as *un-becoming*—the church *failing to thrive*. Christianity resting solely on getting saved, but showing no interest in Matthew-style discipleship, is un-becoming, stuck, stilted, settled. It is guilty of that old monastic sin, *sloth,* failing to get on with the program.

Is it possible that an ever more encompassing social gospel that brings good news to the poor and social justice across the land could result in the reimagination of society to reflect God's vision? That Christians could lead the way, with secular alliances and political activism, in rethinking the commons and achieving a re-enchanted earth? That secular politics is at an impasse and cannot proceed beyond the status quo, but that multiple religious movements could align with progressive politics and proceed beyond an impasse? (This is common in European countries.) Could religious communities join with political communities to reach common goals? Might government instilled with religious values and energy achieve what previously has been impossible, or return to what once had been possible but no longer is (e.g., the New Deal consensus)? Could such communities, such interest groups, come together to create a new tax and regulative structure that corrects gross inequalities and regulates capitalism and markets in ways that make social justice possible? Have we been waiting for coalitions that could meet the needs of the poor and correct the excessive privileging of the wealthy?

All this while responding to the least of these! Dorothy Day, always the purist, insisted that individual Christians feeding the poor was the point, not developing more benevolent and efficient social and economic structures. Point taken. And a proper spiritual discipline achieved. But Martin Luther King's dream imagined a just society, not just individual charity. He spoke of the arc of the moral universe being long, bending toward justice. A collaborative eschatology projects Christians and social justice meeting on the road ahead. In Jesus' story of the last judgment we are *tested on our vision*, our ability to see Christ enthroned by way of the cross. What would the world, government, economics, politics, neighbor-love be like if Christ were acknowledged as King?

Some Christian thinkers today are letting their imaginations, and their cosmologies, run wild as they try to make connections between historical Christian thought and contemporary theoretical physics or "process philosophy." In Roman Catholic scientist Teilhard de Chardin's view,

> the world is not hurtling itself into aimless expansion but is moved by Christ to Christ that God may be all in all. The future of the material universe is intimately linked to the fulfillment of human beings in whom the universe has come to consciousness. What we do matters to the "matter" of the universe, because by our choices we influence the life of the universe. The total Christ is only attained and consummated at the end of universal evolution. That is, the Christ of the physical universe, the Christ of all humanity, the Christ of all religions. In this respect, Christ is not a static figure, like a goal post with a gravitational lure, toward which the universe is moving. Rather, Christ is moving in evolution because we, human and nonhuman creation, are in

evolution. We must take seriously the impact technology and science are causing on the shape of life in the universe.

Consider Teilhard's most famous line: "Someday, after mastering the winds, the waves, the tides and gravity, we shall harness for God the energies of love, and then, for a second time in the history of the world, man will have discovered fire." Do these ideas make your Christian head or heart hurt? Or burn within you?

Eschatology has been the long-standing theological word for reflecting on the final destiny of humans in the universe, and the role God plays in it. Collaborative eschatology is a term adopted in our times to signal that *God's being and human becoming may unite in a joint grand project*. I have allowed myself the fanciful notion that we are joining with God in a "double helix." In an evocative and stunning configuration, two strands of evolution are ascending upward in a diagonal, wrapped around each other, God and humanity in embrace. If God hovers over the earth pulling us along, onward and upward, the least of these will be included too.

THE MATTHEW 25 ALTAR CALL

When I was eighteen and visiting my sister in California and her husband who was a Lutheran pastor in the East Bay, we thought it would be fun to go to a Billy Graham rally in San Francisco. At first I was mildly intrigued. Then it crept up on me, and I thought I should go forward with so many others for the closing altar call. My brother-in-law said, "Donny, Lutherans don't do altar calls; let's head for the parking lot."

Readers, are you prepared to come forward? To respond to the crisis of decision that Jesus' proclamation of the kingdom of God evokes? The prophet Isaiah said the dawning of the messianic age would be good news for the poor. Jesus opened his public ministry preaching on that Isaiah text. The New Testament uses the word *gospel* to mean good news from God—not just good news for the poor but good news for all peoples and shalom for the entire earth. Why don't people, and Americans in particular, welcome a generous God as good news for all and a breakthrough to a new future? Why is a gospel with implications for social justice and the interdependence of the human community so readily *ignored or even suppressed*?

The softer take on sin than rejecting God's call to our own transformation, or the neighbor's need, is the unacknowledged default: the gospel just expects too much of us, in time, attention, commitment, self-giving. (That's why John Wesley decided that the sanctified life would take a *methodical* approach, with his followers calling themselves Methodists.) A liberating God means a *high-maintenance relationship and a changed life*, not just Jesus in the attic of our preoccupied consciousness. Today holding back comes dressed up as *ironic detachment* or disguised as *metaphysical abstention* from postmodernist grand wagers on the meaning of life.

The real conundrum is the number of Christians who cannot accept as good news that the biblical God is liberating and portends a covenanted society that builds in justice for the poor, a new human community, and a re-enchanted earth. Some respectable people are determined to reject the sheer grace of such a God as a *moral hazard*. So the call to "repent and accept the good news" must be perennial. Backsliders will always be with us. Indeed, backsliders are always us.

But the problems for very many American Christians run deeper. Let it be admitted first that they may reject God's liberalism because they do not believe that the Bible proclaims it. Liberation theology is fake news, possibly because it includes gays and elevates women. And "a preferential option for the poor" would be a threat to the American way of life.

So many prefer "another gospel." That might be the American mythology of free-market capitalism as God's plan for humanity and individualist striving and its attendant success as the reliable sign of God's election. Or a conservative ideology that lacks the moral imagination of the neighbor. Social Darwinism and American exceptionalism are also other gospels. MAGA is alternative good news worn on a cocky red cap.

So at the end of this handbook comes the *last call* to sell all and sign on. This book opened presenting the evidence that the God of the Bible is a liberating God, already displayed in exodus theology. The New Testament proclaims that God left heaven to embody this divine good news on earth, in the person of Jesus Christ, God's liberal paradigm in human form. The apostle Paul took a world-friending God public, rendering the Jesus movement a light to the world. What are we going to do with this? I propose this answer: *Yes, I'm joining the Christian movement toward collaborating with God.* As you make your way up to the altar with many others, carry these banners in procession in church and through town:

How beautiful upon the mountains are the feet of the messenger who announces peace, who brings good news, who announces salvation, who says

> to Zion, "Your God reigns." The kingdom of God has come near.
> *Isaiah 52:7*

> Jesus came to Galilee, proclaiming the good news of God, and saying, "The time is fulfilled, repent, and believe in the good news."
> *Mark 1:14*

> Jesus said to them, "Follow me."
> *Mark 1:17*

> You are the light of the world. A city built on a hill cannot be hid.
> *Matthew 5:14*

> Your kingdom come. Your will be done on earth as in heaven.
> *Matthew 6:10*

> If anyone is in Christ, there is a new creation, everything has become new. In Christ God was reconciling the world to himself.
> *2 Corinthians 5:17, 18*

RENOUNCING THE WORLD IN BAPTISM AND RETURNING TO THE WORLD THROUGH BAPTISMAL COMMISSION AND ENGAGEMENT

In comprehensive Christian theology and ethics there is a paradox. In baptism, new Christians momentarily turn their back on the world and renounce all its empty promises, as Jesus did in the temptation stories that follow his baptism in the Gospels. The history of baptismal liturgies follows this pattern. (When I was a boy growing up in the quite Catholic town of Dubuque, Iowa, I often heard boys say: "Cross your heart and spit to the devil," especially when they were coming up to bat.) But then the newly initiated, the baptismal candidates, are commissioned to turn around and seek engagement with the very world they are called to make new, where Christ's kingship is recognized as occupying real earthly territory. The kingdom of God proclaimed in all the Gospels, and especially clearly in Matthew, is not a spiritual idea that takes up no earthly space. It wants to become coterminous with the world itself, leaving no space and no sphere, as especially Calvinists assert, unclaimed by Christ. The

Christian faith must escape isolation in the believer's heart. Here are the New Testament authorizations:

> Go and make disciples of all nations,
> Baptizing them in the name of the Father and of the Son
> and of the Holy Spirit,
> Teaching them to obey everything that I have commanded you.
> Remember, I am with you always, to the end of the age.
> *Matthew 28:19-20*

> You will be baptized with the Holy Spirit.
> *Acts 11:16*

> For all of you who were baptized into Christ have clothed
> yourselves with Christ.
> *Galatians 3:27*

> Having been buried with him in baptism,
> in which you were also raised with him through your faith in the working
> of God,
> who raised him from the dead.
> *Colossians 2:12*

> Baptism now saves you,
> as an appeal to God for a good conscience
> through the resurrection of Jesus Christ,
> Who has gone into heaven and is at the right hand of God.
> *1 Peter 3:21-22*

So step into the exodus waters God is stirring up. And start walking—as civil rights marchers once did. Once your feet are wet, pause to acknowledge the community cheers, renounce the old life, and accept your joyful baptismal commissioning. When I was doing my research on the Christian World Liberation Front, an instance of the Jesus Movement in Berkeley, new Christians would descend into a nearby body of water as a crowd of believers encircled them. As they came up out of the water, Jack Sparks, the leader of the group, would loudly pronounce: "Before the watching world." Baptism is the beginning of the Christian life in the community of the church and the mission to the world and, as Luther saw, the daily reclaiming of our identity.

As Jesus' command began to echo through the life of early Christianity, the meanings of baptism developed in the church's self-understanding and ritual. The early baptismal rites began by renouncing the devil and all his works and ways. Then came the immersion into Christ's own being and a confession of what it means. And then a commission to become a new kind of community on earth.

Adults to be baptized would speak for themselves, while godparents would speak for infants. As the ceremony began amidst prodigious amounts of water, and sometimes immersion, there were allusions to deliverance from Noah's flood. Eventually baptisms were mostly held in church, where a performative liturgy could be staged. Eventually, every Sunday congregants would remember their own baptisms by dipping their fingers into the font and making the sign of the cross on their forehead as they entered the church.

The liturgical revival emerging during the middle of the twentieth century among both Catholics and some Protestants sought to recover liturgical continuities between early Christianity and the needs of contemporary Christianity. Early Christian baptismal rites had been composed of two parts—renunciation (*apotaxis*) of Satan and his dominions, and adherence (*syntaxis*) to the reign of God. The new Christian life was meant to move from the old to the new.

Why, at the dawn of the third millennium, bring back renouncing the devil and all his works and all his ways? Indeed, this book has diagnosed many of them and demythologized them so as to name, unmask, and resist them. Demons in Jesus' time meant cosmic forces so powerful and so arrayed against the reign of God that few people could successfully resist them. But how naïve to imagine that no such powers, any sense of the demonic, could exist in our benign modern age! What about economic systems that systematically enrich the 1 percent and impoverish the great majority, that buy political power in order to ward off movements for social justice in the commons? What about an entire culture arrayed against the recognition of the least of these? What about the casual destruction of the earth and the inability to mourn the lost mother, and the fate of the garden? What about America's "original sin" of racism? What about idolatrous nationalisms and the myth of the state entitled to wreak havoc on neighbors? The biblical witness is a mandate for religious insurgency. A careful catechesis walks all baptismal pilgrims through this expectation.

But wait! In this view of baptism as both a renouncing and commissioning ceremony to empower the Christian community to join God in a collaborative eschatology, the question sometimes arises in theological reflection: *Is one baptism going to be enough?* Only the sixteenth-century Anabaptist movement, the rebaptizers, practiced a second baptism—of adults. They did it as a sign of resistance and nonconformity—so that it would not come to appear that baptism was nothing more than a birth certificate into European civilization. The Anabaptists wanted to call initiates into a self-conscious reidentification with the Way of Jesus. But their penalty for not going with the flow was capital punishment, enthusiastically engaged in by Catholics and many Protestants.

Revisioning baptism to include renunciation and counterculture commissioning brings me to follow the analysis and bibliography of Michael Knippa, "Converted Citizens: From National Allegiance towards Heavenly Adherence" (*Word and World*, Fall 2017), who calls on the modern church to recover lost territory and influence. Likewise, William Cavanaugh's *Migrations of the Holy: God, State, and the Political Meaning of the Church* argues that in recent centuries the state has in fact occupied the sacred and in many ways replaced the cultural role of the church. Cavanaugh believes that the migration of the sacred from the church to the state diminishes the possibilities of a unique Christian culture, the possibilities of resistance and nonconformity and insurgency. While many Christians do not pause to notice, the state increasingly demands first allegiance even from people who are religious. Permission not to participate in the absolutizing of the nation might, as Jehovah's Witnesses discovered, have to go all the way to the Supreme Court. Football players may not sit out the national anthem. The place of the state and of the secular world has displaced the sacred space of the church (or other causes, like Black Lives Matter). The state controls material life and its spaces, while privatized space is conceded to religion.

Similarly, in *The Borders of Baptism: Identities, Allegiances, and the Church*, Michael Budde argues that since the Protestant Reformation, political and economic leaders have fragmented the unity of the church in the interests of nationalism, capitalism, and individualism. In the unacknowledged commitment to white racism, many churches self-segregated for a long time. And so "the bonds of baptism are spiritualized and sidelined in favor of the blood and iron ties of patriotism and ethno-national solidarity." There lies the contemporary decline of moral and spiritual formation, which half-hearted and somewhat rare confirmation classes cannot make up for. The state and national culture become the undefined god. Many Catholic and Orthodox moral theologians and Protestant ethicists have decried the formative and corrosive power of American nationalism upon the church, the absolutizing even by Christians of national, ethnic, political, economic, and cultural values. Indeed, consider the readiness of the secular world to *call any movement towards a Christian culture an unacceptable and dangerous theocratic displacement of the state.* People who do not think this through, especially liberal Christians, are far too ready to make the state their default and to declare unacceptable any assertions from the church in public space. Of course they may see this stand as a distancing from right-wing evangelicals or Islamic sharia law.

In recent decades New Testament scholars have come to see that the designation of Jesus Christ as Lord (*Kyrios*) was *political speech* directed in part as a rejection of the deification and worship of the Roman Caesars. Jesus' ride into Jerusalem on Palm Sunday might be seen as counter to the ceremonial ride-in of Roman troops. Richard Horsley was one of the early leaders of this scholarship, and he noted that St. Paul, a Roman citizen himself, was careful to root the ultimate citizenship of new Christians in the reign of God, not in the Roman Empire. Few contemporary Christians take any notice of these claims. Many Christian pastors and their congregations (often with national flags in their worship space) are pledged to "keep politics out of the pulpit"—not noticing that all speech is political speech, all speech is occupied speech, all speech is connected to power and part of a worldview, all speech and stories have a social location. So I close this book calling for Christians to become movements in new directions, in alternative spaces. The church's mission is to reduce the distance that separates humans from each other and from God.

In Eastern Orthodox depictions of Easter and the resurrection, Christ is never pictured rising alone; he has Adam and Eve in tow—and by implication millions of others freed from the bondage of the old world. In some Orthodox iconography, Jesus' rising up (the Greek word *anastasis*) may be portrayed as rising from sleep or rising up against all the forces that stand in the way of God's eschatological plan for the world. This activist view of the resurrection also comes to mean that Christians too (and all humanity?) are *commissioned in baptism to rise up* from compromised pasts and follow God into new futures. And eventually bring the neighborhood with them. Christians are called to live lives anticipating the final resurrection, reaching down into their own lives, their own neighborhoods, their own societies, the resurrecting power of God who meets us in the world and draws us in God's final direction. God is circling overhead. Prepare the landing strip! God is intending to arrive in the present, not merely the sweet by-and-by. Chasing the Holy Spirit, that whirlwind-maker, provides the power for the triumph of spirit over matter.

A prayer that Christians around the world pray every Sunday of their lives, and perhaps every day, the Lord's Prayer, becomes the energy and direction of the Christian life: "Thy kingdom come, Thy will be done, on earth as it is in heaven." For those empowered by a corporate resurrection, these words become revolutionary and anticipatory. God embraces us from out of the future and together with God we participate in God's ultimate plan. No doubt when Paul says "You have been raised with Christ" he is implying "You should be living risen lives," pointing toward resurrection in the universe.

Collaborative eschatology means that God is joining with us, and we with God, in a renewed heaven and earth together in a final act of repair and restoration. Champions of this view like to quote Augustine: "God without us will not; we without God cannot." What difference would all this make? William James, the psychologist of religious experience, famously asked: "What experiences will be different from those which would obtain if the belief were false? What, in short, is the truth's cash value in experiential terms?" The answer is that if Christ rose, and if we are in on it, and if it becomes the meaning of a future in which God is arriving, then everything about our baptized lives is different.

For a very long time Christians have wanted to think of themselves as God's image-bearers (since we were made originally "in the image of God"). Christian baptism across the ages is the liturgical performance of how we, together with God in Christ, die and rise again. And become new iterations of the social gospel. This is the Christian commission—to invite the world in.

Bibliography

Albright, W. F., and C. S. Mann. *Matthew: The Anchor Bible*. New York: Doubleday, 1971.
Allen, O. Wesley, Jr. *Matthew*. Fortress Biblical Preaching Commentaries. Minneapolis: Fortress, 2013.
Aymer, Margaret, Cynthia Briggs Kittredge, and David A. Sanchhez. *Fortress Commentary on the Bible: The New Testament*. Minneapolis: Fortress, 2014.
Bolz-Weber, Nadia. *Pastrix: The Cranky, Beautiful Faith of a Sinner and Saint*. Brentwood, TN: Worthy, 2021.
Bowler, Kate. *Blessed: A History of the American Prosperity Gospel*. New York: Oxford University Press, 2018.
Bretherton, Luke. *Christ and the Common Life: Political Theology and the Case for Democracy*. Grand Rapids: Eerdmans, 2019.
Brueggemann, Walter. *Virus as a Summons to Faith: Biblical Reflections in a Time of Loss, Grief, and Uncertainty*. Eugene, OR: Cascade, 2020.
Budde, Michael. *The Borders of Baptism: Identities, Allegiances, and the Church*. Eugene, OR: Cascade, 2011.
Bynum, Caroline Walker. *Holy Feast and Holy Fast: The Religious Significance of Food to Medieval Women*. Berkeley: University of California Press, 1988.
Carney, Margaret. *Light of Assisi: The Story of St. Clare*. Cincinnati: Franciscan Media, 2021.
Case, Anne, and Angus Deaton. *Deaths of Despair and the Future of Capitalism*. Princeton: Princeton University Press, 2020.
Cavanaugh, William. *Migrations of the Holy: God, State, and the Political Meaning of the Church*. Grand Rapids: Eerdmans, 2011.
Dorrien, Gary. *American Democratic Socialism: History, Politics, Religion, and Theory*. New Haven: Yale University Press, 2021.
———. *Breaking White Supremacy: Martin Luther King Jr. and the Black Social Gospel*. New Haven: Yale University Press, 2019.
———. *The Making of American Liberal Theology: Imagining Progressive Religion, 1805–1900*. Louisville: Westminster John Knox, 2001.
———. *The New Abolition: W. E. B. DuBois and the Black Social Gospel*. New Haven: Yale University Press, 2018.
———. *Reconstructing the Common Good: Theology and the Social Order*. Maryknoll, NY: Orbis, 1990.
———. *Social Democracy in the Making: Political and Religious Roots of European Socialism*. New Haven: Yale University Press, 2019.

Du Mez, Kristin Kobes. *Jesus and John Wayne: How White Evangelicals Corrupted a Faith and Fractured a Nation.* New York: Liveright, 2020.
Duggan, Lisa. *Mean Girl: Ayn Rand and the Culture of Greed.* Berkeley: University of California Press, 2019.
Duran, Nicole Wilkinson, and James Grimshaw. *Matthew: Texts and Contexts.* Minneapolis: Fortress, 2013.
Dreher, Rod. *The Benedict Option: A Strategy for Christians in a Post-Christian Nation.* New York: Sentinel, 2018.
Emerson, Michael, and Christian Smith. *Divided by Faith: Evangelical Religion and the Problem of Race in America.* New York: Oxford University Press, 2001.
Fea, John. *Believe Me: The Evangelical Road to Donald Trump.* Grand Rapids: Eerdmans, 2020.
France, R. T. *Matthew.* Tyndale New Testament Commentaries. Downers Grove, IL: IVP Academic, 1985.
Friere, Paulo. *Pedagogy of the Oppressed.* Fourth ed. London: Bloomsbury Academic, 2018.
Frykholm, Amy. "A strange humbling ritual." *Christian Century,* March 25, 2020.
Gerson, Michael, and Peter Wehner. *City of Man: Religion and Politics in a New Era.* Chicago: Moody, 2010.
Graeber, David. *Debt: The First 5,000 years.* Rev. ed. Brooklyn: Melville House, 2014.
Graves-Fitsimmons, Guthrie. *Just Faith: Reclaiming Progressive Christianity.* Minneapolis: Broadleaf, 2020
Guinness, Os. *The Dust of Death: The Sixties Counterculture and How It Changed America Forever.* Downers Grove, IL: InterVarsity, 2020.
———. *Last Call for Liberty: How America's Genius for Freedom Has Become Its Greatest Threat.* Downers Grove, IL: InterVarsity, 2018.
Gundry, Robert H. *Matthew: A Commentary on His Handbook for a Mixed Church under Persecution.* 2nd ed. Grand Rapids: Eerdmans, 1994.
Hauerwas, Stanley. *Matthew.* Brazos Theological Commentary on the Bible. Grand Rapids: Brazos, 2006.
Heinz, Donald. *After Trump: Achieving a New Social Gospel.* Eugene, OR: Cascade, 2020.
———. *Christmas: Festival of Incarnation.* Minneapolis, Fortress, 2010.
Hilton, Allen. *A House United: How the Church Can Save the World.* Minneapolis: Fortress 2018.
Hofstadter, Richard. *Anti-Intellectualism in American Life.* New York: Vintage, 1966.
———. *The Paranoid Style in American Politics.* Reprint ed. New York: Vintage, 2008.
Holland, Tom. *Dominion: How the Christian Revolution Remade the World.* New York: Basic, 2019.
Horsley, Richard. *Jesus and Empire: The Kingdom of God and the New World Disorder.* Minneapolis: Fortress, 2002.
———. *Jesus and the Politics of Roman Palestine.* Columbia: University of South Carolina Press, 2014.
———. *Jesus and the Powers: Conflict, Covenant, and the Hope of the Poor.* Minneapolis: Fortress, 2010.
Howe, Ben. *The Immoral Majority: Why Evangelicals Chose Political Power over Christian Values.* Northampton, MA: Broadside, 2019.

Jenkins, Jack. *American Prophets: The Religious Roots of Progressive Politics and the Ongoing Fight for the Soul of the Country.* New York: Harper One, 2020.

Jones, Robert P. *White Too Long: The Legacy of White Supremacy in American Christianity.* New York: Simon and Schuster, 2020.

Keddie, Tony. *Republican Jesus: How the Right has Re-written the Gospels.* Berkeley, CA: University of California Press, 2020.

Kingsbury, Jack Dean. *Matthew as Story.* 2nd ed. Philadelphia: Fortress, 1988.

Klein, Naomi. *The Shock Doctrine: The Rise of Disaster Capitalism.* London: Picador, 2008.

Knippa, Michael. "Converted Citizens: From National Allegiance towards Heavenly Adherence." *Word and World* (Fall 2017) 395–403.

Konczal, Mike. *Freedom from the Market.* New York: The New Press, 2021.

Labberton, Mark, Shane Claiborne, et al., eds. *Still Evangelical?: Insiders Reconsider Political, Social, and Theological Meaning.* Downers Grove, IL: InterVarsity, 2018.

Labberton, Mark. *The Dangerous Act of Worship: Living God's Call to Justice.* Downers Grove, IL: InterVarsity, 2012.

Lehman, Chris. *Money Cult: Capitalism, Christianity and the Unmaking of the American Dream.* Brooklyn: Melville House, 2016.

Lindberg, Carter. *Beyond Charity: Reformation Initiatives for the Poor.* Minneapolis: Fortress, 1993.

Luhrman, T. M. *When God Talks Back: Understanding the American Evangelical Relationship with God.* New York: Vintage, 2012.

Luz, Ulrich. *Matthew 1–7: Hermeneia.* Minneapolis: Fortress, 2007.

———. *Matthew 8–20: Hermeneia.* Minneapolis, Fortress, 2001.

———. *Matthew 21–28: Hermeneia.* Minneapolis: Fortress, 2005.

———. *Matthew in History: Interpretation, Influence, and Effects.* Minneapolis: Fortress, 2007.

MacIntyre, Alasdair. *After Virtue: A Study in Moral Theology.* 3rd ed. Notre Dame: University of Notre Dame Press, 2007.

Mamrak, Robert. *Trump: Evangelical Plague.* N.p.: Pin Oak Bottom, 2018.

Manseau, Peter. *The Jefferson Bible: A Biography.* Lives of Great Religious Books. Princeton: Princeton University Press, 2020.

Mayer, Jane. *Dark Money: The Hidden History of the Billionaires Behind the Rise of the Radical Right.* Norwell, MA: Anchor, 2017.

McGinn, Sheila, Lai Ling Elizabeth Ngan, and Ahida Calderon Pilarski, eds. *By Bread Alone: The Bible through the Eyes of the Hungry.* Minneapolis: Fortress, 2014.

Mayfield, D. L. *The Myth of the American Dream: Reflections on Affluence, Autonomy, Safety, and Power.* Downers Grove, IL: InterVarsity, 2020.

McBride, Jennifer M. *Radical Discipleship: A Liturgical Politics of the Gospel.* Minneapolis: Fortress, 2017.

Mettey, Wendell E. *Are Not My People Worthy? The Story of Matthew 25.* Franklin, TN: Providence House, 2015.

Mitch, Curtis, and Edward Sri. *The Gospel of Matthew.* Catholic Commentary on Sacred Scripture. Grand Rapids: Baker Academic, 2010.

Murray, Charles. *Coming Apart: The State of White America, 1960–2010.* New York: Crown Forum, 2013.

Piketty, Thomas. *Capital and Ideology.* Cambridge: The Belknap Press of Harvard University Press, 2020.

———. *Capital in the Twenty-First Century*. Cambridge: The Belknap Press of Harvard University Press, 2013.

Pinson, Matthew. *Washing of the Saints' Feet*. Nashville: Randall House, 2006.

Posner, Sarah. *God's Profits: Faith, Fraud, and the Republican Crusade for Values Voters*. Sausalito, CA: Polipoint, 2008.

———. *Unholy: Why White Evangelicals Worship at the Altar of Donald Trump*. New York: Random House, 2020.

Putnam, Robert. *Bowling Alone: Revised and Updated: The Collapse and Revival of American Community*. New York: Simon and Schuster, 2020.

Raboteau, Albert. *American Prophets: Seven Religious Radicals and Their Struggle for Social and Political Justice*. Princeton: Princeton University Press, 2018.

Rand, Ayn. *Fountainhead*. Anniversary ed. New York: Signet, 1996.

———. *Atlas Shrugged*. New York: Signet, 1996.

Rodgers, Daniel. *As a City on a Hill: The Story of America's Most Famous Lay Sermon*. Princeton: Princeton University Press, 2020.

Ruse, Austin. *The Catholic Case for Trump*. Washington, DC: Regnery, 2020.

Sandel, Michael. *The Tyranny of Merit: What's Become of the Common Good*. New York: Farrar, Straus, Giroux, 2020.

———. *What Money Can't Buy: The Moral Limits of Markets*. New York: Farrar, Straus, Giroux, 2012.

Schiess, Kaitlyn. *The Liturgy of Politics: Spiritual Formation for the Sake of Our Neighbor*. Downers Grove, IL: InterVarsity, 2020.

Schweizer, Eduard. *The Good News according to Matthew*. Atlanta: John Knox, 1975.

Sider, Ronald J. *Rich Christians in an Age of Hunger: Moving from Affluence to Generosity*. New York: Thomas Nelson, 2015.

Sider, Ronald J., ed. *The Spiritual Danger of Donald Trump: 30 Evangelical Christians on Justice, Truth, and Moral Integrity*. Eugene, OR: Cascade, 2020.

Smith, Christian, and Michael O Emerson, with Patricia Snell. *Passing the Plate: Why American Christians Don't Give Away More Money*. New York: Oxford University Press, 2018.

Smith, James K. A. *Awaiting the King: Reforming Public Theology*. Cultural Liturgies 3. Grand Rapids: Baker Academic, 2017.

———. *Desiring the Kingdom*. Cultural Liturgies 1. Grand Rapids: Baker Academic, 2009.

———. *Imagining the Kingdom: How Worship Works*. Cultural Liturgies 2. Grand Rapids: Baker Academic, 2013.

Stark, Rodney. *The Rise of Christianity: How the Obscure, Marginal Jesus Movement Became the Dominant Religious Force in the Western World in a Few Centuries*. San Francisco: Harper San Francisco, 1997.

Stivers, Laura. *Disrupting Homelessness: Alterative Christian Approaches*. Minneapolis: Fortress, 2011.

Stiglitz, Joseph. *People, Power, and Profits: Progressive Capitalism for an Age of Discontent*. New York: W. W. Norton, 2020.

Sunstein, Cass. "The Siren of Selfishness." *The New York Review of Books*, April 9, 2020.

Taylor, Charles. *A Secular Age*. Cambridge: The Belknap Press of Harvard University Press, 2018.

———. *Sources of the Self: The Making of the Modern Identity*. Cambridge: Harvard University Press, 1992.

Theoharis, Liz. *Always with Us? What Jesus Really Said about the Poor.* Grand Rapids: Eerdmans, 2017.

Vance, J. D. *Hillbilly Elegy: A Memoir of a Family and Culture in Crisis.* New York: Harper Paperbacks, 2018.

Wehner, Peter. *The Death of Politics: How to Heal Our Frayed Republic after Trump.* New York: Harper One, 2019.

Whitehead, Andrew L., and Samuel L. Perry. *Taking America Back for God: Christian Nationalism in the United States.* New York: Oxford University Press, 2020.

Winner, Lauren F. *The Dangers of Christian Practice: On Wayward Gifts, Characteristic Damage, and Sin.* New Haven: Yale University Press, 2018.

Wilson-Kastner, Patricia. *Sacred Drama: A Spirituality of Christian Liturgy.* Minneapolis: Fortress, 1999.

Wink, Walter. *Naming the Powers: The Language of Power in the New Testament.* The Powers 1. Minneapolis: Fortress, 1984.

———. *Engaging the Powers: Discernment and Resistance in a World of Domination.* The Powers 3. Minneapolis: Fortress, 1992.

———. *Unmasking the Powers: The Invisible Forces That Determine Human Existence.* The Powers 2. Minneapolis: Fortress, 1993.

Wright, N. T. *God and the Pandemic: A Christian Reflection on the Coronavirus and Its Aftermath.* Zondervan, 2020.

———. *Matthew: 25 Studies for Individuals and Groups.* Downers Grove, IL: IVP Connect, 2009.

www.ingramcontent.com/pod-product-compliance
Lightning Source LLC
Chambersburg PA
CBHW021914180426
43198CB00035B/540